Inwardness, Individualization, and Religious Agency in the Late Medieval Low Countries

MEDIEVAL CHURCH STUDIES

Previously published volumes in this series are listed at the back of the book.

VOLUME 43

Inwardness, Individualization, and Religious Agency in the Late Medieval Low Countries

Studies in the *Devotio Moderna* and its Contexts

Edited by

Rijcklof Hofman, Charles Caspers, Peter Nissen,
Mathilde van Dijk, and Johan Oosterman

BREPOLS

British Library Cataloguing in Publication Data

A catalogue record for this book is available from the British Library

ISBN: 978-2-503-58539-0
e-ISBN: 978-2-503-58540-6
DOI: 10.1484/M.MCS-EB.5.117902
ISSN: 1378-868X
e-ISSN: 2294-8449

Printed in the EU on acid-free paper

D/2020/0095/55

CONTENTS

List of Illustrations

Figures

PREFACE

By the end of the Middle Ages, an increasingly individualistic attitude towards devotion and the practice of religion can be observed within the context of communal life, both in the lay world and in religious communities. In order to gain more insight into this development, researchers at Radboud University and the Titus Brandsma Instituut, both in Nijmegen, together with a colleague from the Instituut voor Christelijk Cultureel Erfgoed, Rijksuniversiteit Groningen, decided to organize a conference entitled *Devotio: Individualization of Religious Practices in Western European Christianity (c. 1350– c. 1550)*. Thirty-two researchers responded to the *Call for papers* and delivered thought-provoking presentations; they were joined by an attentive audience of a further thirty-four scholars. Each speaker approached the topic from his or her own discipline (history, theology, and literary history and criticism) and/ or specialism (such as material culture, spirituality, or Modern Devotion). Eight papers have been selected for this volume of *Proceedings*, all of them addressing inwardness, individualization, and religious agency in the late medieval Low Countries, most of them with a focus on the *Devotio Moderna*. This narrowing down to a specific region and period has the advantage that all papers speak to each other and that there is a coherence and depth of enquiry to the essays that should make the collection useful for scholars and allow substantive conclusions to emerge. While this collection of essays was being prepared for publication, one of the authors — Anne Bollmann — sadly passed away after a serious illness in November 2018. She is deeply missed by all of us, and we saw it as our duty to publish this last of her publications in this volume as best as we could.

We are most grateful to Nigel Palmer (Oxford) and Marinus van den Berg (Hilversum), for their critical assessment of and valuable remarks on several articles, and to the two anonymous peer reviewers of the volume for their welcome and helpful suggestions. Thanks are due also to Rob Lutton of the editorial board of the series *Medieval Church Studies* as well as to Sarah E. Thomas, Ruth Kennedy and Guy Carney of Brepols Publishing House for processing the volume. And finally, many people at Radboud University provided invaluable assistance in the run-up to the conference in October 2016 and in ensuring that it went smoothly. Special thanks are due to Ria Heerema of the Titus Brandsma Instituut and to the students Nina Brouwers, Klinte de Rijck, and Mariëlle Splint.

Rijcklof Hofman, Charles Caspers,
Peter Nissen, Mathilde van Dijk, Johan Oosterman

Inwardness and Individualization
in the Late Medieval Low Countries:
An Introduction

Rijcklof Hofman*

Both the emergence of 'the individual' and the room for personal options in religious agency — which can be defined as the capacity of individuals to act independently and to make their own free choices in religious matters — have enjoyed considerable attention in scholarly research over the last fifty years. Scholars have explored the personal choices or decisions made by individuals about the manner in which they wish to arrange their relationship with others, but primarily with God or the Divine. The present volume addresses the topic in the specific context of the Low Countries (or more broadly Northwest Europe) in the fourteenth and fifteenth centuries, as the two themes have quite surprisingly rarely been studied in combination in precisely this geographical area in the late medieval period, despite the fact that the interaction between individualization and religious agency has been scrutinized in numerous other books and collections, in particular in relation to the so-called 'Twelfth-century Renaissance',[1] but also with

* I am most grateful to Anna Dlabačová, Nigel Palmer, Maria Sherwood Smith, Koen Goudriaan, Charles Caspers, Peter Nissen, Bernadette Smelik, Mathilde van Dijk, and Johan Oosterman for their comments on this Introduction.

[1] Studies on awareness of the self focus to an astonishing degree on the twelfth and thirteenth centuries, with virtually total disregard of later developments. A characteristic observation is that

Rijcklof Hofman (Rijcklof.Hofman@TitusBrandsmaInstituut.nl) is editor of the *Gerardi Magni Opera omnia* at the Titus Brandsma Instituut, Radboud University, Nijmegen (The Netherlands), edited in the *Corpus Christianorum Continuatio Mediaevalis* series.

Inwardness, Individualization, and Religious Agency in the Late Medieval Low Countries, ed. by Rijcklof Hofman, Charles Caspers, Peter Nissen, Mathilde van Dijk, and Johan Oosterman, MCS 43 (Turnhout: Brepols, 2020), pp. 1–34   BREPOLS 🐝 PUBLISHERS   10.1484/M.MCS-EB.5.119387

a focus on the later Middle Ages and the early modern period.[2] The essays in this volume hope to make a start in filling this gap.

The related concepts 'person' and 'individual' (differentiated below) can be approached from various perspectives. When reflecting about the differences between the two concepts and about the manner in which 'individuals' act in the world at large, it can be said that they are studied from a philosophical perspective, an approach mostly practised at universities — in modern times as well as in the Middle Ages —, and chosen in the volume edited by Aertsen and Speer;[3] another mode of enquiry studies how individuals or persons interpret themselves, how they view their interactions with other people surrounding them (the sociological viewpoint), and how they commit their ideas to writing, either deliberately in autobiographies or 'self-narratives', or in accidentally preserved written documents, such as household books and similar material, an approach chosen in the volume edited by Arlinghaus;[4] the essays in the present volume, as those in the one edited by Melville,[5] however, primarily focus on the manner in which individuals see or interpret themselves in their relationship with others and especially with the Other, in short on their religious agency.

Interiorization of religious routines, as well as their 'individualization', defined below as the process whereby an individual makes deliberate choices in order to distinguish himself or herself from others, is best documented for religious communities.[6] Most of the essays in this collection therefore focus on developments in such communities, or on texts which catered for the needs in

---

of Gert Melville in his general introduction to a recent collection of essays on the 'individual', emerging 'individuality', and related topics (Melville, 'Einleitende Aspekte zur Aporie von Eigenem und Ganzem', p. xvi): 'Überwiegend werden Befunde aus dem Zeitraum zwischen dem 11. und dem 13. Jahrhundert, der Phase des gewiß größten Umbruches in der Geschichte des mittelalterlichen Religiosentums, aufgegriffen'.

[2] Cf. most recently the collection of essays *Forms of Individuality and Literacy*, edited by Arlinghaus, and with a focus on autobiographical texts the collective volume *Von Individuum zur Person*, edited by Jancke and Ulbrich, both with ample references.

[3] Aertsen and Speer, eds, *Individuum und Individualität im Mittelalter*.

[4] Arlinghaus, ed., *Forms of Individuality and Literacy*; on the term 'self-narratives', roughly equivalent to German *Selbstzeugnisse*, cf. Jancke, '"Individuality", Relationships, Words about Oneself', esp. pp. 163–65.

[5] Melville and Schurer, eds, *Das Eigene und das Ganze*.

[6] The observations voiced by Southern, *Western Society and the Church*, pp. 359–60, regarding the difficulties connected with the unearthing of religious agency in lay environments are still pertinent, but progress is possible here also, cf. on the Low Countries for instance several of the essays in Corbellini and others, eds, *Discovering the Riches of the Word*.

such communities. However, awareness of the Divine pervaded medieval society, and by the end of the Middle Ages we come across texts specifically produced for lay readers, or in any case used by lay people. One such text is discussed in the final essay in this collection.

Before embarking on an introduction to awareness of the 'self' in the Low Countries in the later Middle Ages, however, some initial complexities need to be sorted out regarding the appropriateness and use of terminology, and the period in which this awareness emerged.

'Individuality' is in the Eye of the Beholder[7]

Although no two human beings are identical, for many centuries differentiation between humans was not a significant issue in Western thought, in which the focus lay on membership of a (social) group, caste, or a similar collective. Attention on the individual, or more properly 'the self', began to emerge in the twelfth century, with initially very hesitant terminology. To complicate matters still further, medieval terms do not coincide with their modern homophones, and in addition modern terminology is often used in an ambiguous manner.[8] It is therefore necessary to start with a reflection on the usage and meaning of terms such as 'an individual', 'individualization', or 'a person'. The understanding of individual beings within (a) group(s) also needs further clarification.

First of all, 'person' needs to be differentiated from 'individual'.[9] In modern parlance, the notion 'person' fairly straightforwardly refers to an 'individual' human being. Gabriele Jancke conveniently defines a 'person' as 'a basic unit standing beside others and on the same level'. At the same time, 'an aspect such as self- and hetero-reference, requiring demarcation and wholeness as constitutive

---

[7] Adapted from Margaret Wolfe Hungerford ['The Duchess'], *Molly Bawn* (2nd London edition: Smith, Elder & Co., ²1880) p. 142.

[8] This point is most convincingly made by Jancke, '"Individuality", Relationships, Words about Oneself', esp. pp. 156–57, and equally insisted upon by Kramer and Bynum, 'Revisiting the Twelfth-Century Individual', esp. pp. 57–63; cf. also Bynum, 'Did the Twelfth Century Discover the Individual', esp. pp. 85–88; on the divergence between modern and medieval use of terminology, with precise descriptions and definitions of medieval usage, cf. also Iogna-Prat, 'Introduction générale', esp. pp. 25–29 ('Des mots pour le dire') and Barret, 'L'individu en action', pp. 534–43.

[9] The short discussion here of course cannot compete with the collection of essays *Von Individuum zur Person*, edited by Jancke and Ulbrich, where, however, the focus is on autobiographical texts.

markers, makes sense only in relation to units complete by themselves and basically of the same type, coexisting on the same level in a non-hierarchical way'.[10] This means that a person acquires his or her identity by comparison with an 'other', and the notion is used with this connotation throughout this volume. As is set out by Rob Faesen in his contribution to this volume, this aspect of 'relationality' of the notion was first developed by William of St Thierry in the twelfth century, and the notion was so used in spiritual literature throughout the Middle Ages and in the early modern period.

When we encounter its cognate in texts dating from the Middle Ages, we need to be very cautious nevertheless, in order to avoid confusion and mis-understandings, as Sébastien Barret has set out.[11] For people in Antiquity and the Middle Ages Latin *persona* and its vernacular equivalents could refer to either a 'role' in a theatrical performance,[12] in this sense derived from the original meaning 'mask' of an actor, or to each of the three divine entities or consubstantial hypostases of the Trinity (Father, Son, and Holy Spirit). At the dawn of the Middle Ages, Boethius added a further shade of meaning, when he defined 'person' as 'the individual substance of a rational nature'.[13] Effectively, *persona* in one of its senses had thus become an equivalent of *homo* (human being) and of 'individual', and this also applied to the vernaculars.

The related notion 'individual' needs to be defined carefully as well. In the majority of the articles in this volume, 'the individual' is understood in the sense in which it is used in a general sense in sociology, as a human being with

---

[10] Jancke, '"Individuality", Relationships, Words about Oneself', p. 153. The notion in its modern sense is defined differently by Barret, 'L'individu en action', p. 539, as 'Un être humain considéré comme un individu conscient, capable de choix librement consentis et responsables, et issu de la combinaison de ces caracteristiques, de son vécu, et de son action', an adaptation in French from the theory expounded in German in Reinhold and others, *Soziologie-Lexikon*, pp. 485–89.

[11] Cf. Barret, 'L'individu en action', pp. 535–36.

[12] This contrasts with the use of 'role' in the essay by Mertens and Van der Poel in this volume.

[13] Boethius, *Liber contra Eutychen et Nestorium*, chap. 3, ed. and trans. by Stewart and Rand, p. 84. 1–5: 'Quocirca si persona in solis substantiis est atque in his rationabilibus substantiaque omnis natura est nec in universalibus, sed in indiuiduis constat, reperta personae est definitio: naturae rationabilis indiuidua substantia' (Wherefore if person belongs to substances alone, and these rational, and if every nature is a substance, existing not in universals but in individuals, we have found the definition of person, viz.: the individual substance of a rational nature), an often quoted definition, cf. e.g. Aertsen, 'Einleitung', p. xvi; Iogna-Prat, 'Introduction générale', esp. p. 28, and in this volume the contribution of Faesen. Cf. for the reception of *persona* and equivalent notions up to the twelfth century De Bok, 'Richard de St Victor', esp. pp. 123–27.

characteristics which distinguish him or her from fellow human beings, whether or not belonging to the same group or class, but who at the same time functions within a group or collective.[14] These characteristics taken together form the 'self', which is understood as 'the inner landscape of the human being', or his or her inner core.[15]

In a recent collection of essays, it is stressed that these sociologically flavoured definitions do not distinguish sufficiently carefully between the 'individual' as a term in modern, let alone post-modern societies, and the notion as it should be understood in the pre-modern world, including the Middle Ages.[16] For earlier periods in history, the sociological concept of systems theory yields remarkable results. This concept was developed by Niklas Luhmann, and it is presented and summarized conveniently by Franz-Josef Arlinghaus with respect to the Middle Ages (or 'pre-modern period').[17] The term 'systems' refers to mutually distinct spheres of communication, in which individual persons interact with each other. Their communication takes place in various 'systems', among them for instance 'art' or 'religion', or any other situation enabling communicative processes involving distinctions, such as right and wrong in the case of law. Arlinghaus elucidates the theory with the example of a painting, an object which can be discussed in terms of its artistic merit in the domain 'art', but in terms of value in the 'economic sphere'. From this example it is at once clear that 'systems' differ from 'institutions'.

In the modern period, starting in the age of Jean-Jacques Rousseau (1712–1778), each individual person is able to choose more or less freely groups of persons in which he carries out his actions, thus assembling a personal cocktail of social circles in which he can or may participate. Such 'segments' may include a job or profession, a family, a sports activity, a hobby, and so on. In each segment he communicates with different people in a different manner, but he does not belong, neither strives to belong, to a single segment. Luhmann called

[14] This means that, either implicitly or explicitly, most contributors follow Kramer and Bynum, 'Revisiting the Twelfth-Century Individual', pp. 60–61; the term is defined in a similar manner in Barret, 'L'individu en action', pp. 537–38: 'Dans son aspect humain, le concept [*sc.* de l'individu] évolue aussi, de l'individu potentiellement absolu à celui qui ne peut être conçu que dans un ensemble, une société, défini au moins en partie par un jeu de relations'.

[15] Cf. on this issue Bynum, 'Did the Twelfth Century Discover the Individual?', pp. 86–87, where she relies on the argumentation which was later published by Benton, 'Consciousness of Self'.

[16] The following paragraphs rely heavily on Arlinghaus, 'Conceptualising Pre-Modern and Modern Individuality', and Jancke, '"Individuality", Relationships, Words about Oneself'.

[17] Cf. Arlinghaus, 'Conceptualising Pre-Modern and Modern Individuality', pp. 21–25, quoting primarily from Luhmann, *Soziale Systeme* (quotations from the English edition), and from Luhmann, *Gesellschaftsstruktur und Semantik*.

this 'exclusion individuality'.[18] In pre-modern times, the situation was radically different, as each individual then strived as much as he could to belong in a single social group or system, in a society characterized by much stricter, in a way sometimes impenetrable boundaries. His agency is called 'inclusion individuality' by Luhmann. As Arlinghaus puts it,

> The important point of our theoretical approach is the suggestion that pre-modern individuality is grounded in inclusion, and that pre-modern society would offer a specific place for the self. The idea is that groups (families, households, guilds, religious orders, etc. — in Luhmann's terms: segments) work as agents of inclusion, while status is defined through the strata persons belong to.[19]

In addition, for people in the Middle Ages, as distinct from people in the twenty-first century, the primary goal or focus on this 'self' was to become closer to God. Caroline Walker Bynum aptly warns us against the pitfall of anachronism that looms large when we study our predecessors:[20]

> The development of the self was toward God. One might say, to simplify a little, that to the ancients the goal of development is the adult human being, for which one finds a model in the great works of the past; to the twelfth century the goal of development is likeness to God, built on the image of God found in "the inner man"; to the twentieth century the goal is the process itself.

A related notion to 'individual' is that of 'individualization', which can be described as the process whereby an individual makes deliberate choices in order to distinguish himself or herself from others. This notion should be distinguished from 'personalization', the process whereby an act, operation, service, or product is tailored to accommodate a specific individual.[21]

In addition to addressing the notions of 'individual' and 'person', it is necessary to linger very briefly over the cognate and closely related notions of 'individuality' and 'personality'. Aaron Gurevich has defined 'personality' as 'the "half-way house" between culture and society', by which he means 'that part of an individual's awareness which sets him or her apart from other individuals or groups'. For 'individuality', he proposes the characterization 'the unique nature

---

[18] Luhmann, *Gesellschaftsstruktur und Semantik*, chap. 'Individuum, Individualität, Individualismus', pp. 149–258, at p. 158–59, quoted through Arlinghaus, 'Conceptualising Pre-Modern and Modern Individuality', p. 25 fn. 59.

[19] Arlinghaus, 'Conceptualising Pre-Modern and Modern Individuality', p. 27.

[20] Bynum, 'Did the Twelfth Century Discover the Individual?', p. 87.

[21] In his essay in this collection, Rob Faesen refers to Krüggeler, 'Individualization'.

and integrity of the individual'.[22] Gurevich's definitions are still particularly useful when studying religion and religious agency in the late medieval period.

Yet another terminological concept, that of 'individuation', is employed by Goudriaan in his contribution to this volume. He takes the term to refer to the use of external markers — such as name, seal, portrait, or autograph — which identify individuals externally and distinguish them from another one outwardly.[23]

When Did Awareness of 'the Self' Emerge?

Ever since the publication of Richard Southern's *The Making of the Middle Ages* in 1953, a growing body of research has established that awareness of the 'self', or of individual aspects in a person's personality, did not suddenly emerge in Italy in the fourteenth century as a bolt from the blue, as had been the *communis opinio* ever since Jakob Burckhardt published his *Die Cultur der Renaissance in Italien* in 1860. Rather, the increasing interest in the 'self' was a gradual process. Dominique Iogna-Prat has observed about 'la naissance de l'individu et de la conscience individuelle' that 'chaque historien a de bonnes raisons de [la] placer à son époque de prédilection!'.[24] In order to determine whether the beginnings of interest in the 'self' can indeed be positioned so arbitrarily in any given period, it is important to briefly trace the emergence of interest in the 'self' and its historiography. The following questions will be addressed: when and how did the awareness of 'the self' develop, when did it first bear fruit, and how did these developments affect the Low Countries in the later Middle Ages, particularly in relation to the religious life?

[22] Cf. Gurevich, *The Origins of European Individualism*, pp. 13–14.

[23] Essays discussing this type of external differentiating can be found, for instance, in Iogna-Prat and Bedos-Rezak, eds, *L'individu au Moyen Âge*, pp. 33–115, with further references. Such markers, incidentally, were for the first time clearly defined and sorted out by Duns Scotus, cf. Aertsen, 'Einleitung', p. xii. Aertsen defines 'individuation' as 'dasjenige, was ein Einzelnes zum einzelnen macht'. On the relative fluidity of such markers in the late medieval period (when compared to modern usage) cf. Rolker, 'Me, Myself and my Name'.

[24] Iogna-Prat, 'Sujets de discours. Introduction', p. 119.

Heralds of Interest in the 'Self'

Larry Siedentop's *Inventing the Individual* is a convenient initial guide for general orientation, but his overview needs to be supplemented with more specialized studies.[25] He notes (though hardly originally) the influence of St Paul. In and through his letters St Paul, writing in a society which until then had been at heart hierarchical, introduced to Christian beliefs the notion of conscience, and also the basic characteristics of inwardness and personal freedom of choice. Until the emergence of Christianity the Greco-Roman civilization had attached more importance to assumptions about natural inequality and to solidarity with the family, clan, or city state than to the individual members who made up such collectives.[26] Ever since St Paul's letters, the personal relationship of individual souls with God has remained a central theme in Christianity, a view that rests on the tenet that all individual souls are fundamentally equal in the eyes of God, and that each soul is individually accountable to God for his acts in society. Once Christianity had been accepted as the dominant religion in the Roman Empire after Constantine's victory at the Pons Milvius in 312 AD, Christian thinkers were no longer forced to operate somewhat surreptitiously. The literary output of St Augustine (354–430), most notably his *Confessions* (published between 397 and 400), represents an important further development in the emergence of awareness of the individual. His writings opened the way for more intensely experienced self-consciousness and greater acceptance of personal emotions and feelings, as well as for the dominant role attributed to God's grace.[27]

---

[25] Siedentop, *Inventing the Individual*, can suffice for a general overview of the emergence of the individual as the fundamental social role, at least as regards the Middle Ages. For the period under consideration in this volume Siedentop's work presents a reasonably accurate and certainly readable overview. Elsewhere in his account, however, his narrative is unfortunately marred by reliance on older, even antiquated literature and sources. For the period from the fifth to the eighth centuries, for instance, he relies on F. Guizot's *Histoire de la civilisation en France*, published as long ago as 1840, when he would have done better to use either Riché's *Les écoles et l'enseignement* or Brünhölzl's magisterial *Geschichte der lateinischen Literatur des Mittelalters*, among many other overviews. Moreover, he describes the Gregorian Reform in the eleventh century without even mentioning Cowdrey's superb *Pope Gregory VII, 1073–1085*.

[26] Siedentop, *Inventing the Individual*, chap. 4, 'The world turned upside down: Paul', pp. 51–66.

[27] Siedentop, *Inventing the Individual*, chap. 8, 'The Weakness of the Will: Augustine', pp. 100–10, relying mainly but not always appropriately on Brown's 1986 reworking of his *Augustine of Hippo*. The syncretism advocated in Brown's work is put in perspective in Lane Fox, *Pagans and Christians*; cf. very briefly on these opposing interpretations Cantor, *Inventing the Middle Ages*, pp. 362–63.

During the Gregorian Reform of the eleventh century, a series of powerful popes successfully re-established papal sovereignty, a major role being played by Pope Gregory VII (1073–1085).[28] The main concerns of the reform-minded popes can be summarized as addressing abuses in the Church, mainly simony and clerical marriage, and attempting to wrest control of the Church from secular rulers. For the theme of the present book, what is especially important is that the Church regained the final say in appointing members of the clergy, even at the local parish level, and that the moral level of Church officials improved considerably. Also, it was in this period that regular confession of sins to the (parish) priest was finally effectively enforced. After the Fourth Council of the Lateran in 1215, confession became mandatory at least once a year, at the end of the Lenten season. Gradually, this regulation took effect in most dioceses, and eventually confession began to take place even more often.[29] Once this obligatory annual confession had definitively taken root, it turned out to be an effective stimulus for introspection. It is true of course that reflection about one's own deeds need not necessarily be more than just checking off whether one's behaviour is or is not in accordance with collective standards and principles.[30] But such reflection nevertheless could — and often did — encourage greater awareness of the 'self'.[31] These developments provided fertile ground for the emergence of consciousness of the 'self'. At least in theory, if not always in practice, better educated priests now more consciously called their flock to account in matters of self-examination and soul-searching, proper behaviour, and individual conscience, reminding them that God judges all individuals equally.[32]

---

[28] Siedentop, *Inventing the Individual*, chap. 15, 'The Papal Revolution: A Constitution for Europe', pp. 192–207, is quite inadequate on this topic; his study must be supplemented by e.g. Morris, *The Papal Monarchy*, or better still by Cowdrey's *Pope Gregory VII, 1073–1085*, which deals with much more than simply this single pope. It is with much reverence that I once venerated Pope Gregory VII's embalmed body in the cathedral in Sorrento. Mention must be made here also of that other great pope of the later eleventh century, Urban II (1088–1089), best known for his involvement in organizing the first Crusade, but also tremendously important for the improvement of the morality of the clergy. For an assessment of his achievements cf. e.g. Somerville, *Pope Urban II*.

[29] On this and on penitential literature in the high and later Middle Ages cf. Ohst, *Pflicht-beichte*; Goering, 'The Internal Forum and the Literature of Penance and Confession', on its functioning in the Low Countries cf. various essays in Clemens and Janse, eds, *The Pastor Bonus*, most notably those by Ch. Caspers and M. van Dijk.

[30] The almost mechanical aspects involved in confession are emphasized by Arlinghaus, 'Conceptualising Pre-Modern and Modern Individuality', pp. 10–12.

[31] This point is made by Dinzelbacher, 'Das erzwungene Individuum', especially.

[32] Cf. on this issue the collected essays in Boyle, *Pastoral Care, Clerical Education and Canon Law*; on the Low Countries, see Bijsterveld, *Laverend tussen kerk en wereld*.

The Breakthrough of Interest in the 'Self'

The major breakthrough — the discovery of the individual, or perhaps better that of the 'self'[33] — occurred during the course of the twelfth century, when the social landscape changed for good.[34] All the changes that took place in this period have given rise to an overwhelming number of studies during the last five or six decades. It is especially those studies that deal with the emergence of the 'self' in connection with the individual's place in a particular social group, or even in society at large, that are of importance for the present volume.[35] These studies therefore receive more detailed treatment here than those written by scholars whose research focuses on the individual person at the cost of the group he or she belonged to.[36]

Among changes from the twelfth century onward that had an impact on the awareness of the self,[37] we may highlight the manner in which the papal administration in Rome obtained an ever firmer hold over an increasing number of aspects of religious life. Popes asserted their sovereignty by convening no fewer than seven general councils between 1123 and 1312, by ensuring that papal legates implemented and oversaw the local enforcement of decisions taken during the councils and disseminated in papal decrees,[38] and by making their views and

[33] The privileged emphasis on the 'individual', at the expense of the group to which he or she belongs, is propagated especially by Morris, *The Discovery of the Individual*. For a brief historiography of the debate, cf. Kramer and Bynum, 'Revisiting the Twelfth-Century Individual', pp. 57–61; the assessment is perhaps surprisingly fair and balanced given that one of the authors was herself a party in the debate. Cf. for attempts to push back the discovery of the individual even further the essays in Corradini, *Ego Trouble*.

[34] Cf. for a brief outline of changes in religious agency in this period Bynum, 'Introduction: The Religious Revival', pp. 9–21, esp. 11–17. The one pioneering study that still deserves more attention than it nowadays receives is De Lagarde's *La naissance de l'esprit laïque*, vols 1; 3, entitled *Bilan du XIIIᵉ siècle* and *Secteur social de la scolastique*, respectively, which deal with much more than just de thirteenth century.

[35] The classic study is Bynum, 'Did the Twelfth Century Discover the Individual', to be supplemented by Kramer and Bynum, 'Revisiting the Twelfth-Century Individual', esp. pp. 57–63, and by the excellent synthesis and update by Melville, 'Einleitende Aspekte zur Aporie von Eigenem und Ganzem', who stresses that 'self' and/or 'individual' should be studied not only in relation to the group(s) to which they belong, but also from the point of view of their involvement with the Divine.

[36] This view is defended most strenuously by Morris, *The Discovery of the Individual*.

[37] Cf. on this topic more elaborately Bynum, 'Introduction: The Religious Revival', pp. 9–21.

[38] Siedentop, *Inventing the Individual*, chap. 17, 'Centralization and the New Sense of Justice', pp. 225–36.

decisions known through papal correspondence.[39] At the same time, a clergy evolved that 'was set apart much more radically than before from ordinary Christians and was also welded into a hierarchy'.[40] Further, the publication of a coherent body of canon law, compiled by Gratian in Bologna in the 1140s, had a decisive impact on virtually all affairs of the Church, as well as of society at large. In his dialectically arranged *Concordia discordantium canonum*, Gratian set the standard, among others, for 'a law of procedure stressing the legal protection of the individual, the recognition of the person, and the autonomy of the woman in marriage law'.[41] It was in this period also that 'the sacraments were defined, and the penitential system and theory that functioned in the later Middle Ages were established'.[42]

Another very important development in the twelfth century was the emergence of new institutions of higher education, more precisely the universities such as the Sorbonne in Paris. These stood apart from monastic teaching as well as from the earlier cathedral schools, but were nevertheless firmly controlled by the Church.[43] Here the new elite was educated, in order to gain higher positions in both Church and society. A tremendous amount of thinking took place in these institutions in the thirteenth and fourteenth centuries, with much heated debate about issues related to what we now call 'the individual'. Especially important in connection with the defence of personal liberty and responsibility for individual choice are the theories developed by the Franciscan friar William of Ockham.[44] Much of this thinking is documented in the essays on theological and especially philosophical speculation about 'the individual' in the volume edited by Aertsen and Speer, *Individuum und Individualität im Mittelalter*.

Perhaps the single most important new development relevant for religious history and awareness of the 'self' consisted in the remodelling of monastic life

---

[39] The number of papal letters, for instance, increased steadily, from an annual average of thirty-five under Leo IX (1049–1054) to 3646 under John XXII (1316–1324), cf. Southern, *Western Society and the Church*, p. 108, who offers varied and illuminating statistics on the increasing hold of the papal administration over Western society on pp. 104–09.

[40] Bynum, 'Introduction: The Religious Revival', p. 11.

[41] Landau, 'Gratian and the *Decretum Gratiani*', at p. 54. This essay, as well as Weigand, 'The Development of the *Glossa ordinaria* to Gratian's *Decretum*' and Brundage, 'The Teaching and Study of Canon Law', are essential supplements to Siedentop, *Inventing the Individual*, chap. 16, 'Natural Law and Natural Rights', pp. 208–21.

[42] Bynum, 'Introduction: The Religious Revival', p. 11.

[43] A convenient recent introduction to the manner in which the University of Paris was organized and functioned in the Middle Ages is Weijers, *A Scholar's Paradise*.

[44] On Ockham cf. most recently Spade, *The Cambridge Companion to Ockham*; still fundamental are Lagarde, *La naissance de l'esprit laïque*. vols 4–6. *L'individualisme ockhamiste*.

during this period. In earlier centuries, strict schedules were observed, regulating the hours and all other monastic activities. Many changes were introduced in this area in the course of the twelfth century. Richard Southern has this to say:[45]

> There was — men came to feel — something lacking in all this: they wanted more time and room for privacy, for a more intense spiritual or intellectual effort, for friendship of kindred spirits. Meditation and spiritual friendship: these things had never been lacking even in the most busily ordered monastic life, but they had existed in the interstices of scanty leisure; the system, at its most rigorous, had not provided for them. By the end of the twelfth century it is difficult to find any enthusiasm for that ornate and crowded life which a hundred and fifty years earlier had seemed like the doorway to Paradise.

At the same time, individuals opting for a cloistered existence could now choose the form of religious life which suited them best from a wide range of possibilities, as an ever more diverse spectrum of canons regular living by the Rule of St Augustine began to emerge from the twelfth century, and the mendicant orders took off from the beginning of the thirteenth century.[46]

In this context, Gert Melville has taken great steps forward in respect of Southern's initial analysis of the desire for more room for personal choices apparent by the year 1200. Melville points out that this wider range of options meant that the choice to enter a specific order, or to transfer from one order to a more austere one,[47] increasingly became an eminently personal affair, especially as

---

[45] Southern's *The Making of the Middle Ages*, p. 162 (I quote from the 1987 reprint; the quotation occurs at the end of chap. 3.iii.b). It is of course rather trite to state that mountains have been moved in research since the publication of this seminal work. However, Norman F. Cantor, *Inventing the Middle Ages*, pp. 337–51, rightly calls Southern perhaps the greatest medievalist of the twentieth century, assessing his work as follows, in 1991: 'Even today, when it [Southern's *The Making of the Middle Ages*] has been in some respects rendered obsolete by Southern's own later prolific writings, and its portrayal of twelfth-century culture challenged, extended, and modified by the critical and historical literature that *Making* prepared the way for, the book is a powerful, deeply moving performance, the work of a great craftsman and a person of very deep feeling' (p. 338). It is for this reason that some of Southern's concise and fortunate observations have been chosen for quotation here.

[46] This diversification is touched upon briefly by Bynum, 'Introduction: The Religious Revival', pp. 12–16, cf. also in greater detail Constable, 'The Diversity of Religious Life' and Melville, 'Diversa sunt monasteria', in which Southern, *Western Society and the Church*, chap. 6, 'The Religious Orders', pp. 214–99, is updated; for an evaluation of this second best of Southern's books with a more general content Cantor, *Inventing the Middle Ages*, pp. 353–54.

[47] Sometimes, however, a transfer to an order where a stricter rule was observed was not a

entering an order now generally took place in adulthood.[48] These developments turned out to be irrevocable during the later Middle Ages.

Melville, even more than Bynum, stresses that communal life in monasteries and convents, with their busy daily schedules, had unexpected consequences. This way of life facilitated individual spiritual growth through constant involvement with God as the ultimate goal, and through group pressure to focus on the same end: a shared drive towards conformity with the image of God in the 'self'. Communal life also stimulated a mutual sense of belonging, which proved to be highly effective in preventing '*singularitas*', the feeling of being exceptional.[49] In this manner, shared conventual life emerged as the best setting for achieving the individual end of coming closer to God, on condition that the self was made subordinate to the community. While rules and constitutions expected of all members dedication to group life, there was nevertheless room to respect individual ways and idiosyncrasies.[50] Such concern for personal feelings and emotions was perhaps most clearly addressed in Aelred of Rievaulx's *De spirituali amicitia*,[51] and it is evident also in the amicable tone in the correspondence between St Bernard and William of St Thierry.[52] Such views about the value of spiritual friendships soon spread outside the Cistercian order.

This continuous interaction between individual and group, described as an 'apparent aporia' by Melville, was bound together by a third pole, which functioned as a supervising essence: God. It is no coincidence that the twelfth

matter of personal choice, but a disciplinary measure. Thus, Geert Grote (Gerardus Magnus) in his *Simonia beg.* recommends that the offer or requirement of a fee upon entrance into a community of Third Order Franciscan sisters should be punished by a compulsory transfer. He relies for this advice on two *Decretals* issued by Pope Innocent III (1198–1216), first in a letter to the Archbishop of Canterbury, and later during the Fourth Lateran Council (1215), transmitted through Gregory IX's *Decretals* (*Decretales Gregorii Papae IX*, X 5.3.30; 5.3.40, ed. by Friedberg, cols II, 759. 39–57, esp. l. 54–57; 765. 47–66, esp. l. 47–54). Cf. Gerardus Magnus, *Simonia beg.*, p. 331. 49–57, repeated in Gerardus Magnus, *Leeringhe*, p. 337. 113–27.

[48] Melville, 'Einleitende Aspekte zur Aporie von Eigenem und Ganzem', pp. xxx–xxxv.

[49] Melville, 'Einleitende Aspekte zur Aporie von Eigenem und Ganzem', pp. xvi–xx.

[50] Melville, 'Einleitende Aspekte zur Aporie von Eigenem und Ganzem', pp. xviii–xxx.

[51] Edited in Aelredus Rievallensis, *Opera omnia*, I, English translation in Aelred of Rievaulx, *Spiritual Friendship*, French translation in Aelred de Rievaulx, *L'amitié spirituelle*, special attention for awareness of the self in this text in McGuire, 'Aelred's attachments', with further references. On the quite widespread medieval and later dissemination of this work cf. Aelred of Rievaulx, *Spiritual Friendship*, 'Introduction', pp. 23–25, with ref. to the *CCCM* edition, Aelredus Rievallensis, *Opera omnia*, I, pp. 281–83.

[52] Cf. Verdeyen, *Willem van Saint-Thierry en de liefde*.

century saw the emergence of a growing body of manuals on self-knowledge. All manuals prescribe that all members in the group should individually and together strive for a better understanding and knowledge of their own *conscientia* (conscience), for which *scientia cordis* (knowledge of the heart) was used as a synonym. After individual members had come to grips with their conscience, they were better prepared to turn to the ultimate goal of religious life: awareness of the image of himself which God had placed in each of their souls. The aim of preoccupation with the self was therefore ultimately to efface as much of this self as possible, to make room for the 'Other'. In conclusion: this shared interest bound together all individuals of the group, while at the same time it explains the growing awareness of the individual.

Some individuals in particular were indefatigable advocates of this new, more individualized spirituality. Cases in point are Bernard of Clairvaux (1090–1153),[53] and his close friend and follower William of St Thierry. William's *Epistula ad fratres de Monte Dei* (Letter to the brothers in Mont-Dieu), also known as the *Golden Letter*, was among the Modern Devout usually attributed to St Bernard. Other influential thinkers of this age were the Victorines, particularly Hugh and Richard of St Victor. Their teachings and writings had a lasting impact, and also influenced the *Devotio Moderna*. I will come back to this later.

Ordinary People, Religious Agency, and Interiorization in the Low Countries in the Later Middle Ages

Sufficient attention has now been paid to the fundamental changes which occurred in the twelfth and thirteenth centuries. It is therefore time to ask which elements of all of this filtered through to people in the later Middle Ages, especially in regions which are in a way peripheral in relation to the great universities. For this investigation the words written in 1970 by Richard Southern seem a proper point of departure. Is his characterization still — after some fifty years of further research — an accurate description of life in late medieval north-western Europe?

> The Benedictines, the Cistercians, the Augustinian canons, and the Orders of friars between them had filled all the main areas open for development. They met all

---

[53] A recent, complete biography of St Bernard is Dinzelbacher, *Bernhard von Clairvaux*. In this work William also figures prominently. It is not always easy to single out details of Bernard's and William's thoughts on spiritual issues, as the work is arranged strictly along chronological lines, and much attention is devoted to involvement in contemporary politics and Church organization; for a more concise focus on spiritual matters, cf. also the chapters on Bernard and William in Ruh's *Geschichte der abendländischen Mystik*, 1, pp. 226–75; 276–319.

the main spiritual, social, and intellectual needs that could be met by organized religious bodies, and they exhausted all the main sources of support. There was only one further step to be taken, and that was in the direction of greater freedom from social and hierarchical pressures and a greater diversity of individual effort.[54]

Southern then goes on to describe the *Devotio Moderna* as a movement of Brethren of the Common Life, who lived together happily without Rule or binding vow, groups of clerics associating big-heartedly and hospitably with lay helpers.[55] In this manner, they practised the ideas formulated by their founding father Geert Grote in his *Conclusa et proposita, non uota* (Resolutions and intentions, not vows).[56] For their daily subsistence, they engaged in manual work, concentrating on book production since guilds blocked other handiwork. In all of this, the suggestion is implicit that the Brethren were cheerfully and buoyantly preparing the way for the Renaissance.[57] Southern does mention that Grote 'in the last months of his life was engaged in founding a community of Augustinian canons at Windesheim a few miles north of Deventer in the IJssel valley',[58] and also that Thomas a Kempis was 'a canon of Windesheim of the second generation (*sic*)'.[59] Unfortunately, many people still turn to this classic, quoting Southern's sketch without reference to more recent research. Siedentop, for instance, blithely upholds the erroneous view that Thomas was a Brother of the Common Life.[60]

However, some fifty years of further research has seen a shift in emphasis regarding many aspects of religiosity — and of daily life in general — in the late medieval Low Countries. Southern was apparently unaware of the publication

---

[54] Southern, *Western Society and the Church*, p. 300.

[55] Southern, *Western Society and the Church*, pp. 331–58; on the absence of vows, pp. 340–46; on the mixing of clergy and laity, pp. 351–52.

[56] This personal document is only transmitted through Thomas a Kempis, who added it as an appendix to his biography of Grote (edited by Pohl, in Thomas a Kempis, *Vita Gerardi Magni*, pp. 87–107). On Grote's personal programme, cf. further the contribution of Hofman to this volume.

[57] This incorrect assumption is also implicit in Roeck, *Der Morgen der Welt*, in chap. 18 with the programmatic title 'Vor der großen Renaissance', § 'Im Jahrtausend des Odysseus', pp. 427–33, at pp. 429; 431, where the *Devotio Moderna* — together with Wycliffe and his Lollards — is mentioned only in a single passage, in a section further populated by mainly Italian early representatives of the Renaissance.

[58] Southern, *Western Society and the Church*, p. 337.

[59] Southern, *Western Society and the Church*, pp. 353–54.

[60] Siedentop, *Inventing the Individual*, chap. 25, 'Dispensing with the Renaissance', pp. 333–48, at p. 340, with an explicit ref. to Southern.

of Post's *Modern Devotion* two years before he penned his own sketch. Post, in
contrast to Southern, rightly posits that the Modern Devotion was firmly rooted
in tradition, and that none of its adherents wanted to break away from the
Church. Also, we are now more aware that the branch consisting of adherents
living without vows was less important than is suggested by Southern,[61] who
downplays the prime importance of the Windesheim congregation of Canons
Regular of St Augustine (which ultimately comprised 102 convents);[62] the third
main branch of the movement, the Third Order of St Francis, was almost entirely
ignored in Southern's day.[63] Thirdly, Southern nowhere mentions women, let
alone Sisters of the Common Life, whereas we now know that female adherents
constituted a good two thirds of the movement.[64] And finally, it has become clear
that the *Devotio Moderna* was just one form of expression for a much more widely
felt dissatisfaction with developments in the Western Church and society. In
religious matters, this feeling found its expression in a much stricter observance
of the Rules and constitutions in communities of monks, canons, and friars
alike.[65] Also, as in the twelfth and thirteenth centuries, people with an inclination
to the religious life could choose between a great variety of orders and modes of
religious living, greater even than in the earlier period.[66]

---

[61] Cf. on this branch now John van Engen's *Sisters and Brothers of the Common Life*, cited in
virtually all essays in this volume.

[62] For a brief introduction with further references cf. Dlabačová and Hofman, *De Moderne
Devotie*, chap. 36–48, pp. 106–33. A new study of the Chapter of Windesheim replacing
Acquoy's *Het klooster te Windesheim*, dating from 1875 to 1880, still remains a desideratum, as
this branch is not a point of focus in Van Engen's *Sisters and Brothers of the Common Life*. Much
can, however, be found in Lesser, *Johannes Busch. Chronist der Devotio Moderna*.

[63] Serious attention was first drawn to this third branch in Goudriaan, 'De derde orde van
Sint Franciscus', replacing Florence Koorn's study from 1992; cf. further esp. Van Engen, *De
derde orde van Sint-Franciscus*, and very briefly Van Engen, 'Het Kapittel van Utrecht'.

[64] This is immediately clear from the tables recently published in Dlabačová, Goudriaan,
and Hofman, 'Wat is de Moderne Devotie'.

[65] For a recent introduction cf. Van Engen and Verhoeven, eds, *Monastiek observantisme en
Moderne Devotie*, as well as Dlabačová, *Literatuur en observantie*, passim, but esp. pp. 37–42.

[66] Cf. esp. Van Engen, 'Multiple Options'.

Towards a Balanced Analysis of Inwardness, Individualization, and Religious Agency

It is the aim of the essays in this volume to contribute to an improved analysis of inwardness and private devotion in the late medieval Low Countries, which also includes an investigation into whether individualization really played a role in religious agency in this period and region. After the more general remarks so far, it is now time to briefly introduce the essays which make up this volume.

Rob Faesen addresses the complexities of applying essentially modern concepts to the medieval period. He points out that 'personalization' focuses on relationships with others, and ultimately God, whereas individualization is associated primarily with more modern developments, in which individual persons focus on more room for the self, not necessarily on engaging in relationships with others. In order to elucidate this thesis, he concentrates on the ideas developed by religious authorities or in religious texts from three different periods: William of St Thierry (twelfth century), John of Ruusbroec (fourteenth century), and texts written in the sixteenth century, some of them ascribed to Johannes Tauler.

The seven other essays deal with personalities, texts, and ideas. Collections on 'individuality' or 'individuals' tend to include contributions on single, 'outstanding', individuals, conspicuous because of their noteworthy actions or achievements. This collection is no exception: it contains an essay on each of the two individuals often identified as the most noteworthy representatives of the spiritual reform movement of the *Devotio Moderna* — Geert Grote (1340–1384), its initiator, and Thomas a Kempis (1379–1471). **Rijcklof Hofman**, in his essay 'Geert Grote's Choice of a Religious Lifestyle Without Vows' examines the ultimate reason for Grote's criticism of the immoral behaviour of his contemporaries. Hofman contends that Grote's conviction goes back to a personal experience he went through when at the brink of death. Grote realized that he had to regain his worthiness in the eyes of God, and this conviction led to an extremely strict sense of uprightness, and a sincere and upright personal lifestyle, which evolved into a reform programme for a movement of admirers and followers.

The second biographical essay concerns Thomas a Kempis, who spent the greater part of his long life in the Windesheim convent of Augustinian Canons Regular of Mons Sancte Agnetis or Agnietenberg near Zwolle. He surely needs no introduction here as the author of the most influential written legacy of the *Devotio Moderna*, 'the most widely sold religious book after the Bible': *De imitatione Christi*. In her essay '"*Ama nesciri*". Thomas a Kempis's Autobiography Reconstructed from his Works', **Margarita Logutova** provides a stimulating discussion of Thomas's views on his own spiritual growth.[67] Her essay very aptly includes the word 'autobiography' in its title, as her analysis, which displays a thorough familiarity with Thomas's written legacy, is for the most part based on utterances culled from a large variety of texts written by this most famous representative of the *Devotio Moderna*.

To introduce the essays on texts and ideas, we can best begin with the categorical *caveat* against speculative learning that occurs right at the start of Bk. 1 of *De imitatione Christi*, completed by Thomas a Kempis in 1441. He writes:

> Quid prodest tibi alta de Trinitate disputare; si careas humilitate unde displiceas Trinitati? Vere alta verba non faciunt sanctum et iustum: sed virtuosa vita efficit Deo carum. Opto magis sentire compunctionem: quam scire eius definitionem. Si scires totam bibliam exterius et omnium philosophorum dicta; quid totum prodesset sine caritate Dei et gratia?

> (What does it profit you to argue profoundly about the Trinity, if you lack humility, and so displease the Trinity? Truly, deep words do not make a man holy and just. It is a virtuous life that makes a man dear to God. I would rather feel contrition than know the definition of the word. If you know the whole Bible, but merely superficially, and the words of all philosophers, what would all this profit you without the love and grace of God?)[68]

Thomas expresses a similar view in the next chapter:

> Omnis homo naturaliter scire desiderat; sed scientia sine timore Dei quid importat? Melior est profecto humilis rusticus qui Deo servit: quam superbus philosophus qui se neglecto cursum caeli considerat. Qui bene se ipsum cognoscit sibi ipsi vilescit: nec laudibus delectatur humanis. Si scirem omnia quae in mundo sunt, et non essem in caritate; quid me iuvaret coram Deo qui me iudicaturus est ex facto?

> (Every man naturally wants to know, but what is the good of knowledge without the fear of God? Indeed, a humble peasant who serves God is better than a proud philosopher who ponders the course of the sky, but neglects himself. He who knows himself well becomes cheap in his own eyes, and takes no pleasure in the praises of men. If I should know everything in the world, but should be without love, what would it avail me in God's presence, he who will judge me by my deeds?)[69]

---

[67] For a very brief characterization of Thomas and his *Imitatio*, cf. also Caspers, 'Wereldliteratuur die kippenvel bezorgt', and Bodemann-Kornhaas, 'De verspreiding en invloed van de *Navolging van Christus*', both with bibliographical references to further literature.

[68] Thomas a Kempis, *De imitatione Christi*, 1. 1. 7–10, ed. by Pohl, p. 6. 2–11, trans. slightly adapted from Blaiklock, p. 3.

[69] Thomas a Kempis, *De imitatione Christi*, 1. 2. 1–4, ed. by Pohl, p. 7. 5–15, trans. by

In these quotations Thomas stresses the importance of a sincere and inwardly oriented bond between 'individual' beings and God. His counsel fittingly reflects how many of his contemporaries in north-western Europe — lay as well as religious — perceived a proper relationship between their self and their Creator. These and similar recommendations, dispersed throughout the text of Thomas's *Imitatio*, though not always with as much anti-intellectual venom,[70] echo the sentiments and beliefs formulated in the twelfth century, as described above, with strong echoes of St Paul (I Corinthians 13). Thomas originally wrote his manual (finalized in 1441) for his fellow Canons Regular of Windesheim, especially the novices, but even within his own lifetime it spread to a much wider audience, beyond the walls of the Windesheim convents. His *Imitatio* survives today in over 900 manuscripts, and his text knew even wider dissemination once it began to circulate in printed editions. As such, it was immensely influential throughout the later Middle Ages and beyond. The stress on interiority and private devotion within the safe environment of a trusted community — either lay or religious — pervades this spiritual guide, helping its readers with their endeavours to draw closer to the image of God in the self.

The essays in this volume portray the religious agency of the generations immediately before Thomas, his own generation, and those immediately after him. The contents of the essays make clear that in north-western Europe in the fourteenth and fifteenth centuries there were individuals — lay people as well as religious or semi-religious — who either were not aware of the intellectual processes taking place at the universities or who deliberately rejected them, and that the convictions and choices of these individuals did not greatly differ from those of their predecessors in the late twelfth-century world, after the great changes described above had taken effect. In their religious life and in the manuals they put together, they practised a devotion for which Bernd Hamm has proposed the term 'Frömmigkeitstheologie', devotional writing with no theology, standing in opposition to scholastic writing. It would certainly be fruitful to approach their writings with the concepts developed by Hamm in mind, an approach which is beyond the scope of this collection of essays.[71]

Blaiklock, p. 4; Thomas comes back to this theme in Bk. 4 (3). 3. 1–3, ed. by Pohl, p. 146. 5–12.

[70] Exactly the same anti-intellectualism occurs already in a comparable antithesis in the twelfth-century anonymous treatise *Meditationes piissimae de cognitione humanae conditionis* (*PL* 184, cols 485–508), at col. 508: 'Quid prosunt haec scripta, lecta et intellecta, nisi temetipsum legas et intelligas? Da ergo operam internae lectioni, ut legas, inspicias, et cognoscas teipsum', quoted by Melville, 'Einleitende Aspekte zur Aporie von Eigenem und Ganzem', p. xxxvi and n. 94.

[71] Cf. Hamm, *Frömmigkeitstheologie am Anfang des 16. Jahrhunderts*; I owe this suggestion to Nigel F. Palmer.

There were some aspects, however, in which people in the fourteenth and fifteenth centuries differed from their predecessors in earlier centuries. One new phenomenon in the later Middle Ages is the emergence of the veneration of material objects, and especially of animate ones, such as hosts which were actually bleeding, as well as devotion to such objects as material reminders of the full humanity of Christ and of the accessibility of that humanity. The first occurrences of such objects can often be dated to the fourteenth and fifteenth centuries.[72] They are not studied further in this collection, as their importance for processes of increasing inwardness and individualization is limited.

A second new phenomenon in the late Middle Ages was the increased emphasis on identification with Christ. Although meditation on the life of Christ, and in particular on his passion, followed by intense prayer, was already strongly recommended in the spiritual literature produced in the twelfth and thirteenth centuries, works written in the last medieval centuries placed an even greater emphasis on attempts at conformity to Christ. This imitation took various forms, focusing either on the passion or the place of the life of Christ in salvation history, accentuating either ascetic imitation or systematic rethinking. Many aspects of the manner in which such reliving the life of Christ was carried out in the period immediately preceding the *Devotio Moderna* are discussed in **Nigel F. Palmer's** contribution to this volume.[73]

The Devout movement, like other comparable observant movements in the same period, had its university-trained adherents. Some of these, such as Grote's close follower Florens Radewijns, largely rejected the attainments of scholastic theology and philosophy. Others never concealed their university education. This is most evident in Geert Grote himself. While he was fully sincere in his preference for an ascetic lifestyle,[74] he nevertheless loved to show off, so to speak, his versatility in the application of the rules and regulations of canon law, as well as his acquaintance with the works of St Thomas Aquinas.[75] But he is something

---

[72] A detailed analysis of such objects and the way in which they functioned and were worshipped can be found in Bynum, *Christian Materiality*, cf. also Bynum, *Wonderful Blood*.

[73] Cf. below also.

[74] Cf. Hofman's essay in this volume.

[75] Two generations later, when the Devout movement was at its peak, Gabriel Biel (1410–1495) combined a position as an influential professor in theology and scholastic philosophy at the recently founded University of Tübingen with a prolonged residence in the house of the Brethren of the Common Life in Butzbach (Hessen). Cf. on Biel most recently Van Geest, 'Gabriel Biel: op de bres voor de Moderne Devoten?'; more elaborately Faix, *Gabriel Biel und die Brüder vom Gemeinsamen Leben*; on the reform of the South-German Brethren into

of an exception, given that as the initiator of the Devout movement he stands at its very inception.

Others, however, were simply unaware of the complexities taught at universities. This holds true for many men with religious inclinations, but especially for the much more numerous religious women.[76] For them, the spiritual attitude propagated by St Bernard and his fellow Cistercians had a much greater appeal:

> They [the Modern Devout especially] found in Bernard's works many spiritual themes which corresponded to their own religious attitudes: a concentration on inner spiritual development, a personal ideal of a mixed life of action and contemplation, culminating in a mystical union with God, and a devotion to the humanity of Christ which included not only the example of his life and sufferings but also his role in the mystical marriage of union with the Word.[77]

Thomas a Kempis was fond of the writings of St Bernard and William of St Thierry (whose work was often attributed to Bernard),[78] and he was not the only one, as we will see. The views and ideas committed to parchment by other spiritual writers, among them the Victorines, especially Hugh and Richard of St Victor, and Franciscans such as St Bonaventure[79] and David of Augsburg, also fell on fertile ground. This is proved for instance by the upsurge in manuscript copies of their works surviving from the fourteenth and fifteenth centuries, and also by their popularity on the early printing press.[80] Thomas was not the only

the 'Oberdeutsches Generalkapitel' most recently Lim, 'Broeders van het Gemene Leven', more elaborately Lim, *Die Brüder vom Gemeinsamen Leben*.

[76] For the three branches, and the overwhelming majority of women in the movement, see the tables and text in Dlabačová, Goudriaan, and Hofman, 'Wat is de Moderne Devotie'.

[77] Quoted from Constable, 'The Popularity of Twelfth-Century Spiritual Writers', pp. 13–20, here p. 18, who relies heavily on Mikkers, 'Sint Bernardus en de Moderne Devotie'; cf. also Constable, 'Twelfth-Century Spirituality and the Late Middle Ages', and for an update Ruh, *Geschichte der abendländischen Mystik*; 4. *Die niederländische Mystik des 14. bis 16. Jahrhunderts*. On the reception of earlier spiritual writers such as St Bernard, Henry Suso, and others in both art and literature among the Devout cf. most recently Smits, 'Wounding, Sealing, and Kissing'.

[78] Cf. Gleumes, 'Der geistige Einfluß des heiligen Bernhard', and Constable, *Three Studies in Medieval Religious and Social Thought*.

[79] On the reception of Bonaventure in the late medieval Low Countries, and esp. in Thomas's *Imitatio Christi*, cf. De Mons, 'L'influence spirituelle'; on that of David of Augsburg, Pansters, 'Didactiek en dynamiek', and briefly Pansters, 'Een invloedrijk boek over de deugden'.

[80] Constable, 'Twelfth-Century Spirituality and the Late Middle Ages', pp. 6–13. St Bernard was extremely popular on the printing press; with reference to Janauschek, *Bibliographia*

one to rely heavily on these influential twelfth-century authorities. The two widely disseminated spiritual guides written by Gerard Zerbolt from Zutphen at the end of the fourteenth century, for instance, also breathe this same spirit. While Zerbolt relies heavily on Cassian and Gregory the Great, for instance, he nevertheless also often quotes St Bernard and William of St Thierry,[81] and the same is true of the manual compiled by his spiritual mentor Florens Radewijns.[82]

Research on the reception in the Low Countries of similar treatises compiled in the German-speaking world has fared less well. It has so far concentrated mainly on two German writers: Meister Eckhart (*c.* 1260–1328), often transmitted in anonymous form after some of his views were condemned by Pope John XXII in 1329,[83] and the Dominican Heinrich Seuse or Henry Suso (1295–1366).[84] However, the Austin Friar Jordan of Quedlinburg (*c.* 1300–1370) and the Carthusian Ludolph of Saxony are equally important names.[85] A first, yet already fairly effective attempt to mend the underexposure of aspects of the reception is **Nigel F. Palmer**'s contribution to this volume. In his essay '"Antiseusiana". *Vita Christi* and Passion Meditation before the *Devotio Moderna*', he discusses one particular group of meditational aids: sequential prayer cycles. His essay first presents an analysis of the purpose and main structure of (part of) Heinrich Seuse's *Hundert Betrachtungen*, in which he compares this text with passages from one of its sources of inspiration, Bonaventure's *Lignum vitae*. Bonaventure treats the passion in the context of salvation history, while Seuse focuses only on an ascetic reliving of Christ's passion. Palmer compares Seuse's work to two other near-contemporary prayer cycles, Jordan of Quedlinburg's *Meditationes de passione Christi* and Ludolph of Saxony's *Vita Christi*. In Jordan's perspective,

Bernardina. pp. 3–74, Constable, 'The Popularity of Twelfth-Century Spiritual Writers', pp. 12–13, notes: 'Bernard's works alone appeared in almost three hundred printed editions before 1500'.

[81] This is immediately clear from the *indices fontium* in Gérard Zerbolt's *De spiritualibus ascensionibus*, and his *Tractatus devotus de reformacione virium anime*; for a brief overview, cf. Legrand, 'Gerard Zerbolt van Zutphen'.

[82] Cf. the *indices fontium* in Florens Radewijns, *Tractatulus devotus*; for a brief overview, cf. Van Ool, 'Florens Radewijns'.

[83] Cf. Sturlese, 'Acta Echardiana', on Eckhart in the Low Countries most recently Scheepsma, 'Eckhart in den Niederlanden', also 'Das mittelniederländische Nachleben', both with further references.

[84] On the reception of Seuse in the Low Countries cf., in addition to Palmer's essay in this volume, esp. Van Aelst, *Passie voor het lijden*, and Van Aelst, *Vruchten van de passie*.

[85] On Ludolph, research is also underway elsewhere, cf. Scheepsma, 'Alijt Bake' and Van Engen, *The Writings of Alijt Bake*.

meditational practice should interpret Jesus's passion as the culmination of a life of suffering; Ludolph, on the other hand, transforms meditation on Christ's suffering into a message of hope. Palmer concludes that for later audiences Seuse's cycle full of bitterness and pain happily coexisted with other cycles offering a considerably more positive perspective.

At the same time, there was a strong emphasis on the advantages of monasticism, which was still considered everywhere to be the superior ticket to heaven, enabling conventuals to achieve the closest likeness to the image of God in the soul possible on earth. Geert Grote went so far in this respect as to stress that lay people should strive for a religious (i.e. monastic) lifestyle in their daily lives.[86] In this context he defines 'religious life' as the personal intention to serve, honour, and revere God in the best possible manner in all one's activities and actions, in this following St Thomas Aquinas, to whom he explicitly refers.

The Modern Devout in general recognized that a religious lifestyle — whether observed as monks or nuns, as canons or canonesses, or as male or female Third Order Franciscans — was superior to that of lay people, or of people choosing a middle course, such as the Sisters and Brethren of the Common Life. However, as Nikolaus Staubach has stressed, among the Brethren in Deventer a different view nevertheless prevailed, which came down to the idea that voluntary observance of the monastic vows of poverty, chastity and obedience was more difficult for those who had chosen to steer a middle course between monasticism and the lay life, and that for that reason their way of life provided better chances of reaching heaven, with fewer problems along the way. This greater degree of complexity was moreover also acknowledged by leading Windesheim canons regular.[87]

Secondly, in this period nobody questioned the practice of granting or earning indulgences.[88] I mention these issues here as just two examples that clearly show that the *Devotio Moderna*, like other late medieval initiatives to strictly observe the Rule and constitutions of an order, was firmly embedded in medieval culture.[89] Such awareness of the self as can be observed in the later Middle Ages is far removed from the developments in the Reformation period.

---

[86] He presents this view in his vernacular treatise on simony for beguines; cf. Gerardus Magnus, *De simonia ad beguttas*, pp. 359–61. 936–93, esp. 983–91, summarized in English ibid., pp. 130–31. For his view of a lifestyle which is truly religious he relies on Thomas Aquinas, II–II, q. 81 a. 2 co. (T. 9, p. 179, c. 2. 6–8) and q. 81 a. 6 co. (T. 9, p. 183, c. 2. 4–13). Cf. in greater detail the essay by Hofman in this volume.

[87] Cf. Staubach, 'Zwischen Kloster und Welt?', esp. pp. 368–96.

[88] Cf. most recently Caspers, 'Hemel, hel of vagevuur?', with further references.

[89] Cf. on this also Goudriaan, 'Grundmann and the Devotio Moderna', esp. the final

Social Life and Individual Preferences

Four essays, each written from a different perspective, deal with the manner in which individuals shaped communal life in the late medieval period. It becomes evident that the tensions first felt in the twelfth century, on how to combine individual agency with life in a group or community, had not yet petered out by the later Middle Ages. Within their group, individual members in various sectors of society still pursued the same end: a close, yet personal relationship with God. This is further proof that individuals in this final period of the Middle Ages proper were still firmly rooted in tradition, far removed from that true individualization which has been claimed as a hallmark of modernity, or of the Reformation for that matter.[90]

In the first of these four essays, **Koen Goudriaan** studies practices of remembrance. In his contribution, 'Modern Devotion and Arrangements for Commemoration: Some Observations', he sets out that many religious practices within the *Devotio Moderna* were communal, even though they were conceived as contributions to the spiritual growth of the individual, in both religious and secular contexts. Whatever the personal regulations that might be set out for individual cases, the practices were nevertheless carried out during the liturgy in the Church, a pre-eminently communal as well as compulsory affair. Only in the run-up to the Renaissance, at the very end of the Middle Ages, did Erasmus's refusal to participate in communal life in his monastery herald a profound change in the role of the individual in religion.

Thom Mertens and **Dieuwke van der Poel** argue in their collaborative essay, 'Individuality and Scripted Role in Devout Song and Prayer', that devout songs show similarities to prayer, and can even be conceived as forms of prayer: the perspective of an 'I'-persona and the use of the present tense script a role for the person who sings or prays these texts. The authors first observe that meditation can be an active process, which may have a major role in the creation of texts and images. Using the theory of the *Devotio Moderna* on meditation and prayer, as presented in Gerard Zerbolt of Zutphen's *De spiritualibus ascensionibus* (The Spiritual Ascents), they then show, through an analysis of the Middle Dutch song cycle *Die gheestelicke melody* (The Spiritual Melody), how devout song could be used during meditation.

sections, with due emphasis on the innovative character of Post's *The Modern Devotion* in this respect, and further references.

[90] Differently again Ohlig, 'Christentum, Kirche, Individuum'; but this viewpoint may have been influenced by the fact that this contribution is a first small chapter in a volume of more than 600 pages, mostly dedicated to the period after the Renaissance.

Anne Bollmann, in her essay 'Close Enough to Touch. Tension between Inner Devotion and Communal Piety in the Congregations of Sisters of the *Devotio Moderna*', also discusses tensions. In religious communities it was necessary to strike a balance, but there was nevertheless an inevitable tension between the life of dedicated, yet virtuous hard manual work in a community of female Modern Devout on the one hand, and individual spiritual growth on the other. Bollmann opens her analysis with a discussion of passages describing this tension in the *Vivendi formula*, a manual on the mode of life appropriate to female religious communities, written at the end of her life by Salome Sticken (1369–1449), the first prioress of the female Windesheim convent Diepenveen. Bollmann compares the recommendations in the *Vivendi formula* with the treatment of the same topic in the four surviving collections of exemplary *Vitae* of female religious. Such tensions could occasionally lead to serious inner struggle and a confrontation with superiors, as is the case in the early years of Alijt Bake (1415–1455). Bake later became prioress of the Windesheim convent in Ghent, in her day the second largest city in northern Europe after Paris, but was ultimately deposed by the General Chapter of the Windesheim Congregation because of her mystical inclinations and her provocative written legacy. By discussing the spiritual life and growth of this independent spirit, Bollmann simultaneously paves the way for the first English translation of Alijt Bake's work with accompanying elucidatory material relating to this remarkable personality, which has been announced by John Van Engen.[91]

Much of this religious agency took place in monasteries, convents, or houses of the Brethren and Sisters of the Common Life, and many of the texts which served as manuals or instructions were written or composed either in or for religious communities. But from the twelfth century onwards, urbanization took off.[92] It is here that differences between the twelfth century on the one hand and the fourteenth and fifteenth centuries on the other become apparent: by the fifteenth century one third of the population of the Low Countries lived in an urban setting.[93] In the cities, people with various religious callings — most prominently the friars, but also the semi-religious, such as the Sisters and Brethren of the Common Life — lived among and alongside their lay neighbours. In some cities, about fifteen per cent of the population had chosen a religious life, and in ecclesiastical centres such as Utrecht, seat of the bishop, this could rise to one third of the local population.[94] Recent research reveals that literacy was quite

---

[91] Van Engen, *The Writings of Alijt Bake*.

[92] Cf. as an introduction Lobrichon, *La religion des laïcs*.

[93] Cf. now Blondé and others, eds, *City and Society in the Low Countries, 1100–1600*.

[94] Cf. Marnef and Van Bruaene, 'Civic Religion'.

widespread among the laity, and that the same religious literature was read both in convents and by lay people.[95] Thanks to the new medium of the printing press, the availability of religious texts increased dramatically. In a recent article, for instance, Anna Dlabačová has drawn attention to two texts on the use of the distaff that survive only in early printed editions.[96] The main contention of their authors, who both stand at the very end of the period which can properly be called the Middle Ages, is that the distaff is an indispensable tool in the process of spinning, but that its component parts stand metaphorically for events which occurred during Christ's passion. While performing their daily duties, female spinners could continuously meditate on the passion by focusing on the metaphorical message of the distaff. Dlabačová argues convincingly that at least one of these two texts, but most probably both of them, were read and used for meditative purposes by both religious and lay women. Lay use is beyond doubt for the religious texts discussed by the same author in her contribution to this volume.

Anna Dlabačová's contribution 'Illustrated Incunabula as Material Objects: The Case of the *Devout Hours on the Life and Passion of Jesus Christ*' is the final essay in the volume. She focuses on early products of the printing press, dating from the 1480s to 1490s, which by virtue of their presentation of traditional material have very few distinguishing features in themselves. In her case study she analyses one particular collection of devout texts, compiled by an anonymous author-compiler. For the sake of lay people who did not have the time to pray the para-liturgical hours contained in a book of hours, this anonymous author collected seven short 'hours': penitential psalms and prayers for each day of the week.[97] Dlabačová shows that purchasers of such products nevertheless succeeded in individualizing — perhaps 'personalizing' is a more fitting term here — their acquisition, most often by adding colour to the drawings in their copy in accordance with their individual taste, but also by adding personal notes or supplementary material, or by binding their hours with other material as part of a collection.

The essays in this volume help to refine our knowledge of the processes of inwardness and of the gradually progressing individualization of religious practices in the late Middle Ages, both in lay circles and in religious communities. We hope they will contribute to the advancement of further scholarly research on devotion in the late medieval Low Countries.

---

[95] Cf. most recently Corbellini, ed., *Cultures of Religious Reading*, and Corbellini and others, eds, *Discovering the Riches of the Word*, also Lobrichon, *La religion des laïcs*, esp. pp. 153–205.

[96] Dlabačová, 'The Distaff as an Object for Contemplative Meditation'.

[97] Cf. on the same topic Anna Dlabačová, 'Volgens het boekje. Gerard Leeus Neder-landstalige editie van de *Meditationes de vita et passione Jesu Christi*', *Ons geestelijk erf*, 91 (2020) (in press).

Works Cited

Primary Sources

Abelard, Peter, *Ethics*, ed. and trans. by D. E. Luscombe, Oxford Medieval Texts (Oxford: Clarendon Press, 1971)

Aelredus Rievallensis, *Opera omnia*, I, ed. by A. Hoste, C. H. Talbot, R. Vander Plaetse, Corpus Christianorum Continuatio Mediaevalis, 1 (Turnhout: Brepols, 1971)

Aelred of Rievaulx, *Spiritual Friendship*, trans. by Lawrence C. Braceland, intr. by Marsha L. Dutton (Collegeville: Liturgical Press, 2010)

Aelred de Rievauld, *L'amitié spirituelle*, trans. and comm. by J. Dubois (Bruges: Éditions Charles Beyaent, 1948)

Boethius (Anicius Manlius Seuerinus Boethius patricius), *Liber contra Eutychen et Nestorium*, in Boethius, *The Theological Tractates*, ed. and trans. by H. F. Stewart and E. K. Rand, Loeb Latin Series (London: Heinemann; Cambridge, MA: Harvard University Press, 1918)

Decretales Gregorii Papae IX, in *Corpus Iuris Canonici*, Pars secunda, *Decretalium Collectiones*, ed. by E. Friedberg (Leipzig: Tauchnitz, 1879)

Florent Radewijns, *Petit manuel pour le dévot moderne (Tractatulus devotus)*, ed. by Sr Francis-Joseph Legrand, intr. by Thom Mertens (Turnhout: Brepols, 1999)

Gerardus Magnus, *Conclusa et proposita, non uota,* included in Thomas a Kempis, *Vita Gerardi Magni,* [= *Dialogus noviciorum*, Lib. 2], in *Thomae Hemerken a Kempis canonici regularis ordinis S. Augustini Opera omnia*, 7, ed. by Michael Josephus Pohl (Freiburg im Breisgau: Herder, 1922), pp. 87–107

——, *Leeringhe ende onderscheit vander sonden der symonien* [= *Leeringhe*], ed. by Marinus van den Berg, in *Gerardi Magni Opera omnia*, Pars II.2, *Scripta contra simoniam et proprietarios*, Corpus Christianorum Continuatio Mediaevalis, 235A (Turnhout: Brepols, 2016), pp. 369–76

——, *Scripta contra simoniam et proprietarios* (*Opera omnia*, Pars II.2), ed. by Rijcklof Hofman and Marinus van den Berg, Corpus Christianorum Continuatio Mediaevalis, 235A (Turnhout: Brepols, 2016)

——, *De simonia ad beguttas* [= *Simonia beg.*], ed. by Marinus van den Berg, in *Gerardi Magni Opera omnia*, Pars II.2, *Scripta contra simoniam et proprietarios*, Corpus Christianorum Continuatio Mediaevalis, 235A (Turnhout: Brepols, 2016), pp. 329–66

Gérard Zerbolt de Zutphen, *La montée du coeur. De spiritualibus ascensionibus*, ed. by Sr Francis-Joseph Legrand, intr. by Nikolaus Staubach (Turnhout: Brepols, 2006)

——, *Manuel de la réforme intérieure. Tractatus devotus de reformacione virium anime*, ed. by Sr Francis-Joseph Legrand, intr. by José van Aelst (Turnhout: Brepols, 2001)

Guillelmus de Sancto Theodorico, *Epistula ad fratres de Monte Dei*, ed. by Paul Verdeyen, Corpus Christianorum Continuatio Mediaevalis, 88 (Turnhout: Brepols, 2003)

Thomas Aquinas, II-II = *Secunda secundae summae theologiae*, in *S. Thomae Aquinatis doct. ang. Opera omnia iussu impensaque Leonis XIII p. m. edita*, t. 8–10, cura et studio fratrum eiusdem [praedicatorum] ordinis (Roma: Typographia polyglotta s.c. de propaganda fide, 1895–1899)

Thomas a Kempis, *De imitatione Christi quae dicitur libri.IIII.*, in *Thomae Hemerken a Kempis canonici regularis ordinis S. Augustini Opera omnia*, 2, ed. by Michael Josephus Pohl (Freiburg im Breisgau: Herder, 1904), pp. 3–263

——, *The Imitation of Christ*, trans. by E. M. Blaiklock, Foreword by J. John (London: Hodder & Stoughton, 1979)

——, *Vita Gerardi Magni* [= *Dialogus noviciorum*, Lib. 2], in *Thomae Hemerken a Kempis canonici regularis ordinis S. Augustini Opera omnia*, 7, ed. by Michael Josephus Pohl (Freiburg im Breisgau: Herder, 1922), pp. 33–115

Secondary Sources

Acquoy, Johannes Gerhardus Rijk, *Het klooster te Windesheim en zijn invloed*, uitgeg. door het Provinciaal Utrechtsch Genootschap van Kunsten en Wetenschappen (Utrecht: Gebr. Van der Post, 1875–1880)

Aelst, José van, *Passie voor het lijden. De 'Hundert Betrachtungen und Begehrungen' van Henricus Suso en de oudste drie bewerkingen uit de Nederlanden*, Miscellanea Neerlandica, 33 (Leuven: Peeters, 2005)

——, *Vruchten van de passie. De laatmiddeleeuwse passieliteratuur verkend aan de hand van Suso's 'Honderd artikelen'*, Middeleeuwse studies en bronnen, 129 (Hilversum: Verloren, 2011)

Aertsen, Jan A., 'Einleitung: Die Entdeckung des Individuums', in *Individuum und Individualität im Mittelalter*, ed. by Jan A. Aertsen and Andreas Speer (Berlin: De Gruyter, 1996), pp. ix–xvii

Aertsen, Jan A., and Andreas Speer, eds, *Individuum und Individualität im Mittelalter* (Berlin: De Gruyter, 1996)

Arlinghaus, Franz-Josef, ed., *Forms of Individuality and Literacy in the Medieval and Early Modern Periods* (Turnhout: Brepols, 2015)

——, 'Conceptualising Pre-Modern and Modern Individuality: Some Theoretical Considerations', in *Forms of Individuality and Literacy in the Medieval and Early Modern Periods*, ed. by Franz-Josef Arlinghaus (Turnhout: Brepols, 2015), pp. 1–45

Barret, Sébastien, 'L'individu en action. Quelques réflexions autour des coutumes et statuts clunisiens (XIe–XIIIe siècles)', in *Das Eigene und das Ganze*, ed. by Gert Melville and Markus Schurer (Münster: LIT, 2002), pp. 531–62

Benton, John F., 'Consciousness of Self and Perceptions of Individuality', in *Renaissance and Renewal in the Twelfth Century*, ed. by Robert L. Benson and Giles Constable, with Carol D. Lanham (Oxford: Oxford University Press, 1982), pp. 263–95

Bijsterveld, Arnoud-Jan A., *Laverend tussen kerk en wereld. De pastoors in Noord-Brabant 1400–1570* (Amsterdam: VU Uitgeverij, 1993)

Blondé, Bruno, Boone, Marc, and Anne-Laure van Bruaene, eds, *City and Society in the Low Countries, 1100–1600* (Cambridge: Cambridge University Press, 2018)

Bodemann-Kornhaas, Ulrike, 'De verspreiding en invloed van de *Navolging van Christus*', in *De Moderne Devotie. Spiritualiteit en Cultuur vanaf de late Middeleeuwen*, ed. by Anna Dlabačová and Rijcklof Hofman (Zwolle: Wbooks, 2018), chap. 90, pp. 234–35

Boyle, Leonard, *Pastoral Care, Clerical Education and Canon Law, 1200–1400* (London: Variorum Reprints, 1981)

Brown, Peter R. L., *Augustine of Hippo: A Biography* (New York: Dorset Press, rev. ed., 1986)

Brünhölzl, Franz, *Geschichte der lateinischen Literatur des Mittelalters*, 1, *Von Cassiodor bis zum Ausklang der karolingischen Erneuerung* (München: Fink, 1975)

Brundage, James A., 'The Teaching and Study of Canon Law', in *The History of Medieval Canon Law in the Classical Period, 1140–1234: From Gratian to the Decretals of Pope Gregory IX*, ed. by W. Hartmann, K. Pennington (Washington, DC: The Catholic University of America Press, 2008), chap. 4, pp. 98–120

Bynum, Caroline Walker, 'Did the Twelfth Century Discover the Individual?', in Bynum, Caroline Walker, *Jesus as Mother* (Berkeley: University of California Press, 1982), pp. 82–109

——, 'Introduction: The Religious Revival of the Twelfth and Thirteenth Centuries and the Clericalization of the Church', in Bynum, Caroline Walker, *Jesus as Mother* (Berkeley: University of California Press, 1982), pp. 1–21

——, *Wonderful Blood: Theology and Practice in Late Medieval Northern Germany and Beyond* (Philadelphia: University of Pennsylvania Press, 2007)

——, *Christian Materiality: An Essay on Late Medieval Religion* (New York: Zone Books, 2011)

Cantor, Norman F. *Inventing the Middle Ages* (New York: William Morrow, 1991)

Caspers, Charles, 'Hemel, hel of vagevuur?', in *De Moderne Devotie. Spiritualiteit en Cultuur vanaf de late Middeleeuwen*, ed. by Anna Dlabačová and Rijcklof Hofman (Zwolle: Wbooks, 2018), chap. 25, pp. 80–81

——, 'Wereldliteratuur die kippenvel bezorgt', in *De Moderne Devotie. Spiritualiteit en Cultuur vanaf de late Middeleeuwen*, ed. by Anna Dlabačová and Rijcklof Hofman (Zwolle: Wbooks, 2018), chap. 48, pp. 132–33

Clemens, Theo, and Wim Janse, eds, *The Pastor Bonus: Papers read at the British-Dutch Colloquium at Utrecht, 18–21 September 2002* (Leiden: Brill, 2004)

Constable, Giles, 'The Diversity of Religious Life and Acceptance of Social Pluralism in the Twelfth Century', in *History, Society and the Churches: Essays in Honour of Owen Chadwick*, ed. by D. Beales and G. Best (Cambridge: Cambridge University Press, 1985), pp. 29–47

——, 'The Ideal of the Imitation of Christ', in Giles Constable, *Three Studies in Medieval Religious and Social Thought* (Cambridge: Cambridge University Press, 1995, repr. 1998), pp. 143–248

——, 'The Popularity of Twelfth-Century Spiritual Writers in the Late Middle Ages', in *Renaissance Studies in Honor of Hans Baron*, ed. by Anthony Molho and John A. Tedeschi (Florence: Sansoni, 1971), pp. 5–28, repr. in Giles Constable, *Religious Life and Thought* (London: Variorum Reprints, 1979)

——, 'Twelfth-Century Spirituality and the Late Middle Ages', *Medieval and Renaissance Studies*, 5 (1971), 27–60, repr. in Constable, Giles, *Religious Life and Thought* (London: Variorum Reprints, 1979)

Corbellini, Sabrina, ed., *Cultures of Religious Reading in the Late Middle Ages: Instructing the Soul, Feeding the Spirit, and Awakening the Passion* (Turnhout: Brepols, 2013)

Corbellini, Sabrina, Hoogvliet, Margriet, and Bart Ramakers, eds, *Discovering the Riches of the Word: Religious Reading in Late Medieval and Early Modern Europe* (Leiden: Brill, 2015)

Corradini, Richard, and others, eds, *Ego Trouble: Authors and their Identities in the Early Middle Ages* (Wien: Der Österreichischen Akademie der Wissenschaften, 2010)

Cowdrey, H. E. J., *Pope Gregory VII, 1073–1085* (Oxford: Clarendon Press, 1998)

Dinzelbacher, Peter, *Bernhard von Clairvaux: Leben und Werk des berühmten Zisterziensers* (Darmstadt: Primus, 1998)

——, 'Das erzwungene Individuum. Sündenbewußtsein und Pflichtbeichte', in *Entdeckung des Ich. Die Geschichte der Individualisierung vom Mittelalter bis zur Gegenwart*, ed. by Richard van Dülmen (Köln: Böhlau, 2001), pp. 41–60

Dlabačová, Anna, 'The Distaff as an Object for Contemplative Meditation in Netherlandish Religious Culture', *The Medieval Low Countries*, 5 (2018), pp. 177–209

——, *Literatuur en observantie. De Spieghel der volcomenheit van Hendrik Herp en de dynamiek van laatmiddeleeuwse tekstverspreiding* (Hilversum: Verloren, 2014)

——, 'Volgens het boekje. Gerard Leeus Nederlandstalige editie van de *Meditationes de vita et passione Jesu Christi*', *Ons geestelijk erf*, 91 (2020) (in press)

Dlabačová, Anna, Goudriaan, Koen, and Rijcklof Hofman, 'Wat is de Moderne Devotie', in *De Moderne Devotie. Spiritualiteit en Cultuur vanaf de late Middeleeuwen*, ed. by Anna Dlabačová and Rijcklof Hofman (Zwolle: Wbooks, 2018), chap. 1, pp. 12–15

Dlabačová, Anna, and Rijcklof Hofman, eds, *De Moderne Devotie. Spiritualiteit en Cultuur vanaf de late Middeleeuwen* (Zwolle: Wbooks, 2018)

Engen, Hildo van, *De derde orde van Sint-Franciscus in het middeleeuwse bisdom Utrecht. Een bijdrage tot de institutionele geschiedenis van de Moderne Devotie* (Hilversum: Verloren, 2006)

——, 'Het Kapittel van Utrecht: vereniging van de derde orde', in *De Moderne Devotie. Spiritualiteit en Cultuur vanaf de late Middeleeuwen*, ed. by Anna Dlabačová and Rijcklof Hofman (Zwolle: Wbooks, 2018), chap. 57, pp. 154–56

Engen, Hildo van, and Gerrit Verhoeven, eds, *Monastiek observantisme en Moderne Devotie in de noordelijke Nederlanden* (Hilversum: Verloren, 2008), esp. J. A. Mol, 'Epiloog: de Moderne Devotie en de vernieuwing van het kloosterlandschap in Nederland', pp. 213–31

Engen, John van, *Sisters and Brothers of the Common Life: The Devotio Moderna and the World of the Later Middle Ages* (Philadelphia: University of Pennsylvania Press, 2008)

——, 'Multiple Options: The World of the Fifteenth-Century Church', *Church History*, 77 (2008), 257–84

——, *The Writings of Alijt Bake: Teacher, Preacher, Prioress, and Spiritual Autobiographer* (in press, 2019)

Faix, Gerhard, *Gabriel Biel und die Brüder vom Gemeinsamen Leben. Quellen und Untersuchungen zu Verfassung und Selbstverständnis des Oberdeutschen Generalkapitels* (Tübingen: Mohr Siebeck, 1999)

Geest, Paul van, 'Gabriel Biel: op de bres voor de Moderne Devoten?', in *De Moderne Devotie. Spiritualiteit en Cultuur vanaf de late Middeleeuwen*, ed. by Anna Dlabačová and Rijcklof Hofman (Zwolle: Wbooks, 2018), chap. 72, pp. 190–91

Gleumes, Heinrich, 'Der geistige Einfluß des heiligen Bernhard von Clairvaux auf Thomas van Kempen', *Zeitschchrift für Aszese und Mystik*, 13 (1938), 109–20

Goering, Joseph, 'The Internal Forum and the Literature of Penance and Confession', in *The History of Medieval Canon Law in the Classical Period, 1140–1234: From Gratian to the Decretals of Pope Gregory IX*, ed. by W. Hartmann and K. Pennington (Washington, DC: The Catholic University of America Press, 2008), chap. 12, pp. 379–482

Goudriaan, Koen, 'De derde orde van Sint Franciscus in het bisdom Utrecht. Een voorstudie', *Jaarboek voor Middeleeuwse Geschiedenis*, 1 (1998), 205–60

——, 'Grundmann and the Devotio Moderna', in *Between Orders and Heresy: Rethinking Medieval Religious Movements*, ed. by A. Lester and J. Kolpacoff Dean (in preparation)

Guizot, François, *Histoire de la civilisation en France depuis la chute de l'Empire romain*, 2nd revised edn, 3 vols (Paris: Didier, 1840)

Gurevich, Aaron, *The Origins of European Individualism* (Oxford: Blackwell, 1995)

Hamm, Bernd, *Frömmigkeitstheologie am Anfang des 16. Jahrhunderts. Studien zu Johannes von Paltz und seinem Umkreis* (Tübingen: Mohr, 1982)

Hungerford, Margaret Wolfe ['The Duchess'], *Molly Bawn* (2nd London edition: Smith, Elder & Co., ²1880)

Iogna-Prat, Dominique, 'Introduction générale. La question de l'individu à l'épreuve du Moyen Âge', in *L'individu au Moyen Âge*, ed. by Dominique Iogna-Prat and Brigitte M. Bedos-Rezak (Paris: Aubier, 2005), pp. 7–29

——, 'Sujets de discours. Introduction', in *L'individu au Moyen Âge*, ed. by Dominique Iogna-Prat and Brigitte M. Bedos-Rezak (Paris: Aubier, 2005), pp. 119–21

Iogna-Prat, Dominique, and Brigitte M. Bedos-Rezak, eds, *L'individu au Moyen Âge* (Paris: Aubier, 2005)

Jancke, Gabriele, '"Individuality", Relationships, Words about Oneself: Autobiographical Writing as a Resource (Fifteenth-Sixteenth Centuries) – Konrad Pellikan's Autobiography', in *Forms of Individuality and Literacy in the Medieval and Early Modern Periods*, ed. by Franz-Josef Arlinghaus (Turnhout: Brepols, 2015), pp. 151–75

Jancke, Gabriele, and Claudia Ulbrich, eds, *Von Individuum zur Person. Neue Konzepte im Spannungsfeld von Autobiographietheorie und Selbstzeugnisforschung* (Göttingen: Wallstein, 2005)

Janauschek, Leopold, *Bibliographia Bernardina, qua Sancti Bernardi primi abbatis Claravallensis operum cum omnium tum singulorum editiones ac versiones, vitas et tractatus de eo scriptos quot-quot usque ad finem anni* MDCCCXC *reperire potuit, collegit et adnotavit*, Xenia Bernardina, 4 (Wien: Hölder, 1891)

Kramer, Susan R., and Caroline Walker Bynum, 'Revisiting the Twelfth-Century Individual. The Inner Self and the Christian Community', in *Das Eigene und das Ganze*, ed. by Gert Melville and Markus Schurer (Münster: LIT, 2002), pp. 57–85

Krüggeler, Michael, 'Individualization', *Religion Past & Present: Encyclopedia of Theology and Religion*, 6 (2009), pp. 463–64

Lagarde, Georges de, *La naissance de l'esprit laïque au déclin du Moyen Âge*, Vol. 1: *Bilan du XIII*ᵉ *siècle*; Vol. 3, *Secteur social de la scolastique*; Vol. 4–6, *L'individualisme ockhamiste*; Vol. 4, *Ockham et son temps*; Vol. 5, *Bases de départ*; Vol. 6, *La morale et le droit* (Saint-Paul-Trois-Châteaux: Éditions Beátrice/Paris: Librairie E. Droz, 1934; 1942; 1942; 1946; 1946)

Lane Fox, Robin, *Pagans and Christians* (New York: Knopf, 1986)

Landau, 'Gratian and the *Decretum Gratiani*', in *The History of Medieval Canon Law in the Classical Period, 1140–1234: From Gratian to the Decretals of Pope Gregory IX*, ed. by W. Hartmann and K. Pennington (Washington, DC: The Catholic University of America Press, 2008), chap. 2, pp. 22–54

Legrand, C. R. W., Sr Francis-Joseph, 'Gerard Zerbolt van Zutphen: verdediger van het Gemene Leven', in *De Moderne Devotie. Spiritualiteit en Cultuur vanaf de late Middeleeuwen*, ed. by Anna Dlabačová and Rijcklof Hofman (Zwolle: Wbooks, 2018), chap. 19, pp. 64–65

Lesser, Bertram, *Johannes Busch. Chronist der Devotio Moderna. Werkstruktur, Überlieferung und Rezeption* (Frankfurt am Main: Peter Lang, 2005)

Lim C. R. V. C., P. Florian-Maria, *Die Brüder vom Gemeinsamen Leben im 15. Jahrhundert in Deutschland* (Berlin: LIT, 2017)

——, 'Broeders van het Gemene Leven in Zuid-Duitsland?', in *De Moderne Devotie. Spiritualiteit en Cultuur vanaf de late Middeleeuwen*, ed. by Anna Dlabačová and Rijcklof Hofman (Zwolle: Wbooks, 2018), chap. 71, pp. 188–89

Lobrichon, Guy, *La religion des laïcs en Occident XIᵉ–XVᵉ siècles* (Paris: Hachette, 1994)

Luhmann, Niklas, *Gesellschaftsstruktur und Semantik. Studien zur Wissenssoziologie der modernen Gesellschaft* (Frankfurt am Main: Suhrkamp, 1998)

——, *Soziale Systeme, Grundriss einer allgemeinen Theorie* (Frankfurt am Main: Suhrkamp, 1984), English edition *Social Systems*, trans. by John Bednarz, Jr., with Dirk Baecker (Stanford: Stanford University Press, 1995)

Marnef, Guido, and Anne-Laure van Bruaene, 'Civic Religion: Community, Identity and Religious Transformation', in *City and Society in the Low Countries, 1100–1600* ed. by Bruno Blondé, Marc Boone, and Anne-Laure van Bruaene (Cambridge: Cambridge University Press, 2018), pp. 128–61

McGuire, Brian Patrick, 'Aelred's Attachments: Individual Growth in Community Life', in *Das Eigene und das Ganze*, ed. by Gert Melville and Markus Schurer (Münster: LIT, 2002), pp. 439–66

Melville, Gert, 'Diversa sunt monasteria et diversas habent institutiones. Aspetti delle molteplici forme organizzative dei religiosi nel Medioevo', in *Chiesa e società in Sicilia. I secoli XII–XVI*, ed. by Gaetano Zito (Torino: Società editrice internazionale, 1995), pp. 324–45

——, 'Einleitende Aspekte zur Aporie von Eigenem und Ganzem im mittelalterlichen Relgiosentum', in *Das Eigene und das Ganze*, ed. by Gert Melville and Markus Schurer (Münster: LIT, 2002), pp. xi–xli

Melville, Gert, and Markus Schurer, eds, *Das Eigene und das Ganze* (Münster: LIT, 2002)

Mikkers, Edmundus, 'Sint Bernardus en de Moderne Devotie', *Cîteaux in de Nederlanden. Mededelingen over het Cisterciënzer leven van de 12e tot en met de 18e eeuw*, 4 (1953), 149–86

Mons, Symphorien P. de, 'L'influence spirituelle de S. Bonaventure et l'Imitation de Jésus-Christ', *Études Franciscaines*, 33 (1921), 36–77; 235–55; 344–59; 433–67; 34 (1922), 23–66; 158–94; 35 (1923), 279–300; 356–81

Morris, Colin, *The Discovery of the Individual, 1050–1200* (Toronto: University of Toronto Press in association with the Medieval Academy of America, repr. ed., 1987)

——, *The Papal Monarchy: The Western Church from 1050 to 1250* (Oxford: Oxford University Press, 1989)

Ohlig, Karl-Heinz, 'Christentum, Kirche, Individuum', in *Entdeckung des Ich. Die Geschichte der Individualisierung vom Mittelalter bis zur Gegenwart*, ed. by Richard van Dülmen (Köln: Böhlau, 2001), pp. 11–40

Ohst, Martin, *Pflichtbeichte. Untersuchungen zum Bußwesen im hohen und späten Mittelalter* (Tübingen: Mohr, 1995)

Ool, Peter J. M. A. van, 'Florens Radewijns: de organisator', in *De Moderne Devotie. Spiritualiteit en Cultuur vanaf de late Middeleeuwen*, ed. by Anna Dlabačová and Rijcklof Hofman (Zwolle: Wbooks, 2018), chap. 13, pp. 48–50

Pansters, Krijn, 'Didactiek en dynamiek: 'voortgaan in deugden' in de geschriften van de Moderne devoten', *Trajecta*, 16 (2007), 311–34

——, 'Een invloedrijk boek over de deugden', in *De Moderne Devotie. Spiritualiteit en Cultuur vanaf de late Middeleeuwen*, ed. by Anna Dlabačová and Rijcklof Hofman (Zwolle: Wbooks, 2018), chap. 26, pp. 82–83

Post, Reinier R., *The Modern Devotion: Confrontation with Reformation and Humanism* (Leiden: Brill, 1968)

Reinhold, Gerd, Lamnek, Siegfried, and Helga Recker, *Soziologie-Lexikon* (München: Oldenbourg, ³1997)

Riché, Pierre, *Les écoles et l'enseignement dans l'Occident chrétien de la fin du Ve siècle au milieu du XIe siècle* (Paris: Aubier-Montaigne, 1979)

Roeck, Bernd, *Der Morgen der Welt. Geschichte der Renaissance* (München: C.H. Beck, 2017)

Rolker, Christof, 'Me, Myself and my Name: Naming and Identity in the Late Middle Ages', in *Forms of Individuality and Literacy in the Medieval and Early Modern Periods*, ed. by Franz-Josef Arlinghaus (Turnhout: Brepols, 2015), pp. 233–57

Ruh, Kurt, *Geschichte der abendländischen Mystik*, 1, *Die Grundlegung durch die Kirchenväter und die Mönchstheologie des 12. Jahrhunderts*; 4, *Die niederländische Mystik des 14. bis 16. Jahrhunderts* (München: C.H. Beck, 1990; 1999)

Scheepsma, Wybren F., 'Alijt Bake (1415–1455) und die deutschen Prediger des 14. Jahrhunderts', in *Predigt im Kontext*, ed. by Volker Mertens, Hans-Jochen Schiewer, Regina D. Schiewer, and Wolfram Schneider-Lastin (Berlin: De Gruyter, 2012), pp. 379–97

——, 'Eckhart in den Niederlanden. Rezeption und Überlieferung im vierzehnten Jahrhundert', in *Exemplâr. Festschrift für Kurt Otto Seidel*, ed. by Rüdiger Brandt and Dieter Lau (Frankfurt am Main: Peter Lang, 2008), pp. 9–54

——, 'Das mittelniederländische Nachleben der Erfurter 'Reden' Meister Eckharts', in *Meister Eckharts 'Reden' in ihrem Kontext*, ed. by Dagmar Gottschall and D. Mieth (Stuttgart: Kohlhammer, 2013), pp. 131–51

Siedentop, Larry, *Inventing the Individual: The Origins of Western Liberalism* (Cambridge, MA: The Belknap Press of Harvard University Press, 2017)

Smits, Lieke, 'Wounding, Sealing, and Kissing: Bridal Imagery and the Image of Christ', *Medium Aevum*, 88 (2019), 1–23

Somerville, Robert, (in collaboration with Stephan Kuttner), *Pope Urban II, the "Collectio Britannica", and the Council of Melfi (1089)* (Oxford: Clarendon Press, 1996)

Southern, Richard W., *The Making of the Middle Ages* (London, New York: Hutchinson's University Library, 1953; reprinted London: The Cresset Library, an imprint of Century Hutchinson, 1987)

——, *Western Society and the Church in the Middle Ages* (Harmondsworth: Penguin, 1970)

Spade, Paul V., ed., *The Cambridge Companion to Ockham* (Cambridge: Cambridge University Press, 1999)

Staubach, Nikolaus, 'Zwischen Kloster und Welt? Die Stellung der Brüder vom gemeinsamen Leben in der spätmittelalterlichen Gesellschaft. Mit einem Anhang: Neue Quellen zum Grabow-Konflikt', in *Kirchenreform von unten. Gerhard Zerbolt von Zutphen und die Brüder vom gemeinsamen Leben*, ed. by Nikolaus Staubach (Frankfurt am Main: Peter Lang, 2004), pp. 368–426

Sturlese, Loris, 'Acta Echardiana', in *Meister Eckhart. Die deutschen und lateinischen Werke. Die lateinischen Werke. 5, Acta Echardiana* (Stuttgart: Kohlhammer, 2008), pp. 597–605

Verdeyen, Paul, *Willem van Saint-Thierry en de liefde. Eerste mysticus van de Lage Landen* (Leuven: Davidsfonds, 2001)

Weigand, Rudolf, 'The Development of the *Glossa ordinaria* to Gratian's *Decretum*', in *The History of Medieval Canon Law in the Classical Period, 1140–1234: From Gratian to the Decretals of Pope Gregory IX*, ed. by W. Hartmann and K. Pennington (Washington, DC: The Catholic University of America Press, 2008), chap. 3, pp. 55–97

Weijers, Olga, *A Scholar's Paradise: Teaching and Debating in Medieval Paris* (Turnhout: Brepols, 2015)

'Individualization' and 'Personalization' in Late Medieval Thought

Rob Faesen

Introduction

The development of European culture in the later Middle Ages and the early modern period is often characterized with reference to the concept of 'individualization':

> Present-day sociology considers individualization a central feature of modern societies. It is rooted in the process of social differentiation or, more precisely, in the development of functional subsystems that for the most part have their organizational structures. Individuals no longer necessarily belong to every subsystem. Commonly — though not always — membership in subsystems comes through individual choice. Understood in this sense, individualization is 'structural individualization'. It is one of the conditions of modern life. The development of social individualization has been encouraged by the postulates of freedom that came with the Reformation and the Enlightenment, which initiated and in the long term legitimized the process of religious individualization.[1]

While the origins of this 'individualization' were long situated in the Italian Renaissance, scholars have come to locate the beginning of this process in the

[1] This contribution has been translated by John Arblaster. Krüggeler, 'Individualization', p. 463.

Rob Faesen (rob.faesen@kuleuven.be) is Professor at the KU Leuven (Catholic University of Leuven, Belgium), and holder of the Francis Xavier Chair at the University of Tilburg (The Netherlands). He is also a member of the Ruusbroec Institute at the University of Antwerp (Belgium).

Inwardness, Individualization, and Religious Agency in the Late Medieval Low Countries, ed. by Rijcklof Hofman, Charles Caspers, Peter Nissen, Mathilde van Dijk, and Johan Oosterman, MCS 43 (Turnhout: Brepols, 2020), pp. 35–50   BREPOLS 🚢 PUBLISHERS   10.1484/M.MCS-EB.5.119388

Middle Ages, influenced by Colin Morris' 1972 study *The Discovery of the Individual 1050–1200*.[2] 'Individualization' and 'personalization' are often used as synonyms. However, in this contribution I seek to demonstrate that these two concepts are actually different — indeed, according to some medieval thinkers, they are radically different — and that conflating them potentially leads to confusion and misunderstanding. This conflation simply hinders our access to the content of medieval texts.

In order to make my point, I have chosen three points in time, and for each point, I focus my attention either on a single person, or on an interrelated group of persons, texts or treatises addressing the same topic. Therefore, I will proceed in three steps. First, I will examine the work of a thinker who provided an important contribution to this question, namely William of Saint-Thierry, and his debate with Peter Abelard. Secondly, I will discuss the way in which John of Ruusbroec further reflected on William's position, and finally, I will briefly sketch some later developments in the *Devotio Moderna*. It is thus my intention to present some important examples that suggest that this distinction is significant and useful. The relevant authors, as I will demonstrate, were each relatively influential over the course of the following centuries. Nevertheless, these are merely case studies and it is not my intention to present a comprehensive overview, however warranted such research might be.

Peter Abelard and William of Saint-Thierry

Let us begin in the twelfth century with two leading figures who each made fundamental contributions to the history of thought in the Latin West, namely William of Saint-Thierry (1075–1148) and Peter Abelard (1079–1142). With respect to these figures, I follow the careful analysis of a long article that is almost fifty years old, but which is little known, by Thomas Michael Tomasic.[3]

Roughly halfway through the twelfth century, the brilliant thinker Peter Abelard demanded that the archbishop of Sens organize a public confrontation between himself and Bernard of Clairvaux (1090–1153). This confrontation took place on 2 June 1140 in the cathedral of Sens. Abelard was condemned. This condemnation was the result of a profound difference of opinion to which Bernard lent his rhetorical talent, but it was in fact his friend William of Saint-Thierry whose disagreement with Abelard had initiated the debate. At that time, William was a Cistercian in the small, remote abbey of Signy in the French Ardennes.

---

[2] Morris, *The Discovery of the Individual*.

[3] Tomasic, 'William of Saint-Thierry'.

Some years earlier, in about 1138, two novices had brought Abelard's *Theologia summi boni* to William's attention. It incensed him so much that he immediately interrupted the writing of his *Commentary on the Song of Songs* to write one of the most damning critiques of the Middle Ages, the *Disputatio adversus Petrum Abaelardum*. He then appealed to his friend Bernard to intervene. The result was the condemnation of 1140 in Sens.

Too often, Abelard is incorrectly identified as a progressive intellectual while William is characterized as a conservative anti-intellectual. But their difference of opinion concerns a much more fundamental question. Indeed, Thomas Michael Tomasic's analysis highlights that this question in fact concerns the difference between the 'individual' and the 'person'. Following a biblical maxim, the starting point of William's theological reflections is that the human person is 'created to the image of God' (Genesis 1. 26). According to William of Saint-Thierry, this clearly expresses the intentional and relational structure of the human person. The identity of the human person can only be established by the 'other'. Therefore, when the human person finds himself alone, he experiences himself as a riddle to himself, feels isolated, and thus recognizes the necessity of a reciprocal relationship with the other. The affirmation of one's own identity cannot come out of the 'self', but must be given by an 'other'.

This condition does not only concern inter-human relationships, but holds true *a fortiori* with respect to our relationship with God. William develops this insight on the basis of the metaphors of the Song of Songs: the human person is the bride, and God is the Bridegroom. William has a particular preference for this metaphor because it expresses this intentional and relational structure. A bride can only be a bride if she has a Bridegroom. In the following passage, William beautifully describes the joy of the encounter between God and the human person, when the orientation of the one to the other reaches fulfilment:

Sedebat sponsa penes semetipsam, expectans reditum sponsi [...], orans, plorans, desiderans ut rediret. Et subito videtur sibi primo audire quod non videt, et sentire sensu interiori quod non intelligit, praesentiam divinitatis et dicit: 'Vox dilecti mei'. Hilarescunt sensus omnes animae fidelis, et gestit in occursum, cum [...] videt eum [...] supersalientem omnem intellectum, et transsilientem omnem rationem. Et videns eum venientem ad se, ad suscipiendum eum recolligit semetipsam in se, sentiens appropinquantem et stantem post parietem. Vidensque eum [...] semetipsum offerentem desideranti, incipit ipsa experientia intelligere mysteria divini amoris.

(The Bride was sitting all by herself, awaiting the Bridegroom's return [...]; she prayed, wept and longed for him to return. And suddenly she seemed to hear something before she could discern anything with her eyes; she felt the presence of the divinity with her interior sense, although her intelligence could not grasp it. Then she exclaimed: 'The voice of my Beloved!' All the senses of the faithful soul thrill with joyousness, and she springs forward to meet him. [...] As she sees him coming towards her, she recollects herself interiorly so that she may receive him; she feels that he is drawing near her, that he is standing behind the wall. As she sees him [...] offering himself according to her desire, she begins to understand by experience the mysteries of divine love.)[4]

Evidently, we must understand this in the context of the Christian doctrine of the Trinity, i.e. that God is three Persons. Incidentally, it was precisely while reflecting on the triune God that Tertullian, around the year 213, used the term *persona*.[5] This was a very felicitous choice, as the subsequent centuries affirmed, precisely because this is a fundamentally relational term. The Son is only a Son because he has a Father; the Father is only a Father because he has a Son. Furthermore, it goes to the heart of the Trinitarian mystery to say that the Son is never an isolated individual, but that his 'being' is perpetually *in* the Father. The Son is begotten of the Father, and is thus an other, but he is never separated from the Father — a doctrine expressed in the theme of indwelling (*in sinu Patris*). In the Trinity, a person is never outside the relationship with the other; on the contrary, each of the Persons is eternally oriented to the other.[6] As Tomasic says: in William's work

> we find that the divine essence is not realized in each Person taken in solipsistic aloneness or in a summary collectivity; rather essence means to be in another, that is in the mutuality of 'another in self' and 'self in another'.[7]

Boethius' famous definition — *individua substantia rationalis naturae*[8] — is useless in this respect. Indeed, *natura* is not a defining category because the Incarnation reveals that 'person' transcends the limitation of divergent natures. And *individua* is also besides the question since a person is defined by relationship, not by indivisibility.[9] Thus, relationships are not of the order of accidents. On the

---

[4] Cf. William of Saint-Thierry, *Expositio super Cantica Canticorum*, 162, ed. by Verdeyen, p. 112, trans. by Hart, pp. 135–36.

[5] Cf. Tertullian, *Adversus Praxean*, ed. by Kroymann and Evans, passim.

[6] Cf. William of Saint-Thierry, *Aenigma fidei*, 71, ed. by Verdeyen, p. 173.

[7] Tomasic, 'William of Saint-Thierry', p. 65.

[8] Cf. Boethius, *Liber contra Eutychen et Nestorium*, chap. 3, ed. and trans. by Stewart and Rand, p. 84. 1–5; cf. also above, Hofman, 'Inwardness', section 1.

[9] *In-dividuum* (indivisible) is formed by Cicero, *Academicae Quaestiones*, 2, 17, after the example of Greek *a-tomos*: 'ex illis individuis, unde omnia Democritus gigni affirmat'; quotation in Lewis and Short, *A Latin Dictionary*, s.v.

contrary, relationality is the very 'being' of God. William expresses this in his *Aenigma fidei* by saying that there is 'no divisible distinction' between the Persons in the Trinity, but neither is there 'fusion of the Persons'.[10]

It is to this relationality of the Persons in the Trinity that the relational structure of the human person corresponds. And this evidently has far-reaching consequences for the way in which the human person relates to God: to be a person is to be known and to have the inherent possibility of knowing as one is known[11] — namely in reciprocal relationship.

It irritated William greatly that these reflections were absent from Abelard's thought. Indeed, Abelard has a radically individualist conception of person. To him, 'person' is synonymous with 'individual' (*per-se-una*). From this perspective, relationships are secondary. An individual is, first and foremost, an isolated being, and in a second instance chooses either to develop relationships with others or not. This early form of nominalism would later be elaborated upon further and it would go on to form the foundation of the modern conception of the subject.

Abelard does not conceive of relationality as being the foundational category of existence. Rather, the basic category is an individuality that coincides with itself, and this conception would influence his theological method. Indeed, from this perspective, God is not the one who becomes known by entering into the already present relationship with him, but rather becomes an 'object' of human reflection. This is the core of the opposition between William and Peter Abelard. This twelfth-century discussion is thus intimately connected to our question here: is a human being fundamentally a 'person', i.e. essentially a relationship with another, or fundamentally an 'individual', i.e. essentially an isolated 'self' that only engages in relationships in a secondary degree? William radically chooses the former, whereas Abelard opts for the latter. Both William and Abelard were very influential authors in later decades and centuries. William's influential and widely read works were, however, generally circulated under the name of his friend Bernard of Clairvaux, and William's name was therefore not widely known.

To return briefly to the aforementioned study by Morris, it is clear that the distinction between 'person' and 'individual' is profoundly relevant. To take but one example, in his conclusion, Morris writes:

> When we find that Saint Bernard holds that, in the moment of union with God, a man is not absorbed into the divine being but remains himself, held by love in a

---

[10] 'Nulla separabilis distinctio seu personalis confusio', cf. William of Saint-Thierry, *Aenigma fidei*, 36, ed. by Verdeyen, p. 151.

[11] Tomasic, 'William of Saint-Thierry', p. 44.

sort of equality with God, we are confronted by an individualism as extreme as any which one can imagine.[12]

For Bernard, evidently, the human person does *not* remain an 'individual' in the highest union with God, but his conception of union is rather a question of relationality. The partners in this relationship are fully 'persons', just as the three divine Persons in the unity of the Trinity are interpersonal Persons. As mentioned above, this 'personalism' is absent from Abelard's thought.

The general development of Western culture would follow the line of Abelard and nominalism. As I mentioned, this would lead to the modern conception of the individualist subject. Mystical authors, on the other hand, would completely reject this line of thought,[13] as is evident from the position of figures such as John of Ruusbroec.

John of Ruusbroec

John of Ruusbroec (1293–1381) — who was not widely known in later centuries due to the posthumous censure of Jean Gerson, but who nevertheless had a profound indirect influence,[14] and most especially through the *Devotio Moderna* — developed this issue based on the biblical metaphors of the 'friends' and 'sons' of God. Further developing these metaphors, he sketches the different ways of relating to God. Thus, he also clarifies his position with respect to our question. From Ruusbroec's perspective, the 'friends' of God are those who do take the exterior service of God to heart and keep the commandments, but also experience an interior friendship with God. The 'sons' are those who, within this friendship, are entirely lost in God. Ruusbroec specifies that the 'friends' orient themselves to the Other from within their own self; the 'sons', on the other hand, lose all 'ownness' in their loving self-gift to the Other. The latter is important for our concerns here. Let us examine a short passage from Ruusbroec's discussion:

> Ende hier omme es groot ondersceet tusschen die heimelijcke vriende ende die verborghene sonen gods. Want die vrienden en ghevoelen anders niet in hem dan eenen minlijcken levenden opganc in wisen; ende daer boven ghevoelen die sonen eenen eenvuldighen stervenden overganc in onwisen. Dat inwendighe leven der vriende ons heeren dat es opgaende ufeninghe van minnen, daer si altoes in bliven

[12] Morris, *The Discovery of the Individual*, p. 162.

[13] Cf. Bonaventure, *Comm. Sent.*, I, d. 9, art. 1, q. 2, sol. 3, ed. Quarrachi, p. 183: 'persona est ad alium' (a person is 'unto the other').

[14] Ampe, *Ruusbroec*; Andriessen, 'Ruusbroec's Influence'.

willen met eyghenscape; maer hoemen boven alle oefeninghe gode besit met bloter minnen in ledicheiden, des en gevoelen si niet.

(And therefore there is a big difference between the secret friends and the hidden sons of God. For the friends feel nothing but a loving, living ascending within specific manners, but beyond that the sons feel a simple, dying passing over, beyond all manner. The inner life of the friends of the Lord is an ascending practice of love in which they always want to remain in a self-conscious way, but they never experience how one can possess God beyond all practice with naked love in emptiness.)[15]

In fact, Ruusbroec implies here that there is a difference between an 'individual' and a 'person' — though of course he does not use these terms. Indeed, he refers to two ways of being. The first is founded on the 'self'. From within the individuality of the self, this first way develops a friendship with the Other, with God. Ruusbroec says: 'Ende al ghevoelen si hem selven opgherecht te gode in starken brande van minnen, si behouden eyghenheit haers selfs' (And even if they feel themselves raised up to God in a strong fire of love, they always keep their own self).[16] This might serve as a good description of the human person as an individual.[17] The 'sons', on the other hand, *are* relationship with God at the most fundamental level. They live more in the Other than in themselves, 'lose' themselves and live a 'dying life', which implies: 'die wiselose overganc ende dat rijcke verdolen in die overweselijcke minne, daermen nemmermeer inde noch beghin, wise noch maniere vinden en mach' (the modeless passing over and the rich wandering in supra-essential love, in which no end nor beginning, no reason or no manner can ever be found).[18] While the 'friends' are 'individuals', the 'sons' are 'persons' in the deepest meaning. Evidently, Ruusbroec's divisions are not intended to delineate sociological or ecclesiological distinctions — as he himself explicitly states[19] — but only an existential distinction.

---

[15] Jan van Ruusbroec, *Vanden blinkenden steen*, ed. by Noë, trans. by Rolfson, pp. 136–37. 416–23.

[16] Jan van Ruusbroec, *Vanden blinkenden steen*, ed. by Noë, trans. by Rolfson, pp. 134–37. 401–02.

[17] One might wonder whether Ruusbroec does not imply 'identity' here rather than 'individuality', i.e., the distinct characteristics of an individual. This questions certainly arises when Ruusbroec contrasts the *wisen* ('modes') of the 'friends' with the *wiselose* ('modeless') 'sons'. This is, however, a further development of Ruusbroec's insight that the 'friends' develop their friendship more from within their own 'self', while the 'sons' live more in the Other than in themselves.

[18] Jan van Ruusbroec, *Vanden blinkenden steen*, ed. by Noë, trans. by Rolfson, pp. 136–37. 414–16.

[19] Jan van Ruusbroec, *Vanden blinkenden steen*, ed. by Noë, trans. by Rolfson, pp. 140–41. 449–58.

The central point for Ruusbroec is that the latter is the most profound and most fundamental form of existence. The 'friends' are certainly praiseworthy — 'si behaghen gode ende god behaecht hem weder'(they are pleasing to God as God is pleasing to them)[20] —, but they do not live the most essential and fundamental form of 'being'. Indeed, by using the biblical metaphor of the 'son', Ruusbroec alludes to the Trinity. 'Being Son' is the life of the second person of the Trinity. A person who shares in this condition lives the same life as the second person of the Trinity. With respect to the latter point, Ruusbroec adds:

> Want het en es anders niet dan een eewich uutgaen ons selfs met eenen claren voersiene in eene anderheit daer wij ute ons selven in neyghen alse in zalicheden. Want wij ghevoelen een eewich ute neyghen in eene anderheit dan dat wij selve sijn.

> (For it is nothing but an eternal going out of ourselves with clear foresight, to an otherness towards which we are inclined, out of ourselves, as to our bliss; for we feel an inclination for an otherness, other than we are.)[21]

For Ruusbroec, this is a matter of human existence itself: relationality with the other and 'eternally going out of ourselves into the alterity of the Other' is what constitutes human happiness. The individual resting in self-sufficiency is not the greatest happiness. No, that consists in the encounter with the Other in a personal relationship. Love and encounter bring the person happiness precisely because this is what constitutes the core of his or her existence. Ruusbroec describes the development of this relationship as follows:

> Die mensche die ute deser hoocheit van gode neder ghesent wert inde werelt, hi es vol der waerheit ende rijcke van allen doechden. Ende hi en soeket sijns niet, maer des gheens eere diene ghesonden heeft; ende daer omme es hi gherecht ende warechtich in allen sinen dinghen. Ende hi heeft eenen rijcken melden gront die ghefondeert es inde rijcheit gods; ende daer omme moet hi altoes vloeyen in alle die ghene die sijns behoeven, want die levende fonteyne des heilichs gheests, die es sine rijcheit diemen niet versceppen en mach. Ende hi es een levende willich instrument gods, daer god mede werct wat hi wilt ende hoe hi wilt; ende des en dreecht hi hem niet ane, maer hi gheeft gode die eere. Ende daer omme blijft hi willich ende ghereet al te doene dat god ghebiedt, ende sterc ende ghenendich al te dogene ende te verdraghene dat god op hem ghestaedt. Ende hier omme heeft hi een ghemeyn leven, want hem es scouwen ende werken even ghereet, ende in beyden es hi volcomen.

---

[20] Jan van Ruusbroec, *Vanden blinkenden steen*, ed. by Noë, trans. by Rolfson, pp. 138–39. 427.

[21] Jan van Ruusbroec, *Vanden blinkenden steen*, ed. by Noë, trans. by Rolfson, pp. 154–55. 615–19.

(The person who is sent by God down from these heights, into the world, is full of truth and rich in all virtues. And he seeks nothing for himself, but only the honour of the one who has sent him, and therefore he is just and true in all his actions. And he has a rich, generous foundation which is grounded in the wealth of God, and therefore he must always flow into all those who need him, for the living fountain of the Holy Spirit is his wealth which cannot be exhausted. And he is a living, willing instrument of God with which God does what he wants, the way he wants; and he does not claim this for himself, but gives the honor to God. And therefore he remains willing and ready to do all that God commands, and strong and courageous to suffer and bear all that God allows to befall him. And therefore he has a common life, for contemplation and action come just as readily to him and he is perfect in both.)[22]

This description of the 'common person' spontaneously puts us in mind of its later development. Indeed, in the *Devotio Moderna*, the Brethren of the Common Life took their name from precisely this doctrine.[23]

Later Developments

The development sketched above certainly continued in the following centuries, and particularly in the Modern Devotion. Unfortunately, the *Devotio Moderna* has often been misrepresented as anti-intellectual and ascetical — especially after Johan Huizinga's negative image of the movement in his influential study, *The Waning of the Middle Ages*.[24] This position is wrong. Albert Deblaere has shown that prayer life in this movement became profoundly oriented to interiority and contemplation — 'interior life' almost became a synonym for prayer, as is evident from the works of Jan Mombaer and Thomas a Kempis.

The personal character of interior prayer (*conversari cum Deo, familiaritas cum Deo*) is very striking here. This is evident, for example, from the development of so-called *rapiaria*: personal collections of passages from the scriptures or from the writings of spiritual authors that were particularly meaningful to people in the personal development of their relationship with God.[25] From the perspective

---

[22] Jan van Ruusbroec, *Vanden blinkenden steen*, ed. by Noë, trans. by Rolfson, pp. 180–83. 936–49.

[23] Deblaere, 'Fratelli della vita commune'.

[24] Huizinga, *Herfstij der middeleeuwen*, p. 272. The English translation by F. Hopman, published by Penguin Books (first ed. 1955), has omitted most of these observations.

[25] Cf. Deblaere, 'Preghiera tra le beguine e nella "Devotio moderna"'; van Woerkum, 'Het libellus "Omnes, inquit, artes"'; Mertens, 'Lezen met de pen'.

I have outlined, it is clear that such a *rapiarium* is not an 'individual' document, but a 'personal' one. *Rapiaria* are meant to foster and support the growth of the relationship with God, not to reinforce a person's individuality, as it is highlighted, e.g., in Thomas a Kempis's famous dictum: 'Sic accipe librum in manibus tuis ad legendum, sicut Simeon justus puerum Jesum in ulnas suas ad portandum et osculandum' (Take a book that you intend to read in your hands in the same way as the just Simeon took the child Jesus in his arms, to cherish and to kiss it).[26]

The *Spiritual Exercises* of Ignatius of Loyola are likewise telling examples. These exercises are intended to cultivate an inner attitude of conformity to the will of God in a deeply personal manner. Ignatius was a great champion of the personal relationship between the human person and God, of a personal friendship even. The objective of the *Spiritual Exercises* is that the believer encounters God in a very personal way. Or, as Ignatius states literally: 'El colloquio se haze propriamente hablando así como un amigo habla a otro' (A colloquy, properly so-called, means speaking as one friend speaks with another).[27] From Ignatius's perspective, the direct contact between Creator and creature is crucial, to such an extent in fact that he encourages spiritual directors of the *Exercises* to be as reserved as possible:

> El que da los exercicios, no deve mover al que los rescibe más a pobreza ny a promessa, que a sus contrarios, ny a un estado o modo de vivir, que a otro. Porque, dado que fuera de los exercicios líçita y meritoriamente podamos mover a todas personas, que probabiliter tengan subiecto, para eligir continencia, virginidad, religion y toda manera de perfectión evangélica; tamen en los tales exercicios spirituales más conveniente y mucho mejor es, buscando la divina voluntad, que el mismo Criador y Señor se communique a la su ánima devote abraçándola en su amor y alabança, e disponiéndola por la vía que mejor podrá servirle adelante. De manera que el que los da no se decante ny se incline a la una parte ny a la otra; más estando en medio como un peso, dexe inmediate obrar al Criador con la criatura, y a la criatura con su Criador y Señor.

> (The one giving the Exercises ought not to move the one receiving them more to poverty or any particular promise than to their contraries, nor to one state or way of life more than to another. Outside the Exercises it can indeed be lawful and meritorious for us to move all who seem suitable to choose continence, virginity, religious life and every form of evangelical perfection, but during these Spiritual Exercises it is more opportune and much better that the Creator and

---

[26] Cf. Thomas a Kempis, *Doctrinale iuvenum*, c. 5, ed. by Pohl, Vol. 4, p. 186. 21–24.

[27] Cf. Ignatius of Loyola, *Exercitia Spiritualia*, n° 54, ed. MHSI, pp. 282–84; trans. by Munitiz and Endean, p. 269.

Lord communicate Himself to the faithful soul in search for the will of God, as He inflames her in his love and praise, disposing her towards the way in which she will be better able to serve Him in the future. Hence the giver of the Exercises should not be swayed or show a preference for one side rather than the other, but remaining in the middle like the pointer of a balance, should leave the Creator to work directly with the creature, and the creature with the Creator and Lord.)[28]

It was Ignatius' primary intention for the exercises to concern not the 'individual', but the 'person' in his or her fundamental relationality. If we perceive this as individualistic spirituality, we miss the most essential characteristics of the Ignatian *Exercises*.

Another, and even finer example, is the anonymous text *Den tempel onser sielen* (The Temple of Our Soul), written in 1543 — a deeply erudite text that was largely inspired by the Middle Dutch and Rhineland mystical tradition. The *Tempel* describes mystical experience on the basis of the liturgy and the development of the liturgical year. It is precisely this liturgical interpretative key that highlights that these are not 'individualistic' experiences, but 'personal' ones. Indeed, the liturgy is by definition relational because it both expresses and brings about the relationship between the human person and God:

Om desen inwendigen tempel is den uutwendigen tempel ghemaect; ende al dat daerin is gheordineert, en is anders niet dan te comen tot desen inwendigen tempel, al hetghene datmen daerin begheet, dattet al in desen inwendigen tempel volbracht soude werden. Die uutwendighe tempel is van menscheliken handen ghemaect; mer dese is van die handen der eewiger Wijsheyt ghemaect. Die is van onbevoelike steenen; dese is van redeliken levendigen steenen opten onbewegheliken berch der Godheyt ende op den vasten steen Christum ghefundeert, ende is omgemuert met die hemelsche gheesten, die hi als stercke bewaerders deser mueren heeft gheset. [...] In dien werden die dienaers moede; mer in desen so en werden die hemelsce dienaers niet moede, noch God en hout selver niet op, hem selven hierin te loven. Dat orghel wort in dien van menscheliken consten gheregeert, ende al die instrumentent, mer in desen wort dat orgel der sielen ghestelt van die heylige Drievuldicheyt, daer die hemelsche meester der minnen met die aldersoetste melodie in dat alrebinnenste zijn lof volbrenget.

(The exterior temple is made for the inner temple. Everything that is disposed in it has no purpose other than to come to this inner temple, and all that is celebrated in it has no aim other than to be perfected in this inner temple. The exterior temple is made by human hands; this one by the hands of the eternal Wisdom. That one is of

---

[28] Cf. Ignatius of Loyola, *Exercitia Spiritualia*, n° 15, ed. MHSI, pp. 236–38; trans. by Munitiz and Endean, p. 286.

inert stone; this one of the rational, living stones and founded on the immovable
mountain of the Divinity and the unfaltering rock that is Christ; it is protected
by the heavenly spirits whom he has set as strong guards of these walls. [...] In that
one the servants tire, but in this one the heavenly servants do not, and God himself
does not cease to glorify himself there. The organ in the external temple, and all the
instruments, are played by human art, but in this one the Holy Trinity plays the
organ of the soul, where the heavenly master of love brings about his praise, with
the sweetest melody in the innermost part of the soul.)[29]

The most important aspect of this 'interior temple' — which with an architectonic
metaphor is called *sancta sanctorum* — is precisely the relational 'core' of the
human person:

> Dat sanctuarium in desen tempel is die eenicheyt des geests, daer die heylige
> Drievuldicheyt sonder onderlaet in gheëert ende aenghebeden wort. Dat altaer is dat
> verborghen rijcdom des godliken wesens, daer dat onghebeelde godlike afgront in
> aenghebedet wort, daer dat eewige Woort, dat uuten vaderliken herte eewelic sonder
> onderlaet ende inder tijt gheboren wort, opghedraghen wort, ende opgheoffert, daer
> die innighe siel haer selven ende alle ghenade, die si uut God ontfangen heeft, weder
> opdraget totten love Gods in dat heymlike sancta sanctorum.

> (The sanctuary of this temple is the unity of the spirit where the Holy Trinity
> is honoured and worshipped. The altar is the hidden wealth of the Divine
> Being, where the imageless divine abyss is worshipped. There, the eternal Word,
> continuously born in time out of the paternal heart, is dedicated and offered as a
> sacrifice. There, the inner soul dedicates itself, and all the graces that it has received
> from God, to the praise of God in the hidden *sancta sanctorum*.)[30]

An exceptionally popular work compiled in the same period and milieu as the *Den
tempel onser sielen*, the *Institutiones Taulerianae*,[31] develops the insight that this aspect
is fundamentally oriented to community building. This is discussed extensively
in the thirty-seventh chapter, and is formulated concisely in the twenty-sixth:

[29] *Den tempel onser sielen*, ed. by Ampe, p. 280, trans. by Faesen, p. 329.

[30] *Den tempel onser sielen*, ed. by Ampe, p. 236; trans. by Faesen, p. 327.

[31] The so-called *Institutiones Taulerianae* were initially compiled by the young Peter
Canisius, and under Tauler's name published as *Des erleuchten D. Johannis Tauleri, von eym
waren Evangelischen leben, ...*, and shortly afterwards translated into Latin and circulated by
his friend Laurentius Surius as *D. Ioannis Thauleri, sublimis et illuminati theologi, saluberrimae
ac plane divinae institutiones aut doctrinae*. Little research has been conducted on this work,
presumably because its composition and history are exceptionally complex, cf. Ampe, 'Een
kritisch onderzoek'; Gueullette, *Eckhart en France*. A short summary of the various editions is
provided in Gnädinger, 'Tauler (Jean),' cc. 72–75.

Ad haec alia compendiosior via dari vix potest, quam ut homo perpetua se deo subjectione in profunda mentis humilitate, vera sui extenuatione, syncera ac integra suijpsius abnegatione submittat, sese in fundum suum et aeternam originem suam, Deum Optimum Maximum, in quo ab aeterno extitit, immergat. [...] Plane quotquot tales sunt, nobilissimi sunt huius vitae homines, qui una brevi hora plus Ecclesiae sanctae utilitatis adferunt, quam omnes alii extra hos, etiam pluris annis, in hunc namque animae fundum et Deum ipsum vel una introversio, multis extra hunc etiam magnis exercitiis operibusque praeclarior atque praestantior est. In hoc solo fundo vera deiformis vita at pax secura habetur.

(There is no shorter route for a person to achieve this than through a total abandonment to God, in deep interior humility, in genuine annihilation, and in complete and sincere denial of oneself. He will sink into his ground and eternal origin, namely God, in whom he has existed for all eternity. [...] These are evidently the noblest people on earth. In a very short time, these people are more beneficial to the Holy Church than others are over many years. One single interior movement [into the ground of the soul and into God himself][32] is more valuable and praiseworthy than innumerable great works and exercises without this interiority. Only here can one find genuine divine life and true peace.)[33]

'Personalization' is thus not the same as 'individualization'. We may furthermore raise the question whether this aspect is a new development that is particularly characteristic of the 'modern era'. Members of the *Devotio Moderna* were certainly not of that opinion. For example, the prior of Windesheim Willem Vornken (d. 1455) considered the *Devotio Moderna* to be a revival of the original relational core of the Christian life, which was typical of the faith life in the earliest phase of Christianity, but which had been lost in his own age.[34]

Conclusion

As I hope to have shown on the basis of a number of suggestive case studies, it is most important for our research to make a clear distinction between 'personal' experience, which is the central theme of many of the masterpieces in the spiritual tradition, and a different — but contemporaneous — development, namely that of the 'individualistic' subject. The latter has profoundly different implications. Individualization implies 'subjectivization'. This leads religion to become a

---

[32] Addition in the Latin translation by Laurentius Surius, omitted in the vernacular version.

[33] Cf. for the Latin text the edition in *Thauleri institutiones*, p. 54, which translates the vernacular text in *Von eym waren Evangelischen leben*, pp. 308–09. A similar insight is likewise expressed in *Den tempel onser sielen*, ed. by Ampe, p. 297.

[34] *Epistola de prima institutione monasterii in Windesem*, ed. by Acquoy, pp. 235–55.

subjective matter, which is distinct from and occasionally even in opposition to the community. This is the project of the construction of the autonomous subject in Modernity.

These two developments took place at almost exactly the same time. This 'individualization' certainly became mainstream in the project of Modernity, but 'personalization' also continued to exist, and especially in mystical literature. These are two clearly distinct conceptions of the human person, of the community, and in last analysis of 'being' itself. Clearly highlighting and defining this distinction brings to light a remarkably beautiful, but still mostly hidden undercurrent in late medieval culture.

Works Cited

Primary Sources

Alcuinus, *Epistola* 110, ed. by Ernest Dümmler, in *Monumenta Germaniae Historica, Epistolarum tomus IV, Epistolae Karolini Aevi*, t. 2 (Berlin: Weidmann, 1895), pp. 156–59

Boethius (Anicius Manlius Seuerinus Boethius patricius), *Liber contra Eutychen et Nestorium*, in Boethius, *The Theological Tractates*, ed. and trans. by H. F. Stewart and E. K. Rand, Loeb Latin Series, vol. 74 (London: Heinemann, Cambridge MA: Harvard University Press, 1918)

Bonaventura, *Commentaria in quattuor libros sententiarum magistri Petri Lombardi* in *Doctoris seraphici Bonaventurae ... Opera omnia*, vol. 1, ed. by the Fathers of the Collegium S. Bonaventurae (Quaracchi: Collegium S. Bonaventurae, 1882)

Den tempel onser sielen, door de schrijfster der Evangelische Peerle, ed. by Albert Ampe (Antwerpen: Ruusbroecgenootschap, 1968); trans. by Rob Faesen, 'The Temple of Our Soul: Excerpts', in *Late Medieval Mysticism of the Low Countries*, ed. by Rik Van Nieuwenhove, Robert Faesen and Helen Rolfson (New York: Paulist Press, 2008), pp. 323–48

Epistola de prima institutione monasterii in Windesem, ed. by J. Acquoy, *Het klooster te Windesheim en zijn invloed*, vol. 3 (Utrecht: Van der Post, 1880), pp. 235–55

Ignatius of Loyola, *Exercitia Spiritualia*, Monumenta Historica Societatis Iesu. Monumenta Ignatiana, series secunda, tomus unicus (Madrid: MHSI, 1919); trans. by Joseph Munitiz & Philip Endean (Harmondsworth: Penguin, 1996)

Jan van Ruusbroec, *Vanden blinkenden steen*, ed. by Hilde Noë, trans. by Helen Rolfson, Corpus Christianorum Continuatio Mediaevalis, 110 (Turnhout: Brepols, 1991), pp. 99–183

[Ps. Iohannes Tauler], *Des erleuchten D. Johannis Tauleri, von eym waren Evangelischen leben, Götliche Predig, Leren, Epistolen, Cantilenen, Prophetien...* (Köln: Jaspar von Gennip, 1543)

——, *D. Ioannis Thauleri, sublimis et illuminati theologi, saluberrimae ac plane divinae institutiones aut doctrinae, recens inventae ...* (Köln: Ioannis Quentel, 1548)

Tertullianus, *Adversus Praxean*, ed. by A. Kroymann and E. Evans, Corpus Christianorum Series Latina, 2 (Turnhout: Brepols, 1954), pp. 1159–1205

Thomas a Kempis, *Doctrinale iuvenum*, in *Thomae Hemerken a Kempis canonici regularis ordinis S. Augustini Opera omnia*, 4, ed. by Michael Josephus Pohl (Freiburg im Breisgau: Herder, 1918), pp. 179–99

William of Saint-Thierry, *Aenigma fidei*, ed. by Paul Verdeyen, Corpus Christianorum Continuatio Mediaevalis, 89A (Turnhout: Brepols, 2007)

——, *Expositio super Cantica Canticorum*, ed. by Paul Verdeyen, Corpus Christianorum Continuatio Mediaevalis, 87 (Turnhout: Brepols, 1997); trans. by Columba Hart (Kalamazoo: Cistercian Publications, 1968)

Secondary Sources

Ampe, Albert, 'Een kritisch onderzoek van de "Institutiones Taulerianae"', *Ons Geestelijk Erf*, 40 (1966), 167–240

——, *Ruusbroec: Traditie en werkelijkheid* (Antwerpen: Ruusbroecgenootschap, 1975)

Andriessen, Jos, 'Ruusbroec's Influence until c. 1800', in *A Companion to John of Ruusbroec*, ed. by John Arblaster and Rob Faesen (Leiden: Brill, 2014), pp. 286–302

Deblaere, Albert, 'Fratelli della vita comune', in *Albert Deblaere (1916–1994): Essays on Mystical Literature*, ed. by Rob Faesen (Leuven: Leuven University Press & Peeters, 2004), pp. 149–60

——, 'Preghiera tra le beguine e nella "Devotio moderna"', in *Albert Deblaere (1916–1994): Essays on Mystical Literature*, ed. by Rob Faesen (Leuven: Leuven University Press & Peeters, 2004), pp. 317–30

Gnädinger, Louise, 'Tauler (Jean)', *Dictionnaire de Spiritualité*, 15 (1991), pp. 57–79

Gueullette, Jean-Marie, *Eckhart en France. La lecture des 'Institutions spirituelles' attribuées à Tauler 1548–1699* (Grenoble: Jérôme Million, 2012)

Huizinga, Johan, *Herfsttij der middeleeuwen. Studie over levens- en gedachtenvormen der veertiende en vijftiende eeuw in Frankrijk en de Nederlanden* (Haarlem: Tjeenk Willink, 1928)

Krüggeler, Michael, 'Individualization', *Religion Past & Present: Encyclopedia of Theology and Religion*, 6 (2009), pp. 463–64

Lewis, Charlton T., and Charles Short, *A Latin Dictionary* (Oxford: Clarendon Press, 1962)

Mertens, Thom, 'Lezen met de pen. Ontwikkelingen in het laatmiddeleeuws geestelijk proza', in *De studie van de Middelnederlandse letterkunde. Stand en toekomst*, ed. by Frits van Oostrom and Frank Willaert (Hilversum: Verloren, 1989), pp. 187–200

Morris, Colin, *The Discovery of the Individual, 1050–1200* (New York: Harper & Row, 1973)

Tomasic, Thomas Michael, 'William of Saint-Thierry Against Peter Abaelard: A Dispute on the Meaning of Being a Person', *Analecta Cisterciensia*, 28 (1972), 3–76

Woerkum, M. van, 'Het libellus "Omnes, inquit, artes". Een rapiarium van Florentius Radewijns', *Ons Geestelijk Erf*, 25 (1951), 113–58

GEERT GROTE'S CHOICE OF A RELIGIOUS
LIFESTYLE WITHOUT VOWS

Rijcklof Hofman

Geert Grote (1340–1384), the only child of a wealthy cloth merchant and city alderman in the city of Deventer in the valley of the river IJssel,[1] inherited a considerable fortune on the death of his parents from the plague in 1350, when he was ten years old. After he had finished studying at the chapter school in his native city, he used this money to fund a university education in Paris. There he completed his studies in the arts in 1357, and was duly accorded a *licentia ubique docendi* (11 May 1358).[2] He then shifted his attention to the study of canon law and other subjects,[3] without, however,

---

* I am most grateful to Maria Sherwood Smith, who corrected the style and use of the English language in this essay, and to Anna Dlabačová for her pertinent observations.

[1] Cf. on Grote's youth e.g. Épiney-Burgard, *Gérard Grote*, pp. 13–18; Van Zijl, *Gerard Groote*, pp. 35–42.

[2] Relevant entries from the cartulary of Paris University and its supplement (*Auctarium*) listed in Épiney-Burgard, *Gérard Grote*, pp. 20–23, where the date quoted in fn. 13 from the *Auctarium*, T. 1, c. 207, 47, should of course be MCCCLVII rather than MDCCCLVII.

[3] In quotations from law texts in all of his treatises Grote demonstrates a sound knowledge of canon law, but all his allusions to Roman law are quoted at second hand. This suggests that he never studied in Orléans, where Roman law was taught.

Rijcklof Hofman (Rijcklof.Hofman@TitusBrandsmaInstituut.nl) is the editor of the *Gerardi Magni Opera omnia* at the Titus Brandsma Instituut, Radboud University, Nijmegen (The Netherlands), edited in the *Corpus Christianorum Continuatio Mediaevalis* series.

Inwardness, Individualization, and Religious Agency in the Late Medieval Low Countries, ed. by Rijcklof Hofman, Charles Caspers, Peter Nissen, Mathilde van Dijk, and Johan Oosterman, MCS 43 (Turnhout: Brepols, 2020), pp. 51–66   BREPOLS ⛫ PUBLISHERS   10.1484/M.MCS-EB.5.119389

actively participating in teaching and intellectual research.[4] In the 1370s, he was poised to embark on a stellar career among the higher clergy, after a period of study which had lasted some fifteen years.[5]

In 1374, however, this promising young prelate suddenly veered away from the enticing prospects of a leisurely career in the Church. Instead, he opted for conversion to a life of poverty, spent not in a convent, but in a small part of his own house in Deventer. In this decision he followed the example of earlier individuals with a wealthy background, such as St Francis, who had made a very personal choice to forsake the comfortable lifestyle enjoyed by their peers. His decision can be taken as a case of 'individualization', in that he was completely unconcerned about the effects of his decision on contemporaries,[6] while the manner in which he refashioned his life must itself be interpreted as an example of 'inwardness'. In this essay I hope to unravel the reasons for Grote's choice. And secondly, I wish to investigate how exactly Grote's attitude towards life changed because of his conversion, and what the consequences were, for himself, but also for his era and contemporaries.

Towards a Life of Inwardness and Personal Devotion

The story of Grote's conversion, which probably occurred in 1374, has often been told already, but it is nevertheless possible to put forward a new interpretation of some of the details. For this, I am indebted to an insight from Charles Caspers.[7]

Grote's fifteenth-century biographers all recount in jubilant phraseology how 'the Almighty God had decided to free [this erring sheep] from the fetters of this world'.[8] Most biographers include more or less lengthy digressions on friends

---

[4] This seems an inevitable conclusion, as his name is not included in Weijers, *Le travail intellectuel*.

[5] Much of this has most recently been described in greater length in my introduction to the edition of his treatises against simony and proprietarism, in Hofman and van den Berg, *Gerardi Magni Opera omnia*, Pars II.2, pp. 38–49.

[6] This is emphasized for instance in the *Vita* of Grote in Thomas a Kempis's *Dialogus noviciorum*, chap. 5, ed. by Pohl, pp. 40. 5 – 41. 15; 58. 27 – 59. 17.

[7] This insight was published in its most accomplished form in Caspers, 'The Sacrament of the Eucharist', pp. 239–52.

[8] Paraphrase from Thomas a Kempis, *Vita Gerardi Magni*, p. 36, as translated by Van Zijl, *Gerard Groote*, p. 72; cf. on Grote's conversion and the *Conclusa* most notably Épiney-Burgard, *Gérard Grote*, pp. 36–50; Van Zijl, *Gerard Groote*, pp. 72–116; all extant biographies from Devout circles are discussed in Épiney-Burgard, *Gérard Grote*, pp. 2–10; Van Zijl, *Gerard Groote*, pp. 1–30.

who, before the actual conversion, had talked Grote into a decision to convert; however, strikingly such persuaders are absent in the most reliable biography, which was compiled by Rudolf Dier from Muiden (1384–1459). This Rudolf, born in 1384, the year in which Grote fell victim to the plague, belonged to the second generation of Brethren of the Heer-Florenshuis, the first of a gradually increasing number of houses of the Brethren of the Common Life.[9] Rudolf entered the community in 1402 and lived here for the larger part of his life, serving as procurator or financial officer for twenty-eight years.[10] He wrote his biography of Geert Grote near the end of his life, in 1458 or 1459.

I quote Rudolf's account of Grote's conversion in full, followed by the English translation published by my colleague Charles Caspers:

Sed cum pius Dominus eum decreuit trahere ad amorem sui, incidit ipse in grauem infirmitatem. Lecto decumbens intra Dauentriam in domo Iohannis Grote siue Ockenbroeck, in parochie ecclesie sancti Nicolai in monte, venit ad eum dominus Prior, curatus eiusdem ecclesie, portans secum venerabile Sacramentum corporis Dominici, ammonuitque magistrum Gherardum, vt libros combureret artis magice: nam illos libros habuit & artem ipsam didicit, non tamen artem exercuit, licet a non nullis hoc sibi imputetur. Ammonitus autem noluit consentire domino Priori, quare abiit ab eo, non tradito sibi Sacramento corporis Domini nostri Jesu Christi. Post hoc inspexit Magister Gherardus vrinam propriam, quia doctus erat in medicina, & videbatur sibi quod mors erat in propinquo. Fecit ergo, reuocari dominum Priorem cum venerabili Sacramento; abrenunciavit nigromancie; fecit comburi libros suos illius artis in Brincone; Sacramentum Dominici corporis suscepit; & ad vtilitatem ecclesie sue Dominus prestitit sibi [3] pristinam sanitatem. Sanus effectus mutatus est in virum alterum: nam domino Deo adherens, toto desiderio reliquit ea, que sunt mundi.

(After Geert Grote fell ill and was confined to bed, the priest of the parish church came to visit him, bearing with him the venerable Sacrament of our Lord Jesus Christ. The priest admonished Master Geert to burn his books on the magical arts. This he refused to do, however, whereupon the parish priest departed without having administered the Sacrament. Master Geert then analysed his own urine, he had after all studied medicine, and it became clear to him that his death was imminent. He again called for the parish priest with the venerable Sacrament. He had his books on the magical arts burned and subsequently received the Sacrament

[9] Cf. now very briefly on this house Van Engen, 'Het eerste huis van de broeders', in greater detail Van Engen, *Sisters and Brothers of the Common Life*, esp. pp. 69–83.

[10] That he served as procurator at least five years longer than his own biographer Petrus Horn would have us believe is argued convincingly by Van Engen, 'Managing the Common Life', p. 132.

of the Body of the Lord. It was to the Church's great profit that he then regained his former health and it transpired that he had become another man. From then on, he attached himself only to God and left all worldly things behind.)[11]

In his analysis of this account, Charles Caspers writes that Grote fully understood that death was imminent, and that it was inescapable. It was nothing short of a miracle that he nevertheless recovered his health. Until now, this miraculous recovery has generally been interpreted as the reason for Grote's conversion. Charles Caspers, however, suggests to focus on a different detail in Rudolf Dier's account: the priest's refusal to administer viaticum unless Grote burned books that were undesirable in the eyes of God, the books on the magical arts; Caspers is undoubtedly right in this. Grote was less afraid of dying — which was inevitable anyway — than of appearing before God in an unworthy manner, without having received viaticum and without absolution of his sins. During the probably short period between the priest's two visits, Grote came to the conclusion that the only proper relation between a human being and God was an attitude of utmost sincerity and honesty, that the prime condition for such a relationship was man's full and unconditional commitment to serve God, and that no compromise was possible. From this moment on, he was convinced that any decent person had to organize his life in accordance with ethically sound standards. And it was this conviction which he consistently and conscientiously propagated for the rest of his life, after his miraculous recovery: each individual believer should behave sincerely in his personal relationship with God.

Shortly after his recovery, and therefore also shortly after his conversion, Grote composed a series of guidelines for himself, in which he articulated how he wished to shape the rest of his life. These guidelines bear a title which is in itself programmatic: *Conclusa et proposita, non uota* (Resolutions and intentions, not vows).[12] An English translation of the *Conclusa* was published by John

[11] This translation is published in Caspers, 'The Sacrament of the Eucharist', pp. 246–47. The only edition of the text is the one by Dumbar, *Analecta seu vetera aliquot scripta inedita*, Vol. 1, pp. 1–12, at pp. 2–3.

[12] It must, however, also be noted that this personal document is transmitted only through Thomas a Kempis, who added it as an appendix, directly following on his biography of Grote (edited by Pohl, in Thomas a Kempis, *Vita Gerardi Magni*, pp. 87–107). Thomas tended to heavily polish everything he wrote or transmitted, and we cannot therefore be certain that Grote's original autobiographical document has come down to us in the phraseology in which he wrote or intended it himself. However, Thomas probably did not greatly change the actual content of Grote's resolutions, so the document can nevertheless be taken as a correct reflection of Grote's views on ethically sound behaviour. In this connection, Klausmann, *Consuetudo consuetudine vincitur.*, pp. 29–31, rightly stresses that the *Vita* and the 'authentic' documents

Van Engen in 1988. In an introductory note he characterizes the guidelines as follows: 'The document contains a series of relatively disorganized proposals and resolutions, little more than notes and arguments about the way of life he now proposed to adopt and the reasons for doing so', and following Georgette Épiney-Burgard, the best modern biographer of Grote, he writes: 'This document marked in retrospect the beginnings of the movement called the New Devotion'. He also comments that these 'were resolutions and intentions, privately drawn up and adhered to; they were not religious vows publicly professed. Grote and the brothers and sisters who came after him saw themselves pledged in conscience and before God to uphold their resolutions'.[13] This characterization reveals the *Conclusa* to be an apt starting point for an analysis of the manner in which Grote fleshed out his personalized relationship with God. The resolutions are preserved as an appendix to the *Vita* of Grote compiled by Thomas a Kempis as part of his *Dialogus novitiorum*; given the fairly wide dissemination of this work, the resolutions must have been well known among Grote's followers.[14]

Propagation of Grote's Ideas on Inwardness

After Grote had spent a period of reflection and internalization in the Carthusian monastery of Monnikhuizen near Arnhem, where he lived as a paying guest for a period of three years, he must have decided to propagate his new convictions and ideas among his contemporaries. This is clear from the fact that many of the topics first formulated in the *Conclusa* also occur in more or less the same form in his later writings. This claim can be substantiated with several examples, mostly taken from Grote's treatises on simony, edited in volume II.2 of Grote's *Opera omnia*.[15]

Grote was not original in attaching considerable importance to intention in the mind, which precedes actual implementation in the form of an act. One of the many ideas advanced by the twelfth-century theologian Peter Abelard (1079–1142) was a theory about sin and culpability. Relying in part on theoretical assumptions developed by Anselm of Laon and his school, Abelard maintained that the internal intention to sin is even more culpable than

following it are deliberately set up as complementary texts, supplementing each other. This circumstance supports the probable authenticity of the material transmitted in the *Conclusa*.

[13] Quoted from Van Engen, *Devotio Moderna*, pp. 39–40, cf. Épiney-Burgard, *Gérard Grote*, pp. 46–50, quoted reference p. 49.

[14] Cf. on the dissemination of the *Dialogus noviciorum* Van Dijk, *Prolegomena*, pp. 435–40, and Sudmann, 'Der *Dialogus noviciorum* des Thomas von Kempen', esp. pp. 191–93.

[15] Cf. Hofman and Van den Berg, *Gerardi Magni Opera omnia*, Pars II.2.

the actual performance of an outward act in the form of the sin itself.[16] Also, 'since deliberation or consent, which are internal acts, are the critical factors in incurring culpability for sin, confession of merely internal sins is consistent with a theory which interiorizes sin'.[17] I mention Abelard's views here, as this insistence on intention rather than actual performance of sins, as well as compulsory confession to a priest of only internally conceived willingness to sin, is taken up by Geert Grote in exactly the same manner, in two of his *consilia* or advisory treatises on ecclesiastical positions involving pastoral care being acquired through simony.[18] Grote may well have been aware of Abelard's views because of his long sojourn studying in Paris. Significantly, however, and in accordance with his usual practice, Grote conceals his direct source by referring to a *locus* in canon law (an excerpt from a papal decretal written by Pope Gregory IX (1227–1241))[19] to motivate his standpoint, rather than to Abelard (or Anselm of Laon). Since both *consilia* circulated comparatively widely in north-western Europe in the fifteenth century,[20] we cannot rule out the possibility that the views expressed in them were widely known.

This notion of inwardness can be extended to imply that a religiously oriented lifestyle without taking vows, based on private and personal resolutions, is as valid in the eyes of God as a similar lifestyle on the basis of publicly taken solemn vows. We find this thinking reflected in the *Statutes* of the Meester Geerts House, Grote's inherited paternal home.[21] After his conversion, Grote signed

[16] Peter Abelard, *Ethics*, p. 15, quoted in Kramer and Bynum, 'Revisiting the Twelfth-Century Individual', pp. 65–74, at pp. 68–69. Cf. on Abelard's views also e.g. Gurevich, *The Origins of European Individualism*, pp. 126–45, or Marenbon, *The Philosophy of Peter Abelard*, chaps 11–12.

[17] Quoted from Kramer and Bynum, 'Revisiting the Twelfth-Century Individual', pp. 72–73, with ref. to Abelard, *Ethics*, p. 109.

[18] Geert Grote, *Consilium de cura pastorali* [= *Cura past.*], in *Scripta contra simoniam et proprietarios*, pp. 289–90. 169–88, cf. p. 285. 84–91, and *Consilium de locatione cure pastoralis*, [= *Locat.*], pp. 256–58. 362–424, esp. pp. 258–59. 383–419; summary in English of the relevant passages ibid., pp. 92–93 (*Cura past.*); p. 65–66 (*Locat.*).

[19] *Decretales Gregorii Papae IX*, X 5.3.46 (c. II, 767. 44–50). On Grote's use of sources cf. Hofman and Van den Berg, *Gerardi Magni Opera omnia*, Pars II.2, pp. 49–53.

[20] *Cura past.* survives in eighteen extant manuscript witnesses, *Locat.* in thirteen witnesses, cf. Geert Grote, *Scripta contra simoniam et proprietarios*, 'Introduction', pp. 94–105; 69–80.

[21] In this section, I rephrase the introduction by Marinus van den Berg to the most recent edition of the *Statutes*, in Hofman and Van den Berg, *Gerardi Magni Opera omnia*, Pars II.2, pp. 114–20, and also rely on the analysis of the *Statutes* recently published in Van Dijk, *Salome Sticken*, esp. pp. 69–75 and pp. 307–09.

and sealed a transfer charter, on 21 September 1374, in which he changed the designated purpose of his parental home into a place of residence for 'poor people who wish to serve God'.[22] Almost five years after the original transfer charter the *Statutes* of the house were drawn up, and were formally enacted and signed in a document which is still preserved in the Deventer City Archives, and which is dated 13 July 1379.[23] Grote intended the *Statutes* to function as a solid legal basis for his foundation. Even in the first introductory section of these *Statutes*, Grote immediately emphasizes that the prospective female inhabitants of his charitable foundation must lead a religiously and spiritually oriented life, but that he presupposes at the same time that they will not take formal vows and that they are free to leave the institution at any time.[24] Effectively, he therefore requires of

---

[22] The text of the charter is preserved through Dumbar, *Het kerkelijk en wereltlijk Deventer*, I, p. 548, and also available more easily through the transcript of this in Van Ginneken, *Geert Groote's Levensbeeld*, pp. 162–63. The relevant passage reads as follows: 'dat vor ons int gherichte [...] is ghecomen her Gheryt die Groete [...] ende hevet opghedraghen ende verteghen mit sinen vryen ende goeden wille in onsen hande [...] to behoef der arme luden, die Gode dyenen willen nu ende hier na, tot hoerre rechter huesvestighen, herberghen ende woninghen sijn erve ende hues, daer hi nu inne woent' (that has appeared for us in court Sir Geert Grote [...] and that he has renounced and handed over into our hands, of his own free will and benevolence, his property and house, in which he currently lives himself, for the benefit of poor people who wish to serve God now and hereafter, in order to house them properly and to provide accommodation and residence for them); cf. on the context Van Dijk, *Salome Sticken*, pp. 59–65.

[23] The most recent and first critical edition of the two versions of the *Statutes* side by side is the one prepared by Van den Berg in Hofman and Van den Berg, *Gerardi Magni Opera omnia*, Pars II.2, pp. 309–26.

[24] The statutes of the Meester-Geertshuis have come down to us in two redactions, a long one and a short one. The short redaction *L* is a draft version, probably drawn up by city notaries. This draft version was most probably submitted to Grote for approval by the city aldermen. Grote inserted a great number of amendments and modifications, which are preserved in the longer redaction, which he finally signed and sealed personally three times. This longer version therefore preserves his personal views, and it is this version that is quoted and used here. Cf. for a full analysis of the two versions the *Introduction* by Marinus van den Berg accompanying his edition in Hofman and Van den Berg, *Gerardi Magni Opera omnia*, II.2, pp. 114–18, and Van Dijk, *Salome Sticken*, pp. 69–75. However, in the section relevant here the two versions overlap almost verbatim. In the long, authenticated version of the *Statutes* Grote specifies his intention to allocate the larger part of his personal home to poor and (/or) devout (now only:) women as follows: '1. Int ijrste so ist to weten dat hi huse ende erve mit horen begrijpe niet en ghevet noch ghegeven hevet om ienighen nyen gheesteliken stat of nye religio te maken [...], meer tot eenre herberghen joncvrouwen ende vrouwen onghebunden die van armoden der herberghen noet is, of die der herberghen begheren om God ende om Gode te beet te deennene mit oetmoede ende penitencie in der herberghen mitten armen luden. 2. Ende wat lude dat men daerin setten sal, die soelen onghebunden wesen van mannen, noch mit gheenre oerden, noch van religien.

the inhabitants that their decision is taken in the from of a conscious personal choice. Moreover, their willingness to stay on is to depend on a constant scrutiny of the 'self'.

A similar view is put forward in an unfortunately undatable *consilium* (or piece of legal advice) for a community of beguines. This document is written in Middle Dutch, but it goes by the Latin title *Simonia ad beguttas*.[25] In this treatise, Grote inserts a passage of some eighty lines[26] in which he reflects on what can be defined as 'religious life', in part following St Thomas. According to Grote, all those can be characterized as 'religious' who do their utmost to serve God (in behaviour, intention, and thought), in other words all those who practise the virtue of religion, or better, of religious life. This virtue, which manifests itself as an effort to imitate the image of God in the 'self' as closely as possible, unconditionally, can be practised either in a formal monastic setting, or alone, or in family life, or in a community of kindred brothers or sisters.[27] What matters is that the intention is and remains sincere, and that earthly possessions and preoccupations and one's own free will should be renounced and relinquished, as these distract the individual from the required inwardness. Key words in Grote's Middle Dutch here are *puere*, *reyn*, *geistlik* (pure, clean, spiritual),[28] and somewhat further in

---

Ende oec en sal men van enghenen menschen die daer incoemt, lofnisse noch verbunt eyschen of nemen, want si sullen vri bliven weder uet te waren ende hem to verbeteren waer ende waen sie willen.' (1. First of all it should be known that he does not present and has not presented his property and house in order to establish a new spiritual residence or a new religious order, [...] but in order to provide accommodation for young girls and unmarried women who need accommodation because of poverty, or who wish for accommodation for the sake of God and in order to serve God better with humility and penitence in the house, together with poor people. 2. And whatever persons will be placed in it, they should be independent from men as well as from a religious state or order. Also, one shall not ask or demand a promise or commitment from any person who enters the institution, for they must remain free to leave again and to better themselves wherever and whenever they wish (quoted from Grote, *Statuta domus a magistro Gerardo feminis deuotis destinatae*, pp. 309–10, col. 2, l. 5–36 [second redaction]).

[25] The most recent critical edition, by Marinus van den Berg, is published in Hofman and Van den Berg, *Gerardi Magni Opera omnia*, Pars ii.2, pp. 329–66, cf. the introduction to the text ibid., pp. 121–32. This introduction relies heavily on the analysis and summary in Goudriaan, 'Geert Grote, On Simony to the Beguines' (reprinted in Goudriaan, *Piety in Practice and Print*, pp. 74–95).

[26] Geert Grote, *Simonia beg.*, pp. 360–62. 957–1040. I here follow the summary of contents as formulated in the introduction, ibid., pp. 130–31.

[27] The view that a sincere religious life can be practised by lay people just as well as by professed religious is touched upon briefly in ll. 981–86, but defended in greater detail somewhat further in the text, especially in ll. 1059–72.

[28] These terms are found in an essential passage in Geert Grote, *Simonia beg.*, p. 361.

the text *(ghe-)recht* (sincere; p. 362. 1036, twice), and *purliker unde vulcomeliker mit herten* (more purely and perfectly in their heart; p. 363. 1060–1061). The theoretical exposition ends in an unalloyed eulogy of individual religious agency in a communal setting — in poverty, chastity, and obedience, whether with or without vows — where mutual support during moments of weakness or despair is the norm.[29]

This account in eighty lines is an elaboration of a few considerations which were in essence present already in Grote's *Conclusa*, where we read, in John Van Engen's translation, these opening sentences:

> Ad gloriam et honorem et servitium Dei intendo vitam meam ordinare et ad salutem animae meae. Nullum bonum temporale sive corporis sive honoris seu fortunae seu scientiae praeponere saluti animae meae. Omnem aemulationem Dei sequi.

> (I intend to order my life to the glory, honor and service of God and to the salvation of my soul; to put no temporal good of body, position, fortune or learning ahead of my soul's salvation; and to pursue the imitation of God.)[30]

This view is repeated in similar words later in the same section of the *Conclusa*, including in this observation: 'Necessarium est enim ex corde puro omni Christiano se ipsum deserere et se Deo committere' ([For] every Christian with a pure heart must abandon himself and commit himself instead to God).[31] This is a trite platitude of course, but Grote probably really meant it sincerely. In this sentence, the phrase *ex puro corde* (with a pure heart) is used as an almost

---

994–1000, where Grote states: 'Unde so woert de doecht vulcomen de *religio* heit unde puere, unde ere werke reyner unde hogher als inwendighe devocie unde inwendich ghebet, dancken unde loven Gode. Unde voert andere uutwendighe unde inwendighe dade unde werke der religien werden puerer unde geistliker, na den dat em de menschen, inwendich unde uutwendich, meer unde meer afdoet, unde meer verbrant de tijtlike dinge de verganclic sijn.' (And in this manner the virtue called *religio* becomes perfect and pure, and its effects become purer and more exalted, including inner devotion and inner prayer, gratitude to and praise of God. In addition, other external and internal deeds and works in the name of religion become purer and more spiritual, in accordance with the degree to which man internally and externally withdraws more and more, and increasingly burns those temporal things that are transient).

[29] Cf. on this 'apparent aporia' of concentrating on individual spiritual growth in a communal setting the remarks in the introduction, in the section 'An apparent aporia', and in greater detail Melville, 'Einleitende Aspekte zur Aporie von Eigenem und Ganzem', pp. xviii–xxx.

[30] Geert Grote, *Conclusa et proposita, non uota*, [1–5], p. 87. 29–88, 5, ed. by Pohl, trans. by Van Engen, *Devotio Moderna*, p. 65.

[31] Geert Grote, *Conclusa et proposita, non uota*, [71–73], p. 90. 26–29, ed. by Pohl, trans. by Van Engen *Devotio Moderna*, p. 66.

encoded expression to designate that one's dedication to God should be sincerely meant. The phrase is a scarcely veiled allusion to St Paul's *Epistles to Timothy*, in which it either refers explicitly to sincerity, as in the observation 'The goal of this command is love, which comes from a pure heart and a good conscience and a sincere faith' (I Timothy 1, 5), or where sincerity is implied, in the observation 'pursue righteousness, faith, love and peace, along with those who call on the Lord out of a pure heart' (II Timothy 2, 22). This key expression is paralleled in *Simonia beg.*, and it also occurs in other texts by Grote.

A similar insistence on the importance of an honest and sincere personal relationship between each individual and God can be found earlier in the same treatise. Here the stress is on the reward, which is that God protects those who follow him sincerely. A central theme in the treatise on simony written for beguines is the recommendation that a vacant position in a beguinage should be offered to a poor, but just and sincere candidate, rather than to a rich, but insincere one,[32] a recommendation culminating in this key sentence:

> Aldus ist mit uwer stede of provende, de u God bevolen hevet entlike te ghevene denghenen de se eerliker, duechtliker unde vruchtbarliker besit to Gode, te gane na vermoeden uwer consciencien unde na vermoede der lere Cristi.

> (This is the case with your position or prebend. God has strictly ordained that you place it at the disposal of a candidate who possesses it more honestly, virtuously, and profitably in his eyes, in accordance with the assessment of your conscience and with the inferences following from the teachings of Christ.)[33]

Grote justifies this preference by referring to God's own recommendations for good and honest stewardship (I Corinthians 4, 1–2; Luke 12, 42–48).

The connection between sincerity and a life of poverty is articulated elsewhere in his written legacy also, for instance in a sermon on the occasion of Palm Sunday, in which voluntary poverty is the main theme. The purport of the argument in the sermon is that a life of poverty is the only sure course to draw closer to God, as possessions inevitably distract the attention of the faithful. Neither is there need for worry in a life of poverty, as God protects the poor and provides reward, if not in this life, then in any case in Heaven.[34] The intended audience of this sermon was a monastic community, and it should not be ruled out that Grote delivered

---

[32] The passage occurs in Geert Grote, *Simonia beg*, pp. 335–40. 191–363, cf. the English summary ibid., in Hofman and Van den Berg, *Gerardi Magni Opera omnia*, Pars II.2, pp. 126–27.

[33] Geert Grote, *Simonia beg.*, p. 339. 336–39.

[34] This view is formulated most aptly at the beginning of the first subdivision of the second part of the sermon, in ll. 576–625.

it in person at the Cistercian monastery in Kamp in the Niederrhein region.[35] He therefore did not restrict his missionary work to the laity, but also propagated his ideas among monastic audiences.

In the sermon he develops two main subjects: firstly that Christ's life in poverty must be imitated by his followers (elaborated in ll. 249–568), and secondly that the dignity of poverty deserves to be praised (elaborated in ll. 569–1163). This second part is essentially subdivided into two sections, one discussing the connection between poverty and man's relationship with God (ll. 576–770), and the other dealing with the advantages of poverty in the natural world (ll. 771–1163).[36] It is in the first section of the second part that we find elements illustrating Grote's conviction that man's relationship with God should be built on sincerity.

Grote first touches on what he presents as an almost natural interdependence between a sincere lifestyle and poverty in his *Conclusa*. In several passages in the *Conclusa* he stresses that a personal relationship between man and God can only be achieved once man has distanced himself from distracting factors such as worldly ambition, riches, and possessions. Thus, he writes already fairly early on in the *Conclusa*:

> Item quitquid incipiam, in nomine Domini incipiam et spem meam in illa re ponam in Domino ut ipse ad viam salutis meae me in illa re dirigat. […] Item, quid scio si prosperare in via vel in re est mihi utile, immo saepissime inutile: quia saepe angustia saepe tribulatio utilissima est, ergo supponam me ordinationi Dei. Beatus enim homo qui sperat in Deo.

> (Whatever I begin I should begin in the name of the Lord, and place my hope in him to direct me in all matters in the way of salvation. […] Indeed, how is it useful for me to know if I will prosper on some journey or undertaking? Most often in fact it is not useful, because anxiety and tribulation is often more useful. I will therefore subject myself to the will of God, for blessed is the man who hopes in God.)[37]

---

[35] Cf. Hofman, *Gerardi Magni Opera omnia*, Pars II.2, pp. 211–14.

[36] In this second part Grote's arguments are based on views aired by Seneca, more specifically in his moral *Letters to Lucilius*, a source which is quoted by name in the sermon, but which Grote rarely quotes elsewhere in his oeuvre (cf. on this Hofman, *Gerardi Magni Opera omnia*, Pars II.2, pp. 215–17, with reference to *loci* in the *Sermon*). A reference to Seneca's views on a morally sound lifestyle also occurs in the *Conclusa et proposita, non uota*, on p. 92. 4–8 and Seneca's views on abstinence and frugal eating habits are cited on p. 103. 1–4.

[37] Geert Grote, *Conclusa et proposita, non uota*, p. 90. 8–20, ed. by Pohl, trans. by Van Engen, *Devotio Moderna*, p. 66; the last phrase loosely quotes Psalm 33 (34), 9, *Beatus uir qui sperat in eo*. The unconditional trust that God will protect his faithful, yet poor followers, as expressed

All of this is elaborated in a much more polished and detailed form in the first section of the second part of the sermon. Thus, the view expressed in the *Conclusa* is echoed most pointedly in a central passage in this part of the sermon, where Grote states:

> Est igitur pauper in se et ad Deum tanto constrictior quanto ab hominibus corpore et mente separatior, quantoque in rebus collectior. Ideoque corde et mente purior, quia a concupiscentiis et inquinamentis elongatior. *Nam ubi thesaurus tuus, ibi et cor tuum.* Consequenter et in oratione et desideriis sanctis mundior, quia diuina lumina et angelicas impressiones ydola substantie mundi transformant, ad quas et ad Deum intuendas nuda in rebus mens est et paratior et permanentior et fructuosior. Nam *uerbum* Dei auditum intus uel extra *sollicitudo huius seculi et fallacia diuiciarum suffocant, ut sine fructu efficiatur.*

> (Therefore a poor person is more closely attached to himself and to God to the same extent as he is more separated from his fellow men, both physically and mentally, and as he is more concentrated on what matters. Accordingly he is more sincere in heart and mind, because he is further removed from desire and defilement. *For where your treasure is, there will your heart be also* [Matthew 6, 21]. And consequently he is more pure in prayer and in holy desire, because the distortions of the world's substance twist the divine light and the impact of the angels. After all, a mind unimpaired by odds and ends is both more prepared and more intent and more fruitful to perceive these as well as God. For *the care of this world and the deceitfulness of riches choke the word* of God perceived inwardly and outwardly, and such a person *becometh unfruitful.* [Matthew 13, 22].)[38]

Grote also aired such views on sincere and honest behaviour in connection with the correct fulfilment of pastoral office. In the two most recent modern biographies of Grote, his veneration for the priesthood is discussed in great detail,[39] and I therefore limit myself to a brief mention of this topic. In a *consilium* on pastoral care intended for a young prospective parish priest, Grote points out that a priest mediates between man and God. It is therefore vital that he sets an example and behaves absolutely flawlessly in all circumstances.[40] Grote takes up a

in the first line of the quotation, is fully developed in the sermon, pp. 452–54. 690–738, where this trusting conviction is substantiated with a wealth of biblical quotations.

[38] Geert Grote, *Tract. paup.*, p. 450. 635–44.

[39] Cf. Épiney-Burgard, *Gérard Grote*, pp. 226–230; Van Zijl, *Gerard Groote*, pp. 243–53[-61].

[40] This text usually goes by the title *Epistola* 73, most recently edited in Hofman, *Gerardi Magni Opera omnia*, Pars II.2, pp. 281–305. In it, Grote enumerates the five requirements which in his view a conscientious priest needs to fulfil. In my edition, the requirements are summarized

similar position in the introductory chapter of his sermon against priests who do not observe their vow of chastity, delivered during a diocesan synodal assembly held on 14 August 1383. As I have observed elsewhere concerning his position in this sermon:

> In the third element of the introduction to the written sermon, which he has given the title *Recommendatio presbyterorum bonorum et ordinis presbyteralis* (A recommendation of good priests and of the priestly office), Grote defines what a good priest should be like, and after that he elaborates on the sacredness of the priesthood (*Focar.*, 111–210). For him, priests should do their utmost to be pure and unblemished, as they are the direct contact and the mediators between ordinary people and God, a privileged and holy caste. When they pollute themselves with blemishes of any kind, then this has immediate repercussions on the state and well-being of ordinary believers.[41]

In short, Grote's views on this matter boil down to the opinion that if a priest has even the slightest of moral shortcomings, he can no longer honestly and sincerely mediate between God and his own flock. In this connection, it is important also to note that he deemed himself unworthy of the priesthood.

Concluding Remarks

In conclusion it can be observed that Grote's decision to adopt a religious lifestyle without vows was taken after a grave illness, probably in 1374. This individual choice can be taken as a case of 'individualization', especially since many of his contemporaries responded to Grote's step with undisguised mockery. The manner in which he styled the rest of his life, however, can best be described as a good example of a turn towards inwardness, as carried out by this single individual. There cannot be any doubt that his impact on contemporary society, and the spiritual movement which he set in motion, made him a conspicuous individual, but he was just an individual none the less.

Grote's criticism of contemporaries whose behaviour he deemed immoral was the result of the personal experience he underwent when on the brink of death. At that moment he realized that he had to regain his worthiness in the

---

in ll. 78–83 (p. 285). Three requirements are directly relevant in the context of an upright lifestyle: Grote elaborates on the requirement for sincere and upright intention in ll. 84–91 (p. 285); on an exemplary lifestyle in ll. 238–51 (p. 293); and on the need to surpass one's flock in care and conduct in ll. 252–83 (pp. 293–95).

[41] Quoted from my Introduction to Geert Grote, *Sermo ad clerum Traiectensem de focaristis*, p. 105.

eyes of God, a step symbolized for the world through the burning of his books on the magical arts. His biographers and followers were convinced that his earthly life was prolonged due to this inner revitalization, that God's intention was that he should stimulate others to regain their worthiness in a similar manner; and perhaps we should follow their view. This process of conversion resulted in an extremely strict sense of uprightness, and we should therefore take Grote as a man who stood up for his principles, whatever the consequences, who never turned a blind eye. Grote disseminated these honourable views and convictions among his followers, in oral form as well as in writing. In this way, a personal experience which led to a sincere and upright personal lifestyle became a reform programme for a movement of admirers and followers, which did not lose its vigour for a century and a half.

Works Cited

Primary Sources

Abelard, Peter, *Ethics*, ed. and trans. by D. E. Luscombe, Oxford Medieval Texts (Oxford: Clarendon Press, 1971)

Decretales Gregorii Papae IX, in *Corpus Iuris Canonici*, Pars secunda, *Decretalium Collectiones*, ed. by E. Friedberg (Leipzig: Tauchnitz, 1879)

Geert Grote, *Conclusa et proposita, non uota*, included in Thomas a Kempis, *Vita Gerardi Magni*, in *Thomae Hemerken a Kempis canonici regularis ordinis S. Augustini Opera omnia*, 7, ed. by Michael Josephus Pohl (Freiburg im Breisgau: Herder, 1922), pp. 87–107

——, *Consilium de cura pastorali* [= *Cura past.*], ed. by Rijcklof Hofman, in *Gerardi Magni Opera omnia*, Pars II.2, *Scripta contra simoniam et proprietarios*, Corpus Christianorum Continuatio Mediaevalis, 235A (Turnhout: Brepols, 2016), pp. 279–96

——, *Consilium de locatione cure pastoralis* [= *Locat.*], ed. by Rijcklof Hofman, in *Gerardi Magni Opera omnia*, Pars II.2, *Scripta contra simoniam et proprietarios*, Corpus Christianorum Continuatio Mediaevalis, 235A (Turnhout: Brepols, 2016), pp. 240–72

——, *Sermo ad clerum Traiectensem de focaristis* [= *Focar.*], ed. by Rijcklof Hofman, in *Gerardi Magni Opera omnia*, Pars II.1, *Sermo ad clerum Traiectensem de focaristis – Opera minora contra focaristas*, Corpus Christianorum Continuatio Mediaevalis, 235 (Turnhout: Brepols, 2011)

——, *De simonia ad beguttas* [= *Simonia beg.*], ed. by Marinus van den Berg, in *Gerardi Magni Opera omnia*, Pars II.2, *Scripta contra simoniam et proprietarios*, Corpus Christianorum Continuatio Mediaevalis, 235A (Turnhout: Brepols, 2016), pp. 329–66

——, *Sermo in festo palmarvm de paupertate* [= *Tract. paup.*], ed. by Rijcklof Hofman, in *Gerardi Magni Opera omnia*, Pars II.2, *Scripta contra simoniam et proprietarios*, Corpus Christianorum Continuatio Mediaevalis, 235A (Turnhout: Brepols, 2016), pp. 425–73

——, *Statuta domus a magistro Gerardo feminis deuotis destinatatae*, ed. by Marinus van den Berg, in *Gerardi Magni Opera omnia*, Pars II.2, *Scripta contra simoniam et proprietarios*, Corpus Christianorum Continuatio Mediaevalis, 235A (Turnhout: Brepols, 2016), pp. 309–26

Rudolf Dier de Muiden, *Scriptum de magistro Gherardo Grote, Domino Florencio et multis aliis devotis Fratribus*, ed. by Gerhard Dumbar, *Analecta, seu vetera aliquot scripta inedita*, 1 (Deventer: Johannes van Wyk, 3 vols, 1719–1722), Vol. 1 (1719), pp. 1–113, (*Vita magistri Gherardi Grote* on pp. 1–12)

Thomas a Kempis, *Vita Gerardi Magni* (= *Dialogus noviciorum*, Lib. 2), in *Thomae Hemerken a Kempis canonici regularis ordinis S. Augustini Opera omnia*, 7, ed. by Michael Josephus Pohl (Freiburg im Breisgau: Herder, 1922), pp. 33–115

Secondary Sources

Caspers, Charles, 'The Sacrament of the Eucharist and the Conversion of Geert Grote', in *Diligens scrutator Sacri Eloquii. Beiträge zur Exegese- und Theologiegeschichte des Mittelalters. Festschrift Rainer Berndt*, ed. by Hanns Peter Neuheuser and others (Münster: Aschendorff, 2016), pp. 239–52

Dijk O.Carm., Rudolf Th. M. van, *Prolegomena ad Gerardi Magni Opera omnia. Die Forschungslage des gesamten Schrifttums (mit Ausnahme des Stundenbuches)* (= *Gerardi Magni Opera omnia*, I, 1), Corpus Christianorum Continuatio Mediaevalis, 192 (Turnhout: Brepols, 2003)

——, *Salome Sticken (1369–1449) en de oorsprong van de Moderne Devotie*, met medewerking van Rijcklof Hofman, en met een eerste kritische editie van de *Statuten van het Meester-Geertshuis*, bezorgd door Marinus van den Berg (Hilversum: Verloren, 2015)

Dumbar, Gerhard, *Analecta seu vetera aliquot scripta inedita* (Deventer: Johannes van Wyk, 1719–1722; 3 vols)

——, *Het kerkelijk en wereltlijk Deventer*, I (Deventer: Henrik Willem van Welbergen, 1732)

Engen, John van, *Devotio Moderna: Basic Writings* (New York: Paulist Press, 1988)

——, 'Het eerste huis van de broeders', in *De Moderne Devotie. Spiritualiteit en Cultuur vanaf de late Middeleeuwen*, ed. by Anna Dlabačová and Rijcklof Hofman (Zwolle: Wbooks, 2018), chap. 14, pp. 52–53

——, 'Managing the Common Life: The Brothers at Deventer and the Codex of the Household (The Hague, MS KB 70 H 75)', in *Schriftlichkeit und Lebenspraxis im Mittelalter*, ed. by H. Keller, C. Meier and T. Scharff (München: Wilhelm Fink, 1999), pp. 111–69

——, *Sisters and Brothers of the Common Life: The Devotio Moderna and the World of the Later Middle Ages* (Philadelphia: University of Pennsylvania Press, 2008)

Épiney-Burgard, Georgette, *Gérard Grote (1340–1384) et les débuts de la Dévotion Moderne*, Veröffentlichungen des Instituts für europäische Geschichte Mainz, 54 (Wiesbaden: Franz Steiner, 1970)

Ginneken, Jacques van, *Geert Groote's Levensbeeld naar de oudste gegevens bewerkt*, Verhandelingen der Nederlandsche Akademie van Wetenschappen, Afdeeling Letterkunde, N.R., 47.2 (Amsterdam: North Holland Publishing Company, 1942)

Goudriaan, Koen, 'Geert Grote, On Simony to the Beguines, and Church Reform', in *Die räumliche und geistige Ausstrahlung der Devotio Moderna - zur Dynamik ihres Gedankengutes (Die Devotio Moderna. Sozialer und kultureller Transfer (1350–1580)*, Bd. 2), ed. by I. Kwiatkowski and J. Engelbrecht (Münster: Aschendorff, 2013), pp. 115–40

——, *Piety in Practice and Print: Essays on the Late Medieval Landscape*, ed. by Anna Dlabačová and Ad Tervoort (Hilversum: Verloren, 2016)

Gurevich, Aaron, *The Origins of European Individualism* (Oxford: Blackwell, 1995)

Hofman, Rijcklof, and Marinus van den Berg, eds, *Gerardi Magni Opera omnia*, Pars II.2, *Scripta contra simoniam et proprietarios*, Corpus Christianorum Continuatio Mediaevalis, 235A (Turnhout: Brepols, 2016)

Klausmann, Theo, *Consuetudo consuetudine vincitur. Die Hausordnungen der Brüder vom gemeinsamen Leben im Bildungs- und Sozialisationsprogramm der Devotio Moderna* (Frankfurt: Peter Lang, 2003)

Kramer, Susan R. and Bynum, Caroline Walker, 'Revisiting the Twelfth-Century Individual: The Inner Self and the Christian Community', in *Das Eigene und das Ganze*, ed. by Gert Melville and Markus Schurer (Münster: LIT, 2002), pp. 57–85

Marenbon, John, *The Philosophy of Peter Abelard* (Cambridge: Cambridge University Press, 1997)

Melville, Gert, 'Einleitende Aspekte zur Aporie von Eigenem und Ganzem im mittelalterlichen Relgiosentum', in *Das Eigene und das Ganze*, ed. by Gert Melville and Markus Schurer (Münster: LIT, 2002), pp. xi–xli

Sudmann, Stefan, 'Der *Dialogus noviciorum* des Thomas von Kempen. Textgestalt und Textüberlieferung', in *Aus dem Winkel in die Welt. Die Bücher des Thomas von Kempen und ihre Schicksale*, ed. by Ulrike Bodemann and Nikolaus Staubach (Frankfurt am Main: Peter Lang, 2006), pp. 188–201

Weijers, Olga, *Le travail intellectuel à la Faculté des arts de Paris. Textes et maîtres (ca. 1200–1500)*, t. 3. *Répertoire des noms commençant par G*, Studia Artistarum, 6 (Turnhout: Brepols, 1998)

Zijl, Theodore P. van, *Gerard Groote, Ascetic and Reformer (1340–1384)* (Washington, DC: The Catholic University of America Press, 1963)

'Ama nesciri': Thomas a Kempis's Autobiography Reconstructed from his Works

Margarita Logutova

Thomas as Author

The life of Thomas a Kempis was closely connected with the Modern Devotion. He was related with this movement both spiritually and through next of kin. From the age of twelve onwards, Thomas lived first in Deventer, then near Zwolle among persons who shared the views of his elder brother John, one of the movement's initiators. Thus he could observe from the inside the development of this movement, which he described in two (pseudo-)historical works, his *Dialogus noviciorum* and his *Chronica montis Sanctae Agnetis*.[1] Remarks and observations about his interior feelings and life as an individual, how these related to his 'self', and about his relationship as an individual with his fellow monks are scattered throughout both works as well as in the rest of his written legacy. These self-reflections are the topic of the present contribution.

These works contain several autobiographical passages. In the *Dialogus*, written for the edification of novices, Thomas employed an excellent method,

---

[1] See Thomas a Kempis, *Dialogus*, and *Chronica*. On the trustworthiness of Thomas as a historiographer in the *Dialogus* cf. Hofman, 'Thomas als Biograf'. I am most grateful to Nigel F. Palmer and Rijcklof Hofman for remarks and observations about an earlier version of this essay.

Margarita Logutova (m.logutova@mail.ru) (Ph.D. St Petersburg State University 1997) is a curator of Western manuscripts at the Russian National Library St Petersburg. Her areas of research are the Modern Devotion, Thomas a Kempis, and Medieval German and Latin manuscript prayer books.

Inwardness, Individualization, and Religious Agency in the Late Medieval Low Countries, ed. by Rijcklof Hofman, Charles Caspers, Peter Nissen, Mathilde van Dijk, and Johan Oosterman, MCS 43 (Turnhout: Brepols, 2020), pp. 67–86   BREPOLS 🖤 PUBLISHERS   10.1484/M.MCS-EB.5.119390

devised to provide for the education of young monks by means of examples taken from the lives of eminent men of the movement. Styling himself as a tutor answering a hypothetical novice's questions, Thomas writes of the moral purity of Geert Grote, Gerard Zerbolt, Florens Radewijns, and their successors. He knew all of them personally, except for Grote, and tells of their tireless efforts at self-improvement, about their loyalty to the common cause, and their love of books, in particular the Holy Scriptures — in short, he speaks of all those things which formed the spiritual basis of the *Devotio Moderna*. There are certain passages in which Thomas, the experienced educator, recalls Thomas the teenager, or Thomas the young man, recording how he was a witness of and participant in the events narrated. Such passages reveal the inner world of the author. Being arranged in chronological order, these stories, as well as some passages from the *Chronica*, allow us to reconstruct Thomas's curriculum vitae. The outline of events in this biography is not clear, since in many of the episodes Thomas focuses on the words and actions of the people with whom he happens to have been in communication, rather than on his own thoughts and feelings. Nevertheless, this putative autobiography reflects an intense inner life, first that of a boy, then of an adolescent, and finally of a mature person who was now tutor to the novices.

The foundation of Thomas's self-perception was Christian humility, something he had laid down already in his teenage years, and to which he subordinated his actions, his thoughts and his feelings: 'Ama nesciri' (love to be unknown). These were the words he used to sum up how he saw his own life. He used them three times when writing about true knowledge and true benefits. In *De imitatione Christi*, they are used to conclude a passage in which he states that one should not employ one's knowledge to elevate oneself over other people: 'Quid te vis alicui praeferre, cum plures doctiores te inveniantur, et magis in lege periti? Si vis utiliter aliquid scire et discere: ama nesciri et pro nihilo reputari' (Why do you long to be raised above another man when there are many people more learned than you, and more skilled in law? If you wish to know and learn something of value, love to be unknown and to be reputed as nothing).[2] Thomas's *Parvulum alphabetum monachorum*, which is a catena of brief precepts for a young monk, set out in alphabetical order, opens with the same phrase. Here 'Ama nesciri' becomes the first and the main monastic precept: 'Ama nesciri: et pro nihilo reputari. Hoc tibi salubrius est et utilius: quam laudari ab hominibus' (Love to be unknown and to be reputed as nothing. This is more beneficial and useful to you than hearing yourself praised).[3] In the *Chronica* these words occur in the chapter devoted to the

---

[2] Thomas a Kempis, *De imitatione Christi*, 1. 2. 14, vol. 2, p. 8. 4–8.

[3] Thomas a Kempis, *Parvulum alphabetum*, vol. 3, p. 317. 10–12.

doings of the canons who had first built the monastery: 'Inveniebatur plerumque res gesta exterius: et nesciebatur actor operis. Sic ostensa fuit caritas in opera, et humilitas custodita in corde, iuxta illud: Ama nesciri' (It was often found that some task was finished, though nobody knew who had done it. In this way was charity was shown in deed, and humility of heart was preserved, according to the saying: Love to be unknown).[4]

A central element in all of Thomas's works is that 'omnis actio bona Deo ascribenda est: non vestrae industriae nec potentiae' (every good action is to be attributed to God, not to your own industry or power).[5] Thomas was the most prolific author of the Modern Devotion, and yet his literary productivity did not contradict the commandment of monastic humility. For Thomas, the written text had a self-sufficient value regardless of the identity of the author, and therefore he wrote: 'Non quaeras quis hoc dixerit: sed quid dicatur attende' (Seek not to know who said something, but pay attention to what is said).[6] If a person did not write for the sake of vainglory, then he had the right to express his own thoughts, especially concerning the education of the younger generation in the Christian spirit, and it was above all this educational aspect which Thomas's contemporaries discerned in his works. The anonymous author of a continuation to the *Chronica* observed in his obituary of Brother Thomas Hemerken that he 'composuit varios tractatulos ad aedificationem iuvenum in plano et simplici stilo, sed praegrandes in sententia et operis efficacia' (composed various treatises for the education of young people, and although they are simple and clear in style, their content is grandiose and their impact profound).[7]

As a professional writer, Thomas thought carefully about the things he wrote about, and he presented his works in the form most fitting for the chosen subject. Each of the small number of autobiographical passages in his works is carefully formulated, and accurately inserted into the narrative canvas. In the prologue to the treatise *Soliloquium animae ad Deum*, Thomas describes his creative method in the following way: 'Vario etiam sermonum genere, nunc loquens, nunc disputans, nunc orans, nunc colloquens: nunc in propria persona, nunc in peregrina placido stilo textum praesentem circumflexi' (I have modulated my text according to the different types of discourse, sometimes formulating it in the form of a statement, sometimes as a disputation, a prayer, or an exchange of words, and

---

[4] Thomas a Kempis, *Chronica*, c. 3, vol. 7, p. 348. 11–15, trans. by J. P. Arthur, pp. 15–16.

[5] Thomas a Kempis, *Sermones ad novicios regulares*, Serm. 8, vol. 6, p. 57. 7–8, trans. adapted from that by Scully, p. 47.

[6] Thomas a Kempis, *De imitatione Christi*, 1. 5. 6, vol. 2, p. 12. 27–28.

[7] Ps. Thomas a Kempis, *Chronica*, *Cont.*, vol. 7, p. 466. 26–29.

in a pleasing manner — sometimes in the first person, at other times in the third person).[8] When the genre demanded it, he would formulate his narrative 'from the perspective of another person', as he did when presenting details of his own biography in the *Chronica*. However, Thomas wrote more often 'from his own perspective', believing that a personal, confidential mode of address could convey information more easily to the reader's mind and heart. In the introduction to the history of his monastery, Thomas lists the sources from which he drew information, first of all mentioning the events he had witnessed himself:

> Quorundam fratrum nostrorum pius flagitavit affectus, ut de exordio domus nostrae et de prima fundatione monasterii nostri in monte sanctae Agnetis brevem chronicam texerem. [...] pauca de pluribus collegi, quae vel ipse oculis vidi, vel a senioribus nostris didici, aut ex aliorum scriptis accepi.

> (The pious desire of certain of our brothers hath constrained me to put together a short chronicle concerning the beginning of our house, and the first foundation of our monastery on Mount St Agnes. [...] I have gathered together a few things out of many, and these I have seen with mine own eyes, or have heard from the elders of our house, or else have gathered from the writings of others.)[9]

The Formative Years

For the most part he writes in the first person when he tells about people whom he had known personally and whose memory he wishes to preserve. In these passages, there are no autobiographical details in the usual sense of the word, but they highlight the personality of the author, displaying his gratitude and compassion.

Only once does he provide a list of all the members of his family, when he recounts his taking the habit: 'Anno Domini MCCCCVI [...] investiti sunt duo fratres clerici et unus conversus frater Thomas Hemerken de Kempis civitate, dioececis Coloniensis, germanus fratris Iohannis Kempen primi prioris, quorum pater Iohannes, mater Gertrudis vocabatur' (In the year 1406 [...] two clerics and one professed lay brother received the habit, Brother Thomas Hemerken from the town of Kempen, a blood brother of Brother John a Kempis, the first prior of the monastery. Their father's name was Johan and their mother was called Gertrude).[10]

---

[8] Thomas a Kempis, *Soliloquium animae*, vol. 1, p. 191. 18–22.

[9] Thomas a Kempis, *Chronica*, vol. 7, p. 333. 2–12, trans. by J. P. Arthur, p. xv.

[10] Thomas a Kempis, *Chronica*, vol. 7, pp. 371. 25 – 372. 1.

While Thomas mentions his parents nowhere else, a good many pages of the *Chronica* are devoted to his elder brother, the first prior of the monastery of Mount St Agnes, where Thomas himself spent the larger part of his life. In the chronological sequence of Thomas's life, the first piece of information he provides about himself occurs in the *Dialogus*. When he moved from Kempen to Deventer at the age of twelve, with the intention of joining his elder brother John, he did not find him there anymore — John had already become a regular canon at Windesheim. Thomas writes:

Cum igitur studii causa in annis adulescentiae Daventriam pervenissem: quaesivi iter pergendi ad regulares in Windesem. Ibique inventis fratribus canonicis regularibus cum germano meo, hortatu illius inductus sum adire summae reverentiae virum magistrum Florentium Daventriensis ecclesiae vicarium sacerdotemque devotum; cuius fama dulcissima ad partes superiores iam ascenderat, et in amorem sui mentem meam traxerat: quem frequens turba scholarium in divinis rebus agentem recommendare solebat.

(When I came to Deventer in my adolescent years as a student, I was seeking a route that would lead me on to the regular canons at Windesheim. After I had found the regular canons there, among them my brother, I was induced on their advice to approach Master Florens Radewijns, a highly esteemed man, a vicar of the church in Deventer and a pious priest. His good reputation had reached the uplands already, inspiring me to feel love for him. It often happened that a whole throng of schoolboys would praise his religious zeal.)[11]

At an age when teenagers need thoughtful guidance, Thomas found himself in a town which was unknown to him. Florens Radewijns took care of the boy. He sent him to the capitular school attached to the church of St Lebuin and provided him with books.[12] First Thomas lived in the Heer Florens House, later Radewijns arranged accomodation for him in the home of a certain pious woman.[13] The charisma of Radewijns's personality had a decisive influence on

---

[11] Thomas a Kempis, *Dialogus*, L. 4. 1, vol. 7, pp. 214. 25 – 215. 9.

[12] Cf. Thomas a Kempis, *Dialogus*, L. 4. 1, vol. 7, p. 215. 13–17, 'Veniens ergo ad praesentiam patris reverendi, mox pietate motus; aliquantisper me secum in domo tenuit et ad scholas instituit: datis insuper libris quibus me egere putavit' (When I met this reverend father, he kindly provided accommodation for me in his house for some time. He also sent me to school, after he had provided me with the books which in his view I needed). On schoolboys and their housing, see Van Engen, *Sisters and Brothers of the Common Life*, pp. 144–54.

[13] Cf. Thomas a Kempis, *Dialogus*, L. 4. 1, vol. 7, p. 215. 18–21, 'Demum hospitium cum quadam honesta et devota matrona gratis impetravit: quae mihi et aliis multis clericis saepius benefecit' (In the end, he arranged living quarters for me with an honest and pious landlady, who regularly cared for me and many other clerics).

the spiritual formation of the young man. Many years later, Thomas wrote: 'Etsi omnes tacuerint ego non silebo, sed misericordias domini Florentii in aeternum cantabo' (Even if all the others hold back, I will not keep silent, but I shall forever sing of Master Florens's kindness).[14] Thomas also relates an episode during a church service, describing it with careful choice of words, accurately conveying the depth of his love and respect for his tutor:

> Et ego tunc temporis cum aliis scholaribus chorum visitare consuevi sicut iniunctum mihi fuerat a magistro Iohanne Boëme, qui scholas et chorum strenue regebat. Quotiens ergo dominum meum Florentium in choro stantem vidi, licet ipse non circumspiceret: praesentiam tamen eius ob reverentiam status sui metuens, cavebam aliquid fabulari. Et accidit aliquando ut non longe ab eo starem in choro: vertitque se ad librum nobiscum canendo. Et stans retro me manus suas super umerum meum posuit, stetique fixus vix audens me movere: stupens ad tantae dignationis gratiam.

> (At that time I regularly attended the choir together with the other pupils, following the directions of Master Johannes Boëme, the severe school- and choirmaster. Whenever I saw Master Florens standing in the choir, I took care not to chatter, being fearful of his presence out of respect for his status, even when he did not look around. Once it happened that I stood not far from him in the choir. He turned to the book, intending to sing together with us. Standing behind me he put his hands on my shoulder. I stood very quiet, hardly daring to move, astounded by such a sign of favour.)[15]

In the Heer Florens House there was a cook called John Kessel. He was a wealthy merchant, but he wanted to become a priest, and started to learn Latin. However, after having had various discussions with Radewijns he put his Latin manuals aside and begged Florens to take him into his house as a cook. He was an example of humility and sang prayers while he cooked. Kessel turned his kitchen into a chapel, since he knew that God is everywhere, and with his material fire he managed to kindle a spiritual flame.[16] There was a conversation that the schoolboys had with the 'humble cook' John Kessel that took a firm hold in the memory of the young schoolboy Thomas:

> Quodam die sacro cum quidam clerici venissent ad eum de schola: coepit eis dicere aliqua bona, et inter cetera haec ait. 'Bene invenimus in evangelio scriptum, beati pauperes spiritu: quoniam ipsorum est regnum caelorum, sed nullibi legimus, beati magistri artium'. At illi obstupescentes de novitate verborum: cum multa reverentia

---

[14] Thomas a Kempis, *Dialogus*, L. 3. 16, vol. 7, p. 158. 1–3.

[15] Thomas a Kempis, *Dialogus*, L. 3. 11, p. 142. 6–22.

[16] Cf. Thomas a Kempis, *Dialogus*, L. 4. 12, p. 296. 1–6.

eius verba sumpserunt. Quibus etiam declarabat sententiam suam: quia sine humilitate scientia non prodest sed paupertate spiritus id est humilitate regnum Dei veraciter obtinetur.

(Once on a feastday, when certain clergymen came from the school to see Kessel, he began to speak of certain good matters. And among other things he spoke as follows: 'We find written in the Gospel: "Blessed are the poor in spirit, for theirs is the Kingdom of Heaven" [Matthew 5. 3], but nowhere do we read: "Blessed are the Masters of Arts"'. The clergymen listened to him with great reverence, were struck by the originality of these words. Thereupon he explained his idea: without humility learning is of no use, but with poverty of spirit, that is with humility, it is possible to attain the Kingdom of God.)[17]

There cannot be a school where the pupils do not compete with one another, or where they do not give thought to the future application of their knowledge. It seems likely that the pupils at the school of St Lebuin were prepared for further studies at the university and to go on to achieve higher degrees. Grote and Radewijns, so greatly venerated by Thomas, were Masters of Arts. That is why the idea that one should strive to humble oneself before God and to refrain from the acquisition of university learning seemed so strange to the young schoolboy. Perhaps Kessel's words made him give thought to his future — should he go on to the university or enter a monastery? Thomas often returned to this subject in his later writings, and he discusses the matter in detail in the second, third, and fourth chapters of the first book of the *De imitatione Christi*.

During his last year at school Thomas lived again in the Heer Florens House. The memories of the years spent with Radewijns and his circle are permeated with cordiality and gratitude. He acquired from the brothers much knowledge that would become extremely useful for his future life. He learnt to comprehend religious texts when they were read out, to understand them, to read the Holy Scripture on his own,[18] and to write, that is to copy out manuscripts. For the Brothers of the Common Life the copying of books was a major occupation. These books were produced for their libraries as well as for sale.

In the Heer Florens House Thomas shared a room and a bed with another young man, Arnold of Schoonhoven. While Thomas had many contacts with clerics and copyists, which encouraged him in his desire to work as a professional scribe, the initial impulse to do so nevertheless came from his room mate Arnold. This young man from a wealthy family longed to live in the Heer Florens House

---

[17] Thomas a Kempis, *Dialogus*, L. 4. 12, p. 297. 6–19.

[18] Cf. Thomas a Kempis, *Dialogus*, L. 4. 14, p. 319. 3–6, 'Ibi quippe didici scribere et sacram scripturam legere, et quae ad mores spectant: devotosque tractatus audire'.

and to become a full member of the community. Radewijns told him that he had
to learn to work as a scribe in order to achieve this goal:

> Ita dicens ad eum [Arnoldum]: Discatis bene scribere et tunc spes erit de vobis.
> Quo audito tota diligentia nitebatur scribere addiscere: saepe vadens ad unum
> de bonis scriptoribus et petens ab eo plenius informari. Et dixit mihi. O si scirem
> bene scribere: ut possem citius cum domino Florentio habitare. Spero quod bene
> per gratiam Dei vellem passiones meas vincere: si tantummodo scribere scirem. Et
> cum haec audissem, miratus sum probitatem eius et fervorem: quia omni conamine
> satagebat agere quae dominus Florentius dixerat. Et ego versa vice cogitavi mecum
> dicens. Bene vellem addiscere scribere: si scirem me bene emendare.

> (He told him: 'Learn to write well, and then there will be hope for you'. On hearing
> that, he [Arnold] made every effort to learn to write well, and he constantly visited
> one of the experienced scribes seeking to learn as much from him as possible. And
> he said to me: 'Oh, if only I could master the skill of writing, I would soon be able
> to take up lodgings with Master Florens. I hope that by the grace of God I can
> succeed in suppressing my passions, so that I can learn to write well'. When I heard
> that, I was struck by his modesty and fervour, because he was doing his best to
> follow Master Florens's advice. And I for my part reasoned telling myself: 'I shall
> learn how to write well, if I learn how to improve myself'.)[19]

The last phrase shows how subtly Thomas captured the difference between his
classmate and himself with his usual high degree of introspection. Two boys
shared a room and a bed, both trying to absorb the atmosphere of the Heer
Florens House and zealously focused on piety. One of them, however, saw
getting a place as a scribe as the purpose of his life, considering all the rest, such
as conquering his passions, as a means to achieve it. As for Thomas, the focus was
on the struggle for the perfection of his spiritual nature, which he pursued all
his life. Later, in *De imitatione Christi*, he wrote: 'Et hoc deberet esse negotium
nostrum, vincere videlicet se ipsum; et cotidie se ipso fortiorem fieri: atque in
melius aliquid proficere' (And this must be our endeavour, in a word, to conquer
our desires, day by day to gain mastery of the self and make progress towards
something better).[20]

Regarding the copyists' skill, Thomas asked one of the clerics, the priest
Lubbert Berneri (Lubbert ten Bosch), to make some writing samples for him.
When he gave the finished samples to the young man, Lubbert told Thomas
that with such long and soft fingers he would surely learn to write well. Thomas
adds: 'Et Deo cooperante verum prophetavit' (And with God's help he predicted

---

[19] Thomas a Kempis, *Dialogus*, L. 4. 14, p. 323. 1–19.

[20] Thomas a Kempis, *De imitatione Christi*, 1. 3. 19, vol. 2, p. 10. 3–6, trans. by Blaiklock, p. 7.

rightly).[21] Afterwards scribal work became one of the main occupations in his life. In his last year at school in Deventer, Thomas copied books for sale, as did other pious clerics. He put the money he earned into a collective moneybox, but since that was not enough to pay his keep, Radewijns, who took fatherly responsibility for the boy, paid the rest for him. Thomas responded with the highest measure of love and respect. True friendship in dealing with other people was Radewijns's distinctive feature, arising from his deep and active faith in God. His dealing with this extraordinary man awakened in the young Thomas the desire to follow his example. This as yet quite child-like desire to imitate a senior gradually came to be transformed into a conscious programme of self-discipline, what Thomas called in his memoires 'studying at the school of Christ':

> Tristibus et temptatis hilarem se exhibuit et solaciosum, ut si quis offensus fuisset et turbatus eo viso et secum parum loquente: mox bene pacatus et consolatus ad sua cum gaudio remearet. Hoc saepissime expertus sum in me ipso et sociis meis devotis, qui eius consilio eruditi sumus: et in schola Christi optimis collationibus informati.

> ([Radewijns] displayed good cheer and kindness in dealing with those who suffer sorrow and illicit temptations, such that if someone became annoyed and angry, having seen and spoken with him for a time, they would return home rejoicing. This is something that both I and my devout companions had often experienced ourselves, we who had been moulded by his good counsel and educated in the debating chamber of the school of Christ.)[22]

It may have been from Radewijns that Thomas took over this sincere and convincing tone of confidential conversation, which sprang from the heart and typified the senior, wise, and experienced man in his dealings with younger pupils. This tone is characteristic of all Thomas's works, most notably in the four books of the *De imitatione Christi*.

The whole manner in which the brothers' way of life was organized, their daily conversations with each other and with others, left its mark on his soul. Thomas came to understand that each of them had found himself and his place in this world. Thomas recalled:

> Adiunctus itaque tam devoto viro et fratribus eius cotidie devotam eorum conversationem attendi et inspexi: et gavisus sum ac delectatus in bonis moribus eorum et in verbis gratiae quae de ore humilium procedebant; quia numquam prius tales homines tam devotos et ferventes in caritate Dei et proximi me vidisse

---

[21] Thomas a Kempis, *Dialogus*, L. 4. 4, p. 242. 4–12; on Lubbert cf. also Post, *The Modern Devotion*, esp. pp. 205–06.

[22] Thomas a Kempis, *Dialogus*, L. 3. 15, vol. 7, pp. 153. 30 – 154. 7.

memini, qui inter saeculares viventes de saeculari vita nihil habebant: nihilque de terrenis negotiis curare videbantur.

(Thus, being so close to a pious man [Radewijns] and to his brethren, I watched and carefully followed their devout way of life from day to day, and I found joy and pleasure in their good conduct and in the gracious words which came from their humble lips. For I do not remember ever before having seen people so pious and zealous in their love for God and their neighbour, people who, though living among the laity, had nothing in common with the secular life, and who seemed not to care about worldly things.)[23]

Thomas was very much aware that he owed much to the Brothers of the Common Life, and to Radewijns above all. In the introduction to Master Florens's biography he lists in a short and precise way those steps by which this priest from Deventer guided Thomas himself and his schoolmates. Thomas exclaimed: 'Denique durum et ingratum mihi indigno videtur, si tam dilecti patris virtutes reticerem: qui mihi et multis aliis benefecit in vita et primo traxit ad Dei servitium ac tandem direxit ad monasterii portum' (It seems to me, unworthy as I am, shameless and ungrateful to remain silent about the virtues of such a beloved father, who promoted me and many others in our life, who brought me first of all into the service of God, and then led me to the monastery gates).[24]

Houses of the Common Life served for these young men as a stepping stone to the monastic path. They gave them the opportunity to assess their strengths and to evaluate whether they were able to renounce the world. 'Non enim omnibus datum est, ut omnibus abdicatis saeculo renuntient: et monasticam vitam assumant'. (For it is not given to just anyone to abandon everything, to renounce the world and take up the monastic life),[25] wrote Thomas later. We can suppose that in the Heer Florens House he was trying to test himself out for a monastic life.

The Choice of a Monastic Life

When he left Deventer in 1399, Thomas left behind his childhood and his youth. Reading between the lines of the *Dialogus*, one can perceive the spiritual search of a young man, finally leading him to the gates of the monastery. By the end of his stay in Deventer, Thomas's character was quite fully formed, he was a man in

---

[23] Thomas a Kempis, *Dialogus*, L. 4. 1, vol. 7, pp. 215. 21 – 216. 1.

[24] Thomas a Kempis, *Dialogus*, L. 3, Prol., vol. 7, p. 118. 20–25.

[25] Thomas a Kempis, *De imitatione Christi*, 4 (3). 10. 11, vol. 2, p. 163. 5–7, trans. by Blaiklock, p. 90.

his twenties. He had a clear idea of the purpose of his life and possessed the moral and spiritual means to achieve it.

Thomas joined the regular canons in their monastery at the Agnietenberg near Zwolle in 1399. In that year, a papal indulgence was promulgated by Boniface IX, on the occasion of the consecration of the Chapel of the Virgin:

> Eodem anno [sc. Anno Domini MCCCXCIX] ego Thomas Kempis, scholaris Daventriensis, ex dioecesi Coloniensi natus veni Zwollis pro indulgentiis. Deinde processi laetus ad montem sanctae Agnetis et feci instantiam pro mansione in eodem loco; et fui misericorditer acceptatus.

> (In this same year [1399], I, Thomas of Kempen, a schoolboy in Deventer, but born in the Diocese of Cologne, came to Zwolle to receive indulgences. Then I went on, glad at heart, to Mount St Agnes, and applied to be allowed to abide there, and I was received sympathetically.)[26]

His entry into the monastery marked the beginning of his adult life, some episodes of which he recounts in the *Chronica montis sanctae Agnetis*. The history of Agnietenberg is presented by Thomas in the context of the Modern Devotion and the progressive development of the Chapter of Windesheim. The narrative begins with a story about Geert Grote's relationship with the house of the Brothers of the Common Life in Zwolle. Then Thomas writes about the first prior of the community, his elder brother John:

> Anno Domini MCCCXCIX post pascha frater Iohannes Kempis, conventualis in Windesem, electus est in priorem domus montis sanctae Agnetis. Hic primus prior Deo auxiliante statum domus cum multa et paupere familia annis novem strenue ac religiose gubernavit: et tam in aedificiis, quam in libris et aliis necessariis bona monasterii commendabiliter melioravit. [...] Non est facile dictu, quanto labore et sudore locus ille montuosus et arenosus in ubertatem fructuum et planitiem terrae sit deductus. [...] Tempore vacante lectionibus sacris insistebat: et saepe libris scribendis vel illuminandis operam dedit. Plures libros pro choro et pro armario scribi fecit; et nihilominus quia pauperes adhuc erant, aliquos fratres pro pretio scribere ordinavit, sicut ab antiquis temporibus consuetum erat.

> (In the year 1399, after Easter, John of Kempen, one of the community of Windesheim, was chosen to be prior of the house of Mount St Agnes. By the help of God, he, the first prior, did govern the affairs of the house, with the many poor inmates, zealously and devoutly for nine years. Also he added to the possessions of the monastery in laudable wise, providing buildings and books and other things

---

[26] Thomas a Kempis, *Chronica*, c. 8, vol. 7, p. 368. 11–17, trans. adapted from that by J. P. Arthur, p. 37.

needful. [...] It is not easy to tell with what toil and sweat this mountainous plain was turned into a level plain, and this sandy soil made abundantly fruitful. [...] When he had leisure, he devoted himself to reading holy books, and often worked at writing or illuminating. He caused several books to be written for the choir and the library, and because they were poor he appointed certain brothers to write for sale, as was the custom of old time.)[27]

At the monastery Thomas was accepted first as a donate.[28] In 1406, he took the monastic habit as a regular canon.[29] In his *Chronica* Thomas covered the events of his own life in a very selective way, there are no descriptions of his own thoughts and feelings, which is what makes the *Dialogus noviciorum* so attractive. It was required both by the strict conventions of the genre of monastic chronicles and by the fact that in the monastery Thomas was already an adult person, a senior member of the monastic community. Everything personal was excluded from the narrative. He remains silent on such a significant event for himself as his ordination to the priesthood. The date of his ordination, in 1413 or 1414, is something we learn from his obituary.[30]

In 1425 the election of new priors for Windesheim and Agnietenberg became a most important event for the inhabitants of the monastery of Mount St Agnes. The prior of Agnietenberg, William Vornken, became the new head of Windesheim, and Agnietenberg was headed by its former subprior Dirc of Cleves.[31] The chronicle does not mention that Brother Thomas a Kempis was appointed to the vacant position of subprior. Nevertheless that appointment meant a lot in Thomas's life, for in the Windesheim monasteries subpriors were also tutors for the young monks. His responsibilities as tutor allowed Thomas to pass on his knowledge and his experience. Thomas resigned his role as subprior in 1431, since he had been summoned to care for his sick brother John, who had been appointed as rector and confessor to the sisters in the newly founded

---

[27] Thomas a Kempis, *Chronica*, c. 8, vol. 7, pp. 365. 25–366. 6; 366. 23–26; 367. 25–368. 8, trans. adapted from that by J. P. Arthur, pp. 35–37.

[28] Cf. Thüss, 'De geschiedenis van het klooster op de Agnietenberg', p. 93.

[29] Cf. Thomas a Kempis, *Chronica*, c. 10, vol. 7, p. 371, 'Anno Domini MCCCCVI in die Sacramenti, quae tunc fuit in profesto Barnabae, investiti sunt duo fratres clerici et unus conversus, frater Thomas Hemerken de Kempis civitate' (In the year of our Lord 1406, on the feast of Corpus Christi, which fell in that year on the day before the feast of St Barnabas, two brothers that were clerks, and one that was a professed lay brother, were invested. The latter one was Thomas Hemerken from the town of Kempen).

[30] Thomas a Kempis, *Chronica, Cont.*, vol. 7, p. 466. 15–16.

[31] Thomas a Kempis, *Chronica*, c. 20, vol. 7, p. 397. 5–20.

monastery of Bethania near Arnhem. During John's illness Thomas helped him with his pastoral duties, and he was present at his bedside during his last hours. In the obituary devoted to his brother, Thomas wrote:

> Anno Domini MCCCCXXXII [...] obiit frater Iohannes Kempis, primus rector et confessor sanctimonialium in Bethania prope Arnhem, anno aetatis suae sexagesimo septimo. Hic in diversis locis et novis domibus rector aut prior fuit. [...] Tandem in Bethania quae interpretatur domus oboedientiae, vitam in oboedientia et bona senectute feliciter finivit sepultus intra clausuram post horam vesperarum, ubi tunc praesens fui et oculos eius clausi. Nam per visitatores pro socio sibi deputatus fui et uno anno et duobus mensibus secum steti.

> (In 1432 [...] died Brother John of Kempen, the first rector and confessor to the sisters at Arnhem, being in the sixty-seventh year of his age. He had been rector or prior in diverse places and houses that were newly founded. [...] At last he ended his life happily after Vespers in a good old age and in obedience in Bethany, which is by interpretation 'the House of Obedience', and he was buried within the cloister. I was with him and I closed his eyes, for I had been sent by the visitators to keep him company, and I dwelled with him for a year and two months.)[32]

His brother John and Florens Radewijns were the people closest to Thomas. Both occupy a significant place in the pages of his works, yet the narrative style differs in the discussion of these two persons. The passages devoted to his brother sound quite reserved when compared to the expression of affection and gratitude shown towards Master Florens. Perhaps Thomas was trying not to show his love and affection for his brother. He was twelve years old when he came to Windesheim, and there he found canons, 'among them his brother'.[33] When he had completed his studies, Radewijns sent him to his elder brother at Mount St Agnes. There Thomas took his vows and assumed the monastic habit at the time of his brother's priorate. He was close to his brother when John needed his assistance at the end of his life. When he died, it was Thomas who closed the dead man's eyes. In the obituary Thomas particularly emphasizes that John had been sent again and again by the General Chapter to newly founded men's and women's convents, where his diligence and organizational skills had swiftly helped to establish the normal rhythm of monastic life.

From 1432 until 1448 Thomas served as procurator, the official in charge of the common economic affairs of the monastery,[34] but in the *Chronica* there is

---

[32] Thomas a Kempis, *Chronica*, c. 24, vol. 7, pp. 407. 12 – 408. 8, trans. adapted from that by J. P. Arthur, p. 82.

[33] Thomas a Kempis, *Dialogus*, L. 4. 1, vol. 7, p. 214. 29.

[34] Thüss, 'De geschiedenis van het klooster op de Agnietenberg', p. 111.

not a single word about this. In 1448 Thomas was appointed to the vacant place of subprior. Having passed over his first appointment in silence, he describes the second one in some detail. This last story that he tells about himself in the *Chronicle* is marked by extreme humility:

> [F]acto brevi scrutinio electus est et nominatus frater Thomas Kempis, unus de senioribus LXVII. annorum: qui praeteritis temporibus huic officio deputatus fuit. Et quamvis se ineptum sciret et excusaret, tamen oboedientia iubente humiliter se subiecit consilio fratrum, non recusans laborem propter eos subire amore Iesu Christi, petens intime sociorum ac fratrum suorum orationes, plus gratiae Dei quam sibi confidens.

> (Brother Thomas of Kempen was nominated and elected after a brief scrutiny. He was one of the elders, being sixty-seven years of age, and in past times had been appointed to this office, and albeit he knew himself to be insufficient and would have made excuse, yet he did submit himself humbly to the assembled Brothers, for his obedience bade him to do so; neither did he refuse to undergo toil on their behalf for the love of Christ Jesus, but earnestly besought the prayers of his comrades and Brothers, for he trusted rather in the grace of God than in himself.)[35]

In the treatise *Soliloquium animae* there is one more autobiographical passage. It is fundamentally different from all those we find in the *Dialogus noviciorum* and in the *Chronica* in that here Thomas slightly lifts the veil on his creative process. The prologue to this work begins with reference to a book dear to his heart — his *rapiarium*. *Rapiaria* or florilegia were widespread in the later Middle Ages. They were booklets containing collections of excerpts taken from Holy Scripture, from the writings of the Church Fathers, and from other pious books. In the circles of the Modern Devotion *rapiaria* numbered among the main instruments of personal self-perfection, and such a collection was an obligatory accessory for each Brother of the Common Life and for every literate inhabitant of the Windesheim convents.[36] The selection of texts and extracts assembled in a book of some kind, and their constant rereading constituted a process of assiduous self-reflection. Such books, with favourite citations of personal significance, were always kept close at hand and provided spiritual food for a believer, face to face with his conscience and with God. Thomas dedicated heartfelt lines to his *rapiarium*:

> Consolationis gratia aliquas sententias devotas in unum coacervavi libellum: quem meo pectori carius committere volui; et quasi quoddam delectabile pratum

---

[35] Thomas a Kempis, *Chronica*, c. 26, vol. 7, pp. 423. 22–424. 2, trans. adapted from that by J. P. Arthur, pp. 98–99.

[36] Cf. Mertens, 'Lezen met de pen'.

variis arboribus consitum: pulchrisque venustum floribus habere disposui; ubi ad legendum speculandumque optabiles materias tempore necessitudinis pro fovendis animis taedio vel maerore obtectis quandoque introirem. Ut autem lucide et prompte invenirem sub qua arbore requiescerem, vel qui ad legendum flos gratior esset: singula capitulorum loca rubricatis titulis praefulgere feci. Vario etiam sermonum genere, nunc loquens, nunc disputans, nunc orans, nunc colloquens: nunc in propria persona, nunc in peregrina, placido stilo textum praesentem circumflexi.

(For my consolation, I gathered together some pious sentences that I was rather eager to commit to memory into a single booklet. And I arranged them as in a delightful meadow planted out with all sorts of trees and lovely flowers, where I could come any time, in moments of need, to read and contemplate whatever I might desire to uplift the spirit when worn down by weariness or sorrow. And in order to find readily and quickly the tree under which I could rest or the flower that might be more appealing, I took care to mark some passages with red headings so they would stand out. I have modulated my text according to the different types of discourse, sometimes formulating it in the form of a statement, sometimes as a disputation, a prayer, or an exchange of words, and in a pleasing manner — sometimes in the first person, at other times in the third person.)[37]

The last two sentences give us grounds to suppose that his *rapiarium* served Thomas not only for spiritual consolation. His booklet of extracts provided him with the themes necessary for his creative work and with precise quotations. Perhaps the themes for the *Soliloquium* were also drawn by Thomas from his *rapiarium*, and that is why he thought it appropriate to tell about this book in the prologue. He also talks about professional techniques employed to avoid monotony in the narration, and thus to keep the reader's attention and interest.

The theme of mystical experience is only rarely discussed in Thomas's treatises. Only twice, in his historical works, does he dare to mention with utmost caution his personal experience. In the *Chronica* we find the description of the prophetic dream which he experienced in the main monastery of the congregation. The story is told in the third person:

Contigit ante paucos obitus sui dies infra octavam sancti Martini episcopi, ut duo fratres de monte sanctae Agnetis ad colloquendum priori in Windesem venirent. Tunc unus illorum eadem nocte tale somnium habuit, praesagium futurorum. Vidit namque in caelestibus concursum spirituum fieri et quasi ad obitum alicuius festinare. Statimque tabulam quasi pro exitu morientis in somnis audivit pulsare, ut inde expergefactus evigilaret. Surgens ergo de lecto et volens ire visum, quid esset, neminem percepit. Erat enim mane ante quintam horam, et fratres adhuc

---

[37] Thomas a Kempis, *Soliloquium animae, Prol.*, vol. 1, p. 191. 3–22.

quiescebant. In se reversus tacitus cogitare coepit, quia forte in brevi pater noster prior de saeculo migrabit. Nulli tamen in domo illa quidquam de visione retulit: sed uni clerico de Brabantia venienti et in via secum pergenti secrete ait: Dicatis domino Hermanno Scutken, qui moratur in Thenis, si velit patri nostro in Windesem loqui, quod cito veniat: quia aestimo, quod non diu erit, si vera est visio, quam quidam hac nocte vidit. Post haec quindena peracta pater reverendus obiit infra summam missam die praefata.

(Now it came to pass a few days before his death [of the Windesheim superior prior John of Heusden], and within the octave of St Martin the Bishop, that two Brothers came from Mount St Agnes to Windesheim to commune with the prior. And one of them had that very night a dream after this wise, which vision did foretell the prior's death; for he saw the spirits gathered together in heaven and hastening as if to the death-bed of some one, and straightway he heard a bell toll as if for the passing of a dying man, and the sound hereof aroused him, and he awoke. So rising from his bed and desiring to go to see what had happened, he perceived no man, for it was before the fifth hour in the morning, and the brothers were yet asleep. So, returning to himself, he kept silence, and the thought came to him that our father the prior should soon depart hence. Yet he told naught of this vision to any that were in the house, but to a certain clerk that was coming from Brabant and journeying in his company he said privately: 'Tell Herman Scutken, who sojourneth at Thenen, to come quickly if he would speak with our father at Windesheim, for if the vision that one hath seen this night is true, I think that he shall not long abide here'. So when fifteen days were passed this reverend father died on the day aforesaid after high Mass.)[38]

Fifteen days later, on 2 December 1424, John of Heusden died. This event is almost literally retold in the *Chronikon Windeshemense* by Johannes Busch, a historiographer of the Modern Devotion, who reports the name of the brother who had experienced the vision: 'Frater Thomas de Kempis vir probate vite, qui plures devotos tractatulos composuit, videlicet 'Qui sequitur me' de imitacione Christi cum aliis' (Brother Thomas a Kempis, a fine man, who wrote many devout treatises, among them 'He who follows me' on the Imitation of Christ).[39]

The second mention of a mystical experience, this time formulated in the first person, is found in the *Vita Lidewigis virginis*. Lidewiga or Liduina (1380–1433), who was a contemporary of Thomas and a native of Schiedam, had a tumble when skating at the age of fifteen and broke a rib. This left her disabled and she spent

[38] Thomas a Kempis, *Chronica*, c. 19, vol. 7, pp. 394. 30–395. 26, trans. by J. P. Arthur, pp. 67–68 (slightly adapted). Hermann Scutken was John of Heusden's confessor, cf. Busch, *Chronicon Windeshemense*, p. 59 n. 1.

[39] Busch, *Chronicon Windeshemense*, p. 58.

thirty-five years in her bed.[40] Lidewiga could do without any sleep and food, and almost without drinking. Spiritual exercises, to which the invalid girl devoted herself zealously, brought it about that 'quandoque ab angelo sancto ad loca terrae sanctae rapiebatur: in quibus Salvator noster nascendo, conversando et patiendo, sacramenta humanae salutis operatus est' (sometimes an angel would take her to the Holy Land, where our Lord was born, conversed, and suffered, and where he enacted the sacrament of man's salvation).[41] The angel also took her to hell, purgatory, and paradise. Bearing in mind Lidewiga's visions, Thomas writes in the introduction to her *Vita*: 'Sunt tamen fere omnia omni admiratione digna, meam experientiam excedentia: quae maioribus iudicanda committo' (Almost all these things are worthy of admiration, but they surpass my own experience: I leave it to the discretion of more experienced people to judge).[42] After the girl's death, pilgrims started to come to her tomb expecting a miracle, and the town authorities built a chapel over the tomb. Thomas tells of three miracles performed by Lidewiga after her death in 1448, though according to him, many more regularly happened.[43]

An unknown monk, who wrote a continuation of the *Chronica*, wrote in his obituary that Thomas a Kempis 'sustinuit ab exordio monasterii magnam penuriam, temptationes et labores' (from the early days of the monastery endured great poverty and many labours and temptations).[44] As befitted a spiritually mature man, Thomas never complained in his works about any circumstances. His moral position was expressed in *De imitatione Christi*:

Non est parvum in monasteriis vel in congregatione habitare, et inibi sine querela conversari: et usque ad mortem fidelis perseverare. Beatus qui ibidem bene vixerit: et feliciter consummaverit.

(It is no small thing to dwell in monasteries or in a religious community, and therein to live without complaint and to continue faithfully to death. He is a blessed man who has lived well there, and happily reached the end.)[45]

---

[40] On Liduina see most recently Caspers, *Een bovenaardse vrouw*. On the basis of an anlysis of her skeletal remains, some modern scholars have identified her disease as multiple sclerosis, cf. Medaer, 'Does the History of Multiple Sclerosis Go Back'.

[41] Thomas a Kempis, *Vita Lidewigis virginis*, c. 2. 2, vol. 6, p. 373. 7–11.

[42] Thomas a Kempis, *Vita Lidewigis virginis, Prol.*, vol. 6, p. 318. 17–20.

[43] Thomas a Kempis, *Vita Lidewigis virginis*, c. 2. 33, vol. 6, p. 453. 6–15.

[44] Thomas a Kempis, *Chronica, Cont.*, vol. 7, p. 466. 22–24, trans. by J. P. Arthur, p. 143.

[45] Thomas a Kempis, *De imitatione Christi*, 1. 17. 2, vol. 2, pp. 28. 29–29. 5, trans. by Blaiklock, p. 22.

Thomas finished his life happily. After his death in 1471, the continuer of the
Chronica wrote:

> Eodem anno [1471] in festo sancti Jacobi maioris post completorium obiit
> praedilectus frater noster Thomas Hemerken de Kempis natus, civitate dioecesis
> Coloniensis, anno aetatis suae XCII, et investitionis suae LXIII, anno autem
> sacerdotii sui LVIII. Hic in iuvenili aetate fuit auditor domini Florentii in
> Daventria et ab eo directus est ad fratrem suum germanum, tunc temporis priorem
> montis sanctae Agnetis, anno aetatis suae XX, a quo post sex annos probationis suae
> investitus est. Et sustinuit ab exordio monasterii magnam penuriam, temptationes
> et labores. Scripsit autem Bibliam nostram totaliter et alios multos libros pro domo
> et pro pretio. Insuper composuit tractatulos ad aedificationem iuvenum in plano et
> simplici stilo, sed praegrandes in sententia et operis efficacia. Fuit etiam multum
> amorosus in passione Domini et mire consolativus temptatis et tribulatis. Tandem
> circa senium suum vexatus hydropisi in cruribus obdormivit in Domino, sepultus
> est in ambitu orientali ad latus fratris Petri Herbort.

> (In the same year, after compline on the feast of St James the Less, died our most
> beloved Brother Thomas Hemerken, who was born in the town of Kempen, in the
> diocese of Cologne. He was in the ninety-second year of his age, and this was the
> sixty-third year after his investiture; likewise he had been a priest for above fifty-
> seven years. In the days of his youth he was a hearer of Florentius at Deventer, by
> whom also he was sent, when twenty years old, to his own brother, who at that time
> was Prior of Mount St Agnes. From this same brother he received his investiture
> after six years of probation, and from the early days of the monastery he endured
> great poverty and many labours and temptations. Moreover, he wrote that complete
> copy of the Bible which we use, and also many other books for the use of the House,
> and for sale. Likewise he composed diverse little books for the edification of the
> young, which books were plain and simple in style, but their content is grandiose
> and their impact profound. The thought of the Lord's passion filled his heart with
> love, and he was wondrous comfortable to the troubled and the tempted; but as age
> grew upon him he was vexed with a dropsy in the legs, and so fell asleep in the Lord
> and was buried in the eastern cloister by the side of Brother Peter Herbort.)[46]

Conclusion

Thomas a Kempis did not leave us his curriculum vitae, but nevertheless his
biography can be reconstructed with sufficient completeness from three dozen
autobiographical passages scattered throughout his writings. In most of these he
appears as a witness and not as a participant in events. For this reason, he often

---

[46] Thomas a Kempis, *Chronica, Cont.*, vol. 7, pp. 466. 10–467. 7, trans. adapted from that
by J. P. Arthur, pp. 143–144.

does not write about himself, but about other people, and in the depiction of these people he invariably takes a positive line of approach. These fragments might have served just as edifying *exempla*, aimed at providing a model of godly behaviour, if it were not for one thing. In the reminiscences presented in the *Dialogus noviciorum* Thomas shows himself to be a sensitive, observant, and grateful teenager. His precocious self-reflection enabled him to capture his thoughts and feelings, to evaluate them and draw lessons from the behaviour of the people around him. These are stories exemplifying how first a teenager, then a young man had been working hard to improve his soul, mind, and behaviour, his own 'ego' or 'self'.

The religious ethics of the Modern Devotion take on a quite obvious personal colouring. The requirement of an individual approach to the reading of Holy Scripture, to meditation, and to prayer led to the individualization of other activities, especially creative activities. Autobiographical passages dispersed throughout these works give focus to the moments that display the formation of Thomas a Kempis's personality. Despite all his endeavours to play down his individuality, it was Thomas's profoundly personal attitude to God and to the truth of the Christian faith that created the synthesis of thoughts and feeling which pervades all his books.

Works Cited

Primary Sources

Busch, Johannes, *Chronicon Windeshemense*, ed. by Karl Grube, *Des Augustinerpropstes Iohannes Busch Chronicon Windeshemense und Liber de reformatione monasteriorum* (Halle: Otto Hendel, 1886), pp. 1–375

Thomas a Kempis, *Chronica montis sanctae Agnetis*, in *Thomae Hemerken a Kempis canonici regularis ordinis S. Augustini Opera omnia*, 7, ed. by Michael Josephus Pohl (Freiburg im Breisgau: Herder, 1922), pp. 331–525

——, *The Chronicle of the Canons Regular of Mount St Agnes*, translated by J. P. Arthur [= John Arthur Pott] (London: Kegan Paul, Trench, Trübner, 1906)

——, *Dialogus noviciorum*, in *Thomae Hemerken a Kempis canonici regularis ordinis S. Augustini Opera omnia*, 7, ed. by Michael Josephus Pohl (Freiburg im Breisgau: Herder, 1922), pp. 1–329

——, *De imitatione Christi quae dicitur libri.IIII.*, in *Thomae Hemerken a Kempis canonici regularis ordinis S. Augustini Opera omnia*, 2, ed. by Michael Josephus Pohl (Freiburg im Breisgau: Herder, 1904), pp. 3–263

——, *The Imitation of Christ*, translated by E. M. Blaiklock, rev. ed., with a foreword by J. John (London: Hodder & Stoughton, 2009)

——, *Parvulum alphabetum monachi in schola Dei*, in *Thomae Hemerken a Kempis canonici regularis ordinis S. Augustini Opera omnia*, 3, ed. by Michael Josephus Pohl (Freiburg im Breisgau: Herder, 1904), pp. 317–22

——, *Sermones ad novicios regulares*, in *Thomae Hemerken a Kempis canonici regularis ordinis S. Augustini Opera omnia*, 6, ed. by Michael Josephus Pohl (Freiburg im Breisgau: Herder, 1905), pp. 3–314

——, *Sermons to the Novices Regular*, trans. Vincent Scully (London: Kegan Paul, Trench, Trübner, 1907)

——, *Vita Lidewigis virginis*, in *Thomae Hemerken a Kempis canonici regularis ordinis S. Augustini Opera omnia*, 6, ed. by Michael Josephus Pohl (Freiburg im Breisgau: Herder, 1905), pp. 317–453

——, *Soliloquium animae*, in *Thomae Hemerken a Kempis canonici regularis ordinis S. Augustini Opera omnia*, 1, ed. by Michael Josephus Pohl (Freiburg im Breisgau: Herder, 1910), pp. 189–346

Secondary Sources

Caspers, Charles, *Een bovenaardse vrouw. Zes eeuwen verering van Liduina van Schiedam*. Thomas van Kempen, *Het leven van de heilige maagd Liduina*, trans. by Rijcklof Hofman (Hilversum: Verloren, 2014)

Engen, John van, *Sisters and Brothers of the Common Life: The Devotio Moderna and the World of the Later Middle Ages* (Philadelphia: University of Pennsylvania Press, 2008)

Hofman, Rijcklof, 'Thomas als Biograf', in *Kempener Thomasbeiträge*, ed. by U. Bodemann-Kornhaas (Kempen: Thomas-Archiv im Kulturforum Franziskanerkloster, 2002), pp. 21–31

Medaer, R., 'Does the History of Multiple Sclerosis Go Back as far as the 14th Century?', *Acta Neurologica Scandinavica*, 60 (1979), 189–92

Mertens, Thom, 'Lezen met de pen. Ontwikkelingen in het laatmiddeleeuws geestelijk proza', in *De studie van de Middelnederlandse letterkunde. Stand en toekomst*, ed. by Frits van Oostrom and Frank Willaert (Hilversum: Verloren, 1989), pp. 187–200

Post, R. R. *The Modern Devotion: Confrontation with Reformation and Humanism* (Leiden: Brill, 1968)

Thüss, B. J., 'De geschiedenis van het klooster op de Agnietenberg', in *Een klooster ontsloten. De Kroniek van Sint-Agnietenberg bij Zwolle door Thomas van Kempen*, ed. by Udo de Kruijf and others (Kampen: IJsselacademie, 2000), pp. 81–111

'ANTISEUSIANA': *VITA CHRISTI* AND PASSION MEDITATION BEFORE THE *DEVOTIO MODERNA*

Nigel F. Palmer

C hrist's humanity and his suffering, and his exemplarity and his virtues, are central themes of the devotional literature of the later Middle Ages. They were an essential point of focus in devotional practice as well. And yet they called for different responses, from the individual devotee in search of an intimate relationship with God, and in the literary and theological texts that set out the principles of meditation and prayer they were combined in different ways. It may be useful, in approaching this subject, to begin with a simple opposition. First, a programme of passion meditation from a fourteenth-century German text:

> Entwúrt der Ewigen Wisheit: Es mag nieman komen ze gŏtlicher hocheit noch ze ungewonlicher sŭzikeit, er werde denn vor gezogen dur daz bilde miner menschlichen bitterkeit. So man ane daz durchgan miner menscheit ie hŏher uf klimmet, so man ie tieffer vellet. Min menscheit ist der weg, den man gat, min liden ist daz tor, durch daz man gan mŭz, der zŭ dem wil komen, daz du da sŭchest. Dar umbe tŭ hin dines herzen kleinheit und tritte zŭ mir in den ring ritterlicher vestekeit, wan dem knecht gezimt nit wol zartheit, da der herre stat in stritberlicher kŭnheit. Ich wil dir minú wafenkleit an legen, wan alles min liden mŭz von dir nah dinem vermugenne werden gelitten.[1]

---

[1] Suso, *Deutsche Schriften*, ed. by Bihlmeyer, p. 205. Cf. the Latin rendering of this passage

---

Nigel F. Palmer (nigel.palmer@seh.ox.ac.uk) is Emeritus Professor of German Medieval and Linguistic Studies at the University of Oxford and Emeritus Fellow of St Edmund Hall. His main areas of research are Medieval German and Latin religious literature, Palaeography and Codicology, and Early Printing.

Inwardness, Individualization, and Religious Agency in the Late Medieval Low Countries, ed. by Rijcklof Hofman, Charles Caspers, Peter Nissen, Mathilde van Dijk, and Johan Oosterman, MCS 43 (Turnhout: Brepols, 2020), pp. 87–119   BREPOLS ⚓ PUBLISHERS   10.1484/M.MCS-EB.5.119391

(Eternal Wisdom's reply: 'No one can rise up to the heights of divinity or experience that exceptional sweetness without first being drawn through the image of the bitterness I suffered as a man. The higher one climbs without having passed through my humanity, the further one will fall. My humanity is the path to take, my suffering is the gateway through which you must pass if you wish to attain what you are seeking. Therefore lay off your faintheartedness, and come and join me on the battlefield of knightly steadfastness, for meekness does not become the servant when the lord is displaying valiant courage. I will clothe you with my armour, for you must suffer again everything that I suffered, in so far as you are able'.)

'Suffering again the sufferings of Christ' in the search for God in his divinity is achieved, according to Eternal Wisdom in this passage from the *Büchlein der Ewigen Weisheit* (Little Book of Eternal Wisdom) of Henry Suso (Heinrich Seuse), through the enacting of a double allegory: the man who lays off his faintheartedness and joins the Lord in battle like a knight, clad in the armour (suffering) of his Lord; the man who climbs upwards on the path (of Christ's humanity) and enters through the gate (of Christ's bitter passion) in order to achieve the sweet goal of his desire. The imaginative act required of the devotee is described as being 'drawn through' an image of the bitter suffering Christ endured, entering through the gateway of his passion.

Suso's experiential encounter with the image of Christ's suffering from about 1330 stands in sharp contrast to the rather differently constructed engagement with the image of Christ proposed some sixty years earlier in a Latin text primarily addressed to Franciscan novices:

> In omnibus virtutibus et bonis moribus propone tibi semper clarissimum speculum et totius sanctitatis perfectissimum exemplar, scilicet vitam et mores Filii Dei, Domini nostri Iesu Christi, qui ad hoc nobis de caelo missus est, ut ostenderet et aperiret nobis viam virtutum et legem disciplinae suo exemplo daret nobis et erudiret nos per semetipsum, ut sicut ad imaginem eius naturaliter creati sumus, ita ad morum eius similitudinem per imitationem virtutum pro nostra possibilitate reformemur, qui eius imaginem in nobis foedavimus per peccatum. Quantum enim quisque se ei in virtutum imitatione hic conformare studuerit, tantum ei in patria, in gloria et claritate propinquior et similior erit.[2]

in Suso, *Horologium sapientiae*, ed. by Künzle, p. 388. For an English translation of the German text, see Suso, *The Exemplar*, trans. by Tobin. For an English translation of the *Horologium sapientiae*, see Suso, *Wisdom's Watch*, trans. by Colledge. All translations of German and Latin texts in what follows are my own.

[2] David of Augsburg, *De exterioris et interioris hominis compositione*, Quaracchi edn, p. 25.

(With regard to all the virtues and good practices, always keep in mind that brightest of mirrors and most perfect exemplar of all sanctity, the life and habitual practices of the Son of God, our Lord Jesus Christ, who was sent to us from heaven so that he might show and open up to us the path of the virtues, provide us by his own example with the law of Christian conduct, and teach us by his own actions how just as we were created naturally in his image, so too we who defiled God's image in ourselves through sin might be morally re-formed in his likeness by imitation of his virtues, in so far as we are able. The more a man endeavours to conform himself to Christ by imitating the virtues, the closer he will be to him and the more like him in the heavenly fatherland, in glory, and in brightness.)

This statement is then followed, in David of Augsburg's *De exterioris et interioris hominis compositione*, by a long list of Christ's virtues, human qualities, and his habitual behaviour, but with just a brief mention in passing of the passion and how it was out of love for mankind that he wanted to become incarnate and die. The novice should inscribe all these things on his heart and should endeavour always to be thinking of some aspect of Christ's life, he should always be meditating and ruminating on him, making Christ his exemplar and his 'forma vitae'. The material which David offers for meditation is not, however, a list of events from the life of Christ, but a meditational programme based on concepts, and one in which the passion and crucifixion play little part.[3]

My concern in this paper is to comment on some aspects of the literary history of meditation and prayer in the later thirteenth and fourteenth centuries, paying particular attention to texts that were influential in north-western Europe, establishing a tradition on which the meditational practices promoted by the *Devotio Moderna* could draw. This is a subject that it is at present impossible to deal with definitively for want of adequate research into the whole range of sources that exist, in Latin and the vernacular languages. And with this in mind, I propose to concentrate on just one group of texts, namely those extensive cycles of prayers and meditations that offer the devotee an ambitious programme based on the passion, the life of Christ, or salvation history as a whole. This is just one element in a much more complex story, and it is immediately obvious that there are other categories which can be placed alongside the material selected for discussion here, for example sets of prayers structured in the form of offices, as in books of hours (Latin, French, Dutch, even German),[4] the nuns' personal

---

[3] For a discussion of this passage, see Steer, 'Die Passion Christi', pp. 57–62, 70–71. For Christ as mirror and exemplar, see Constable, 'The Ideal of the Imitation of Christ', pp. 234–35.

[4] See, for example, Reinburg, *French Books of Hours*; Hindman and Marrow, eds, *Books of Hours Reconsidered*.

prayer books in vernacular languages,[5] or thematically based collections of Latin prayers based on material from the Gospels and the lives of the saints.[6] The prayer cycles that I have in view circulated mostly in Italy, the German lands, and the Low Countries, and the perspective adopted is much indebted to my attempt to understand a cycle of German prayers from about 1480, written in Strasbourg, those of the so-called *Begerin Picture Cycle and Prayers*, and a study of their Latin sources, which are essentially the product of literary traditions established in the later thirteenth and fourteenth centuries.[7] It is not this German text, however, that I wish to foreground in this contribution, but rather what goes before, and in particular the texts and religious practices from just before the period that saw the rise of the different branches of the *Devotio Moderna* in the Low Countries, and which came to be influential throughout the Central Rhineland and Netherlands during the period which we associate with names such as Geert Grote, Florens Radewijns, Gerard Zerbolt van Zutphen, and Johannes Mauburnus.

With the exception of the writings of Henry Suso, who wrote in both Latin and the vernacular, the works chosen for discussion were all composed in Latin, but in view of the fact that the practice of meditation on the life of Christ and the passion which these writers aimed to stimulate was not just to be practised by monks, but also by nuns and laypeople, it will be necessary to keep the vernacular reception in Medieval German and Middle Dutch constantly in sight. I have not attempted to extend this study to include Italian, English, and French, although such an extension would certainly be desirable. The life of Christ and passion devotions are almost invariably formulated in the first-person singular. The devotee presents him- or herself (generally ungendered) as an individual person fervently regretting their state of sinfulness, the specifics of which are never clearly set out, seeking protection from adversity and tribulation or wrongdoing (such as duplicity or causing offence to others), assistance in the practice of virtues such as wisdom, reason, patience, compassion, and love (often conceived as imitating the virtues of Christ), urged on by fear of hell and damnation, seeking to be empowered to show penitence and remorse, and above all hoping for a 'good death' and to be counted among 'the chosen'. Despite the first-person perspective, the personal situation and aspirations of the devotee are presented using the

---

[5] For the German lands, see Ochsenbein, 'Deutschsprachige Privatgebetbücher vor 1400'; Cermann, *Katalog der deutschsprachigen illustrierten Handschriften*, vol. 5, fasc. 1/2.

[6] See, for example, the prayers of Heinrich Arnoldi, prior of the Basel Charterhouse, from the 1470s; Achten, 'Die Meditationes und Orationes des Arnoldi von Alfeld'; Hogg, 'Arnoldi, Heinrich, von Alfeld'.

[7] Hamburger and Palmer, *The Prayer Book of Ursula Begerin*.

traditional topoi of Christian prayer and the Psalter, and what could, from a modern point of view, be read as individual experience is thus absorbed, in the medieval texts, into a continuum of engagement with God, a construction of self that is subordinated to the continuity of the struggle of the Christian community to find a solution to the Fall. The prayers and meditations are private devotions, presented as being absolutely central to the religious life of the individual, but with no specified context within the established structures of religious life such as were provided by the Office and the Mass for monks and nuns. Where they are divided up according to the canonical hours, this symbolizes the centrality of Christocentric devotion to the Christian life, and is unlikely to have been intended as a programme of prayer that was to be executed in practice every day.

The hypothesis I wish to advance is that in the analysis of systematically constructed prayer cycles and meditations from the third quarter of the thirteenth century onwards, we should begin by focusing on the differences that exist between salvation history cycles, *Vita Christi* cycles, and cycles based on the passion, a triad that corresponds to what Giles Constable memorably presented as a chronological sequence of the imitation of the divinity of Christ, the humanity of Christ, and of the body of Christ,[8] and then also on the interaction between the different types of meditational practice to which these literary forms testify. One could go further and ask how they relate to other categories of medieval prayer. The *Hundert Betrachtungen* (Hundred Meditations) of Henry Suso constitute the major example of such a passion cycle in this period, and may well be the dominant representative of this type in Western Europe during the later fourtenth and fifteenth centuries, but in order to see the *Hundert Betrachtungen* in the round attention needs to be paid to important alternative traditions in which the passion occupies a different position, what I am calling 'Antiseusiana'. This approach is not entirely new. The German art historian Fritz Oskar Schuppisser takes full account of both types in a fine article dating back to 1993, José van Aelst presents a subtle and detailed picture of late medieval passion literature in her two volumes on the reception of Suso's *Hundert Betrachtungen* in the Netherlands (2005/2011), and I have attempted an overview in my part of Hamburger and Palmer, *The Prayer Book of Ursula Begerin* (2015).[9]

Suso's *Hundert Betrachtungen* had a precursor in Bonaventure's *Lignum vitae* (Tree of Life, from the 1260s), and yet there are also very considerable differences to be observed between these two 'classics' of late medieval

---

[8] Constable, 'The Ideal of the Imitation of Christ'.

[9] Schuppisser, 'Schauen mit den Augen des Herzens'; Van Aelst, *Passie voor het lijden*; Van Aelst, *Vruchten van de passie*; Hamburger and Palmer, *The Prayer Book of Ursula Begerin*.

meditational literature: Dominican and Franciscan, German and Italian, vernacular and Latin, passion meditation and *Vita Christi*/salvation history meditation. The *Lignum vitae* is a coherent meditational ensemble, as distinct from being a cycle of individual prayers, in which the devotee is invited to perform a series of forty-eight meditations that can be held in the mind on the basis of the mnemonic image of a tree, whose branches, flowers, and fruit are inscribed with verses which when put together constitute the poem 'O crux frutex salvífica'.[10] The forty-eight meditations, which are all about one small page in length, are arranged sequentially, chronologically, in three groups of sixteen, devoted to the life, passion, and glorification of Christ. Each meditation is divided into two sections. In the first, an event or individual moment in the salvation history narrative is rehearsed, corresponding to what has been called the *narratio* or *rememoratio* in descriptions of the literary structure of prayers.[11] In the second section, a response from the individual soul is articulated, often expressed in the form of exclamations or apostophe addressed to oneself, man in general, Christ, or Mary. Only occasionally is this second section formulated as a prayer constituting a petition. Numerous large blocks of text employed by Bonaventure in the *Lignum vitae* are borrowed directly from two twelfth-century sources, the *De institutione inclusarum* by the English Cistercian Aelred of Rievaulx and the *Meditatio de humanitate Christi* by the German Benedictine Ekbert of Schönau, both of which Bonaventure attributed to Anselm.[12] Bonaventure must have been aware that he was repackaging well established and traditional meditational material, quite possibly texts that he had recited in his own devotions, and placing them in a new and theologically distinctive literary structure.

The passion occupies a central place in the *Lignum vitae*, literally, in that following on from the divine origin, birth, and ministry of Christ, which occupy exactly one third of the work, a second group of meditations, nos. 17–32, is devoted to events from the Betrayal through to the Entombment, before the transition to the third and final group of sixteen chapters on the Resurrection,

---

[10] Bonaventura, *Lignum vitae*, Quaracchi edn; cf. Bonaventura, *Opera omnia*, vol. 8, pp. xxxix–xlix, 68–87. See the fundamental study by O'Connell, 'The "Lignum vitae" of Saint Bonaventure', and for more recent accounts Karnes, *Imagination, Meditation, and Cognition*; Preisinger, *Lignum vitae* (with a discussion of representations in the visual arts); Hamburger and Palmer, *The Prayer Book of Ursula Begerin*, vol. 1, pp. 419–22.

[11] Cf. Palmer, 'Allegory and Prayer'.

[12] See O'Connell, 'The "Lignum vitae" of Saint Bonaventure', and in particular his articles, 'Aelred of Rievaulx' and 'Eckbert of Schönau'.

the Ascension, and the events at the end of the world. The preface sets out a programme for the devotee, stating that in order to be perfectly conformed, 'configured', to Christ crucified he must carry the cross continually, both in mind and body, metaphorically. But he must not only hold in his memory the passion, he must also contemplate the whole range of hardships, sufferings, and love from the entire life of Christ, focusing on them with the powers of his soul. This statement is then followed by a reinterpretation of Bernard's famous account, in sermon 43 of his *Sermones in Cantica Canticorum* (Sermons on the Song of Songs), where he describes his devotional practices as a novice when he collected a bundle of myrrh, events and experiences selected from the life of Christ, which he could constantly keep between his breasts.[13] Bonaventure proposes to reformulate these briefly in memorable words structured according to the origin and life of Christ, his passion, and his glorification, later referred to as the 'status, dignitates, virtutes et opera' (conditions, dignities, virtues, and acts) of Christ.[14] The cross provides a focal point, and achieving conformity with Christ crucified is shorthand for what has been called a 'progressive assimilation' to Christ,[15] leading to an existential, experiential awareness of the process of redemption, which can be achieved by means of the literary form of serial meditations on salvation history in which the passion and crucifixion are placed at the centre, but not at the expense of the broader context in salvation history. The *Lignum vitae* is offered not just as a text, but as a meditational practice involving memory and visualization in the form of an image of the Tree of Life, of which numerous visual representations have been preserved as panel paintings, frescoes, and manuscript illuminations. The Latin poem that structures the meditations was more than once set to music.

The *Hundert Betrachtungen* provide a second major example of a cycle of sequential meditations.[16] Suso's Hundred Meditations, or 'articles' as they are

---

[13] Bernard of Clairvaux, *Sermones in Cantica Canticorum*, 43. 2. 3, in Bernard of Clairvaux, *Opera*, ed. by Leclerq and others, vol. 2, p. 42 [*PL* 183, col. 597]. See my discussion in Hamburger and Palmer, *The Prayer Book of Ursula Begerin*, vol. 1, pp. 402–03.

[14] Bonaventura, *Lignum vitae*, Prol. 4, Quaracchi edn, p. 171. Cf. *Opera omnia*, vol. 8, p. 69.

[15] O'Connell, 'The "Lignum vitae" of Saint Bonaventure', p. 190. This unpublished dissertation by Patrick O'Connell from 1985, available from University Microfilms International, offers a quite exceptionally sophisticated and nuanced literary and theological analysis of the *Lignum vitae* which has not been surpassed in the more recent literature.

[16] Suso, *Deutsche Schriften*, ed. by Bihlmeyer, pp. 314–22. For Suso, see Michel, 'Seuse als Diener' (pp. 344–55 for the *Hundert Betrachtungen*); Haas and Ruh, 'Seuse, Heinrich'; Haas, *Kunst rechter Gelassenheit*; Ruh, *Geschichte der abendländischen Mystik.*, vol. 3, pp. 417–75; McGinn, *The Harvest of Mysticism*, pp. 195–239. For the *Hundert Betrachtungen*, see Van Aelst,

often called, are presented not just as a literary text, but also, like Bonaventure's *Lignum vitae*, as a devotional practice, a devotional ritual to be performed. Just as the *Lignum vitae* demands of the devotee that he should not just read the text, but meditate on it with reference to a visual representation of the Tree of Life (for example a wall painting), Suso's text is also presented as the textual basis of a practical, performative devotion, not necessarily in this case with a visual point of reference,[17] but involving the recitation of the hundred articles from memory and accompanied by genuflections and prayers. The difference between the two works is not only to be sought in their theology, but also in the way in which the incarnation and passion of Christ are presented as quite differently structured programmes of systematic meditation and prayer, with different emphases, with a different developmental structure throughout the cycle,[18] and with differently constructed meditations. In the case of Bonaventure these are skilfully formulated literary texts, most likely to be recited verbatim, whereas with Suso they are short 'articles' to be memorized, more as ideas than as texts, and as a basis for meditation 'nach den sinnen, die in den kurzen worten sint begriffen' (on the basis of the ideas expressed in the brief formulations).[19]

The text of the *Hundert Betrachtungen* exists in three distinct authorial versions, first as Part III of the *Büchlein der Ewigen Weisheit* (Little Book of Eternal Wisdom), then as an individual text copied on its own, and thirdly in a Latin rewriting of articles 1–10 in Suso's *Horologium sapientiae* (Clock of Wisdom), Book II, *materia* 6.[20] There is a complex manuscript tradition in several languages preserved in more than 500 copies. Rüdiger Blumrich identified over a hundred manuscripts of the German *Büchlein* that contain the *Hundert Betrachtungen* and refers to at least 248 manuscripts of the text on its own (a number which includes the 220 Dutch manuscripts noted by Deschamps), to which seventy manuscripts of the two Latin translations may be added (Van Aelst); Pius Künzle, in 1977, made a catalogue of 233 Latin manuscripts of the *Horologium sapientiae*, to which must be added at least twenty manuscripts of the Dutch translation

Passie voor het lijden; Van Aelst, *Vruchten van de passie*; Hamburger and Palmer, *The Prayer Book of Ursula Begerin*, vol. 1, pp. 432–36.

[17] For the very considerable significance of images in Suso's piety, see Hamburger, *The Visual and the Visionary*, pp. 197–232 (notes pp. 522–23); Haas, *Kunst rechter Gelassenheit*, pp. 152–54; Falque, '*Daz man bild mit bilden us tribe*'.

[18] For the structure of the cycle of articles in the *Hundert Betrachtungen*, see Enders, *Das mystische Wissen*, pp. 309–13.

[19] Suso, *Deutsche Schriften*, ed. by Bihlmeyer, p. 314. 15.

[20] Suso, *Horologium sapientiae*, ed. by Künzle, pp. 585–87.

from the Latin (not including excerpts) and ten Latin printed editions from the sixteenth century.[21]

In the late 1320s, Suso composed his *Büchlein der Ewigen Weisheit*, which consists of a preface and three parts, the first two of which are constructed as dialogues between the Servant, who represents Suso himself, and Eternal Wisdom, who represents Christ. These two parts offer chapters on love and suffering, focusing on man's obligation to re-live what Christ suffered out of love for man, the Last Things, Mary, an *ars moriendi*, the Eucharist, and a number of other religious topics. Part I begins with an account of the divine revelation in which Suso was taught by God to perform the devotion of the Hundred Meditations, followed in the second chapter by a detailed first-person narrative, spoken by Eternal Wisdom, of Christ's passion from Gethsemane onwards, describing the mystical process by which the devotee must 'suffer again' the passion of Christ, blow by blow, if he is to penetrate into the heights of Christ's divinity. As presented in Part I, Chapter 13, of the *Büchlein* passion devotion requires of the devotee that he should take delight in the most terrible physical suffering imaginable, a horrific ascetic programme that at this stage of the argument is presented as a goal in itself. This is Suso's *Leidenstheologie*, but perhaps not yet *Leidensmystik*.

The *Hundert Betrachtungen* make up the whole of Part III of the *Büchlein* and present a hundred brief articles for memorization, one hundred single moments or aspects of Christ's suffering in the course of the passion which the devotee should call to memory (*rememoratio*) as a basis for meditation. These are divided up into thematically related groups of five or ten in such a manner that each such group is followed by a prayer, formulated as a petition, that relates back to the whole set of five or ten articles. A brief preface states that anyone who desires to meditate on Christ's loving suffering ('betrachten nah dem minneklichen lidenne'), which is the basis of our salvation, and to give thanks for it, should commit the following hundred meditations to memory and work through them every day, accompanying them by a hundred genuflections, each to be followed by a *Pater noster* or, if there is reference to Mary in the respective article, a *Salve regina* or *Ave Maria*. It is then stated that the hundred articles were revealed by God to a Dominican preacher as he stood praying in a state of melancholy before a crucifix, lamenting to God his inability to contemplate Christ's sufferings

---

[21] Blumrich, 'Die Überlieferung der deutschen Schriften Seuses', p. 193; Van Aelst, *Passie voor het leiden*, p. 1; Suso, *Horologium sapientiae*, ed. by Künzle, pp. 103–200; Hoffmann, 'Die volkssprachliche Rezeption', pp. 211–13. See also Hofmann, 'Seuses Werke in deutschsprachigen Handschriften', pp. 149–54 nos. 154–214; Deschamps, 'De Middelnederlandse vertalingen'; and the critical comments by Ruh in Haas and Ruh, 'Seuse, Heinrich', cols 1114–17.

adequately, as he found them so painful. The petitions that follow the articles were not part of the divine revelation, it is said, but were added by the monk as a guide for those devotees who might wish to formulate their own personal prayers, according to their individual disposition.[22] This brief account of the divine revelation in the preface to Part III is a repetition of the rather fuller account of the same visionary experience reported in the preface to the *Büchlein der Ewigen Weisheit* at the beginning of the work, and the hundred articles cover exactly the same material as was revealed by Eternal Wisdom to the Dominican monk in Part I of the *Büchlein*, sometimes with overlap in the wording. The impression is thus created that the *Hundert Betrachtungen* provide us with a copy of the actual document which the anonymous Dominican (whom we are intended to understand to be the author, Henry Suso) is said to have written down 'in German as they were revealed to him', as an aid to any person who might have similar problems of his own in the contemplation of Christ's bitter suffering.[23] In the preface to Part III it is claimed that the Hundred Meditations have been taken out or extracted ('die hie nach usgenomenlich stant'), underlining the idea that they constitute an independent textual item, repeating the narrative material presented earlier at greater length, but now in the form of a list of short articles for memorization. They are thus at once independent of the main text of the *Büchlein* and part of it, and we cannot be sure if the special status accorded to the *Hundert Betrachtungen* is part of a strategy to create a sense of verisimilitude, or if it is a genuine document of the textual history.

The whole of the *Büchlein der Ewigen Weisheit* was later incorporated, unchanged and including the *Hundert Betrachtungen*, into what is called the *Exemplar*, the illustrated compendium containing a number of his German writings that Suso put together some thirty years later, in 1362–1363,[24] but it is the separate text of the *Büchlein der Ewigen Weisheit*, containing the full text of the *Hundert Betrachtungen* as Part III, that enjoyed an enormous circulation as one of the most widely read German texts of the Middle Ages.[25]

Whereas it is expressly stated in the *Büchlein* that the *Hundert Betrachtungen* may be excerpted and copied independently of the main text,[26] it is not clear and,

[22] Cf. 'dar umbe daz ieder mensch im selber ursach vinde ze begerenne, als er denne gemût ist'; Suso, *Deutsche Schriften*, ed. by Bihlmeyer, p. 314. 25–26.

[23] Suso, *Deutsche Schriften*, ed. by Bihlmeyer, p. 197. 6–11.

[24] For the manuscript transmission, see Blumrich, 'Die Überlieferung der deutschen Schriften Seuses', pp. 190–91.

[25] It is not known just how many manuscripts have been preserved that contain the German text of the *Hundert Betrachtungen* on its own.

[26] It is stated in the epilogue of the *Büchlein* that scribes should always copy the work in

in view of the fidelity with which the texts were copied, can probably never be determined, if the hundred articles were conceived separately and subsequentely integrated into the *Büchlein*, or if it was the other way round. The only variation seems to be in the formulation of the title, insofar as a title is present. Sometimes the *Hundert Betrachtungen* are referred to in the manuscripts as 'vermanunge' (reminders) — underlining how the devotee is invited to recall and imagine the events of the passion ('dis sind die hundert vermanung'), sometimes as 'articles' — most commonly in the Netherlandish transmission ('Hier bighinnen die hondert articulen'), or as 'betrahtunge und begerunge' (meditations and petitions) — employing terms used in Suso's preface.[27] In the *Hermetschwiler Gebetbuch*, written in the first quarter of the fifteenth century, the title is 'Dis sint die hundert betrachtunge und die hundert manung mit kurtzen worten, alse man si alle tag mit andacht sprechen sol' (These are the hundred meditations and the hundred reminders, expressed briefly, as they should be spoken devoutly every day).[28]

The Latin transmission presents a quite different picture. The revised excerpt of articles 1–10 from the *Hundert Betrachtungen* is contained in Suso's Latin work, the *Horologium sapientiae*, which was composed some time after the *Büchlein*, at the beginning of the 1330s, and completed *c.* 1334. This is a rewriting of the *Büchlein der Ewigen Weisheit* in Latin, with numerous additions and modifications, in which the text of the *Hundert Betrachtungen*, apart from the first ten articles, is said to have been omitted in order to save space ('causa brevitatis').[29] The context is a discussion of how the contents of the book can be communicated to different types of recipient, in the course of which the passion devotions in particular are commended and exemplified by the passages cited, which present a short sequence of narrative episodes beginning with the Sweating of Blood in Gethsemane, extending only as far as the Condemnation.

---

its entirety and 'sol nút sunders dar us schriben, denne die hundert betrahtung ze hindrost; die schrib dar us, ob er well'; Suso, *Deutsche Schriften*, ed. by Bihlmeyer, p. 325. 22–23.

[27] St. Gallen, Stiftsbibl., Cod. Sang. 479, fol. 168^r; Utrecht, Museum Catharijneconvent, BMH h 53, fol. 123^v; Suso, *Deutsche Schriften*, ed. by Bihlmeyer, p. 314. For the regular use of the term 'articulus' in the Dutch and Latin translations, see Van Aelst, *Passie voor het lijden*, pp. 282, 299, 322, and further examples in the appendices in Van Aelst, *Vruchten van de passie*. The term 'begerunge' (petition) is employed by Suso in the final sentence of the preface to Part III.

[28] Sarnen, Benediktinerkollegium, Cod. chart. 208, fol. 48^r; *Das Hermetschwiler Gebetbuch*, ed. by Wiederkehr, p. 325. I have not been able to establish whether a standard title was employed in the independent German copies of the *Hundert Betrachtungen*.

[29] Suso, *Horologium sapientiae*, ed. by Künzle, p. 369. 16–17. This passage in the preface to the *Horologium sapientiae* contains one further account of the divine revelation in which the Hundred Meditations were communicated to the Servant.

In the German text the first ten articles are presented as follows:

I. Eya, Ewigú Wisheit, min herze ermanet dich, als du nah dem jungsten nachtmale uf deme berge von angsten dines zarten herzen wurd hinvliezende von dem blůtigen sweize,

II. Und als du wurde vientlich gevangsen, strenklich gebunden und ellendklich verfůret;

III. Herre, als du wurde in der nacht mit herten streichen, mit verspôizenne und verbindenne diner schônen ôgen lasterlich gehandelt,

IV. Frúje vor Cayphas versprochen und in den tôd vúr schuldig ergeben,

V. Von diner zarten můter mit grundlosem herzleide an gesehen.

VI. Du wurd vor Pylato schamlich gestellet, valschlich gerůget, tôtlich verdampnet,

VII. Du, Ewigú Wisheit, wurd vor Herodes in wissen kleidern torlich verspottet,

VIII. Din schôner lip wart so gar leitlich vor dien ungezognen geiselschlegen zerfůret und zermůstet,

IX. Din zartes hôpt mit spitzigen dornen durstochen, da von din minneklichs antlúte mit blůt waz verrunnen,

X. Du wurd also verteilet ellendklich und schamlich mit dinem krúze us in den tôt gefůret.

Ach, min einigú zůversiht, dez siest du ermanet, daz du mir våtterlich ze hilf komest in allen minen nôten. Enbinde mich von minen sůntlichen sweren banden, behůt mich vor heinlichen súnden und offenbarem laster. Beschirme mich vor dez viendes valschen reten und vor ursach aller súnden; gib mir dins lidens und diner zarten můter leides ein herzklichs enphinden. Herr, rihte ab mir an miner jungsten hinvart erbarmherzklich, lere mich weltlich ere versmahen und dir dienen wislich. Alle mine gebresten werden in dinen wunden verheilet, min bescheidenheit in dem sere dins hôptes vor aller anvechtunge gesterket und gezieret, und alles din liden nach minem vermugenne von mir ervolget.[30]

(I. O Eternal Wisdom, my heart calls out and reminds you how after the Last Supper, on the mount, you were drenched in bloody sweat because of the anguish of your gentle heart.

II. And how you were taken captive by your enemies, roughly bound, and led off in misery.

III. And how, Lord, during that night, you were shamefully abused with harsh

---

[30] Suso, *Deutsche Schriften*, ed. by Bihlmeyer, p. 315. 1–33. My translation draws on that in Suso, *The Exemplar*, trans. by Tobin, pp. 294–95.

blows, were spat upon, and your fair eyes were ignominiously blindfolded.

IV.   How in the morning you were falsely charged before Caiaphas and condemned to death as guilty,

V.   And how your gentle mother looked upon you with immense sorrow.

VI.   How you were shamefully brought before Pilate, falsely charged, and condemned to death.

VII.   Eternal Wisdom, how you were mocked as a fool, dressed in white clothing, before Herod.

VIII.   Your fair body was so agonizingly beaten and smashed by the frenzied lashes of the scourge.

IX.   Your gentle head was punctured by sharp thorns so that blood ran down over your dear face.

X.   Thus you were condemned, and led forth to your death carrying your cross in misery and shame.

O my only hope, remember all this so that you might come to my aid as a father in all my distress. Free me from the heavy bonds of my sins. Protect me from secret sins and public vice. Guard me against the deceitful counsels of the enemy and against the originator of all sins. Let me feel compassion in my heart for your suffering and for the sorrow of your gentle mother. Lord, judge me with mercy on my final journey, teach me to scorn worldly honour, and to serve you in wisdom. May all my failings be healed in your wounds, my reason be strengthened and embellished by virtue of the pain of your head in the face of all temptations, and all your suffering, insofar as I am capable of it, be compensated for.)

In this, the original version, meditation on the first ten articles forms the basis for a prayer asking that the Lord might help the devotee in his own distress, that on the basis of Christ's bondage he might be freed from the bonds of sin, that as a response to the way Christ was falsely charged before Caiaphas, he might be granted help in resisting the false counsels of the devil. He prays that just as Mary felt compassion when she saw Christ's suffering (an apocryphal motif), he himself might be empowered to feel compassion with Christ and Mary; that Christ, who was taken on the journey from Pilate to Herod to Calvary, should show him mercy on his own final journey when he dies; and teach him to scorn worldly honour and to display wisdom, as a response to the way Christ himself was treated with dishonour and as a fool. He asks that his own sins might be healed on the basis of Christ's wounds, referring to those incurred by the scourging, and that his reason when confronted by temptations might be reinforced on the basis of the wounding of Christ's head by the crown of thorns. Finally he pleads that he might be empowered to compensate[31] Christ for his suffering. The devotee, as constructed in the German text, is a man plagued by suffering on account of his sins and the demands and temptations of the devil, in search of modesty, wisdom, and reason, seeking mercy from the Lord at the time of his death, and hoping that he will be helped in pursuing these goals by emotional engagement with Christ and Mary, in compassion. His devotion, as summed up in the last sentence, is founded on a response to Christ's suffering which he describes as 'compensating' Christ, fulfilling his obligations as a man to subject himself to suffering in response to Christ's suffering, a concept which is in line with Suso's doctrine expressed elsewhere concerning the value of a life totally committed to internalizing the imitation of Christ.[32] This is not unlike Bonaventure's concept of a life 'configured' to Christ crucified, but with greater stress on the ascetic aspect of such a regime. It is only in two of the ten articles in this section of the *Hundert Betrachtungen* that the *rememoratio* forms the basis for a response in which the configuration of one's life in imitation of Christ crucified plays a direct part, namely in the compassion with Mary and Christ in their suffering in article 5, and in the idea of paying compensation for Christ's suffering (*ervolgen*) in article 10. The other components are standard elements in Christian prayer, pinning hope on combatting sin, self-improvement through the virtues, and a plea for salvation. *Leidenstheologie* is thus by no means the only item on Suso's agenda.

Suso's own Latin reworking of this material is very different from his German text, placing much greater stress on Christ as an exemplar of the virtues. This can be illustrated from the presentation of articles 1–4 in the *Horologium sapientiae*:

> Materia illa superius posita, ubi divina sapientia inchoat discipulo pro ipsius fervore excitando suam passionem explicare, taliter est ad populum ordinanda:
>
> j. Siquidem Christus Dei Filius imminente sibi passione horrenda, cum prae angustiis superventurae in proximo mortis guttas sanguineas sudando funderet in terram, nihilominus tamen libere suam voluntatem Patris voluntati commisit, et quod coeperat, devote perfecit. Sic quilibet devotus in omni adversitatis pressura et tribulationis angustia, licet forte naturam habeat reluctantem, se paternae voluntati committat et devote hoc suscipiat, quod occurrit.

---

[31] The German word is *ervolgen*, which Willem Jordaens was later to translate as *rependere*; Van Aelst, *Passie voor het leiden*, p. 302. 32.

[32] Haas, *Kunst rechter Gelassenheit*, pp. 162–68 (with reference to the *Vita*). See also Ulrich, 'Zur Bedeutung des Leidens', especially pp. 129–31, who stresses that Suso moves on, in his later writings, to a rather different concept of suffering that goes beyond the external ascetic practices that focused on the *imitatio Christi*.

ij. Et sicut Christus fuit captivatus et vinculatus, ne quo vellet posset abire; sic homo se ipsum debet captivare, ne sequatur concupiscientias carnis ac sensualitatis appetitum ad nociva trahentem.

iij. Item eadem nocte omnes sibi illusiones factas ac verecundias illatas ab iniquis patienter sustinuit; sic homo omnia verba contumeliosa et turbativa atque opprobria et cuncta mala irrogata a malis et importunis hominibus patienter ferat amore sui redemptoris similia vel potius multo maiora propter ipsum patientis.

iiij. Deinde in mortis discrimine ad Caipham adductus veritatem non deseruit, sed maledicentem et condemnantem se Dei Filium cum omni modestia confessus fuit. Sic verus ipsius servus propter nullum temporale periculum debet veritatem deserere, sed usque in mortem constans perdurare.

[...]

Itaque simili modo his decem articulis faciendum est in omnibus consequentibus materiis, quae sunt de Christi passione.[33]

(The matter set out above, where Divine Wisdom begins describing her passion to the Disciple in order to stir up his fervour, should be presented to the people as follows:

1. Even though Christ, the Son of God, as his horrific passion approached, sweated and poured out drops of blood onto the ground out of fear at what was shortly to come, and yet nonetheless freely accomplished what he had begun, so every devotee, when faced with all the pains of adversity and the anguish of tribulation, even if he might well feel reluctant, should entrust himself to the will of the Father and devoutly accept whatever may happen.

2. And just as Christ was arrested and bound to stop him going wherever he wanted, so a man should hold himself captive and abstain from the pleasures of the flesh and sensual appetite that might put him in harm's way.

3. And then, as that same night he bore mockery and shameful attacks from wicked men with patience, in the same way a man should suffer all the wild abusive language and taunts, and all the insults heaped on him by evil and malicious men with patience, for love of his redeemer, who suffered such things, or indeed even much worse things, for his sake.

4. And then, as when he was led to Caiaphas, in mortal danger, he did not forsake the truth, but calmly confessed that he was the Son of God, thereby compromising

---

[33] Suso, *Horologium sapientiae*, ii. 6, art. 1–4, ed. by Künzle, pp. 585. 23–586. 16; 587. 16–17.

and condemning himself, so his true servant should never forsake the truth on account of any earthly danger, but should remain steadfast even to the point of death.

[...]

And one should respond in a similar fashion to all the rest of these matters that relate to the passion of Christ.)

Just as Christ, as summoned to mind in article 1, sweated blood out of fear and thereby subordinated his will to that of the Father, it is stated, so the devotee should subject his will to that of the Father and accept whatever hardships he is subjected to. Just as Christ, in article 2, was captured and bound, so a man should take a grip on himself and bind himself to guard against sensual desires. In a similar manner each of the first ten articles is presented as a stimulus to observe a particular virtue, namely steadfastness in adversity, self-control when faced with temptation, patience when under attack, truthfulness, compassion, facing accusations with equanimity, putting up with mockery, restraint through self-chastisement, calmly accepting one's lot. Finally the sentence of death imposed in article 10, and the manner in which Christ is led to Calvary like a malefactor, is said to mean that the true imitator of Christ should engage in self-abnegation, taking up the cross of Christ and focusing on Christ's death in such a way as to experience the life of Christ in his own body. As in the German text, the formulation of the tenth article offers the idea of self-configuration on the model of Christ crucified, but it is made clear in the *Horologium sapientiae* that meditation on the passion achieves this 'self-configuration' on the basis of the almost stoic imitation of Christ's virtues and not principally through engagement with the process of redemption as with Bonaventure, or as in Suso's own *Leidenstheologie* by suffering again what Christ suffered.

Wherein exactly do the differences lie between the *Hundert Betrachtungen* and Bonaventure's *Lignum vitae*? Let us consider Bonaventure's meditation no. 31 'Iesus cruore madidus' (Jesus, dripping with blood), the fourth of a set of meditations on the passion and crucifixion, and look at it in comparison with Suso's articles 76–80, which refer to the wound in Christ's side, from which blood and water poured after his death on the cross.

> *Jesus, cruore madidus.* Cruentatus enim Christus Dominus sanguine proprio, primum sudore, dehinc flagellis et aculeis, post clavis et tandem lancea copiose effuso, ut apud Deum esset copiosa redemptio, vestem pontificalem habuit rubricatam, quatenus vere rubrum appareret indumentum ipsius, et vestimenta eius quasi calcantium in torculari. Et sic, vero Ioseph in veterem dimisso cisternam, tunica ipsius intincta sanguine hoedi, propter similitudinem scilicet carnis peccati, approbationis notitia discernenda mitteretur ad Patrem.

Cognosce igitur, clementissime Pater, tunicam praedilecti filii tui Ioseph, quem invidia fratrum secundum carnem tanquam fera pessima devoravit et conculcavit in furore vestimentum ipsius et omnem decorem illius reliquiis cruoris inquinavit; nam et quinque scissuras lamentabiles in ea reliquit. Hoc enim est, Domine, vestimentum, quod in manu meretricis Aegyptiae, synagogae videlicet, innocens Puer tuus sponte dimisit, magis eligens, spoliatus a carnis pallio, in carcerem mortis descendere, quam adulterinae plebis acquiescendo voci temporaliter gloriari. Nam et proposito sibi gaudio, crucem sustinuit, confusione contempta. — Sed et tu, misericordissima Domina mea, aspice illam dilecti Filii tui sacratissimam vestem de castissimis membris tuis Spiritus sancti artificiositate contextam et una cum ipso confugientibus nobis ad te veniam postula, ut digni habeamur effugere ab ira ventura.[34]

(*Jesus, dripping with blood*. Christ the Lord was stained with his own blood, which flowed profusely: first from the bloody sweat, then from the lashes and the thorns, then from the nails, and finally from the lance. And so that with God there might be plenteous redemption (Psalms 129. 7), he wore a priestly robe of red; his apparel was truly red and his garments like those that tread the wine press (Isaiah 63. 2). As in the case of Joseph who was thrown into an ancient pit, his tunic was dipped in the blood of a goat (Genesis 37. 24; 31) — that is, because of the likeness of sinful flesh (Romans 8. 3) — and he was sent to the Father for his recognition and acceptance.   Recognize, therefore, O most merciful Father, the coat of your beloved son Joseph, whom the envy of his blood brothers has devoured like a wild beast and has trampled upon his garment in rage, befouling its beauty with the vestiges of blood, for it has left in it five lamentable gashes. For this is indeed, O Lord, the garment which your innocent Son willingly gave over into the hands of that Egyptian prostitute, that is to the Synagogue, choosing to be stripped of the mantle of his flesh and to descend into the prison of death rather than to seek temporal glory by acquiescing to the shouts of the adulterous mob. For when joy was set before him, he endured the cross, despising the shame (Hebrews 12. 2). But you also, my most merciful Lady, behold that most sacred garment of your beloved son, skilfully woven by the Holy Spirit from your most chaste body; and together with him beg forgiveness for us who take refuge in you that we may be found worthy to flee from the wrath to come (Matthew 3. 7).)

In Bonaventure's text the context presents meditation no. 31 as one of a series of passion meditations, nos. 25–32, devoted to Christ's maltreatment by the soldiers, being nailed to the cross, crucified alongside robbers, his last words 'Sitio' and 'Consummatum est', followed by Christ's death on the cross, being pierced with the lance, and the Entombment. In the first part of this meditation it is stated that his bleeding is five-fold, caused by the bloody sweat at Gethsemane,

---

[34] Bonaventura, *Lignum vitae*, Quaracchi edn, pp. 204–05. Cf. *Opera omnia*, p. 80.

the whiplashes, the crown of thorns, the nails, and the lance, a mnemonic list that may have been intended to assist the devotee in thinking through Christ's sufferings systematically, but presented without commentary. It is followed, still in the first section, the *rememoratio*, by typological references to God as the workman treading the wine press from Isaiah and the story of Joseph's coat of many colours from Genesis, which are used to deepen the theological significance of Christ's blood-stained body and to present it as the fulfilment or antitype of Old Testament events.

The *rememoratio* is followed by a response, in this case formulated as a prayer, which begins by addressing God the Father, calling on him to recognize in Christ's body an allegorical realization of Joseph subjected to maltreatment as the result of the envy and rage of his brothers, his beauty defiled, and leaving five symbolic gashes in his coat. This is followed by an allegorical reading of the story of Joseph and Potiphar's wife from Genesis Chapter 39, which is interpreted as pointing forward to Christ willingly suffering death at the hands of the Jews, choosing shame and crucifixion, and then descending into hell. The addressee of the prayer now switches to Mary, and the devotee asks her to call to mind Christ's sacred body, referred to metaphorically as a garment woven from her own body, before moving on to a petition asking that she and Christ should together seek forgiveness from God the Father for those who take refuge in Mary from God's anger at the Last Judgement.

The prayer for protection and salvation spoken on behalf of the devotee himself and his companions is thus based on a meditation summoning to memory individual moments of Christ's passion and crucifixion. These ideas are developed on the basis of typological allegory that places the events of the crucifixion in the context of a discourse about subjects such as redemption, the relationship between the Son and the Father, Mary's motherhood, and her role when the sinner is brought before the Last Judgement. It is about understanding the passion in a salvation history context, a process founded on memorizing individual moments from the life of Christ. In this section of Bonaventure's work this certainly means meditation on the passion, but it is all about understanding, not about engaging in a life totally committed to experiential conformity with Christ crucified, such as was set out in the prefaces to the *Lignum vitae*.

Bonaventure's treatment of this episode from the passion narrative can be compared to articles 76–80 in Suso's *Hundert Betrachtungen*:

I.   Ach herr, gedenke, wie daz scharphe sper durch din gŏtlichen siten wart gestochen,

II. Wie daz rŏsvarw kostber blŭt dar us trang,

III.   Wie daz lebende wasser dar us ran,

IV.   Owe, herr, und wie sure du mich hast erarnet,

V.   Und wie vrilich du mich hast erlôset!

Minneklicher herr, din tieffú wunde behûte mich vor allen minen vienden, din lebendes wasser reine mich von allen minen súnden, dins rôsvarwes blůt ziere mich mit allen gnaden und tugenden. Zarter herre, din sures erarnen binde dich zů mir, din vriliches erlôsen, verein mich eweklich mit dir.[35]

(I.   O Lord, remember how that sharp lance pierced your divine side,

II.   How the rose-red precious blood spurted out,

III.   How the living water poured out,

IV.   O Lord, and how bitterly you paid for me,

V.   And how generously you redeemed me!

Dear Lord, may your deep wound preserve me from all my enemies, your living water cleanse me of all my sins, your rose-red blood embellish me with all your grace and the virtues. Gentle Lord, may your bitter payment bind you to me, and your generous salvation unite me with you eternally.)

In this case the five articles that form the meditation call upon the Lord to remember how he was pierced with the lance, the outpouring of blood, and then water, and the opposition between how bitterly he had to pay, and how generous he was in bringing about man's salvation. The keywords, which have a mnemonic function, are the sharp lance, the red blood, the living water, paying bitterly, and the generosity with which man was redeemed. The listing of the articles is followed by a prayer to the Lord, formulated as a petition seeking protection from his enemies on the basis of the side-wound, the purging of sin by means of the living water, and the bestowal of the grace of God and the virtues through the red blood. Finally he pleads for a bond to be established between God and himself through Christ's bitter payment, and for eternal union with Christ in the next world through the generosity of redemption. There is not always such a close fit between the prayer and the elements of the meditation as here, but in this case each article is associated with one particular idea. Being washed with water is a metaphor for the purging of sin. That the body is covered with blood is a metaphor for being decked out with God's grace and the virtues. In each case what is said of Christ in the *rememoratio* forms the basis of a petition for what the devotee desires for himself. The first petition, namely the request that

---

[35] Suso, *Deutsche Werke*, ed. by Bihlmeyer, p. 320. 16–26.

remembrance of how Christ's divine side was pierced might form the basis of a plea that the wound so incurred might protect the devotee from his enemies, has no self-contained logic. It depends on the association between the side-wound and the blood and the water of the second and third articles, as these signify God's grace and the virtues, as well as the purging of sin through which the devotee can be protected from his enemies, the devils. The side-wound would thus seem to be emblematic of God's protection. Finally the prayer is concluded with a plea that the bitter payment and the generous salvation might bring about a bond between the devotee and God and their eternal union. Clear conceptual links are thus established between specific elements of suffering in the crucifixion of Christ and the content of the following prayer, in this case the piercing of the dead body, the suffering Christ had endured, and its result in terms of man's redemption. But the petition itself is only loosely associated with the theme of suffering: the devotee is presented as a sinner in need of protection from the devils, who hopes to be granted God's grace and to come into possession of the virtues, desirous of a bond between himself and God, and hoping for eternal union with Christ in the afterlife. It is not suggested that these things might be obtained by reliving Christ's suffering. Passion meditation here takes on a didactic aspect, and just as it would be quite wrong to think of Suso's version of meditation on Christ in his humanity as being exclusively concerned with imagining in emotional terms just the gory aspects of Christ's passion and crucifixion, it would be equally wrong to think of it as being exclusively concerned with what Suso conceived elsewhere, in more strictly theological terms, as a penitential process of engagement with redemptive suffering.

Both Suso and Bonaventure have an overall theological concept of how devotion to the passion works. For Suso, this entails suffering again what Christ suffered, the essential gateway to the heavenly feast through which the devotee has to pass and a process that, in the *Büchlein* and the *Hundert Betrachtungen*, is presented as an ascetic, performative practice. For Bonaventure it is the Franciscan idea of self-configuration on the model of Christ, the experiential awareness of the process of redemption achievable by continual mental concentration on the 'conditions, dignities, virtues and acts' of Christ, suffering in the Bernardine sense, suffering what Christ endured simply by virtue of his humanity — given focus in the passion and crucifixion, but by no means just in these events. Notwithstanding the similarities, their positions differ fundamentally in the scope they allow for the practice of *imitatio Christi*, and in the way in which allegorical, typological, metaphorical, tropological, and even didactic interpretation is given a place in Christ-centred meditation. They differ even more in the literary structures of the meditational cycles they created. In the case of Bonaventure we have forty-eight serial meditations structured according to salvation history, with the passion at the centre, and in the case of Suso one hundred meditations focused entirely on individual articles of the passion, and only that.

Where does the literary history of meditational cycles take us next? Suso's *Hundert Betrachtungen* originated about 1330, but as far as we know its widespread dissemination does not really begin until the 1360s, when it was published as part of the *Exemplar*, which appears to have provided the main impetus for the dissemination of the *Büchlein der Ewigen Weisheit* and the separately transmitted *Hundert Betrachtungen* devotion.[36] The next landmarks in the history of prayer cycles based on the life or passion of Christ are the *Meditationes de passione Christi* (Meditations on the Passion of Christ) by the Austin Friar Jordan of Quedlinburg and the *Vita Christi* of the Strasbourg Carthusian Ludolph of Saxony, both of which I need to complete my story. I will deal with them more briefly.

Jordan of Quedlinburg, an exact contemporary of Suso's, was an Austin friar in Erfurt and Magdeburg and prior provincial of the Saxon-Thuringian province of his order in the third quarter of the fourteenth century.[37] Jordan's *Meditationes de passione Christi* (also known as the *Articuli LXV de passione Christi*: Sixty-Five Articles on the Passion of Christ), which is first encountered in the section for Good Friday in his *Opus postillarum et sermonum de tempore*, datable to about 1365, is structured on the basis of sixty-five short prayers addressed to the Lord and presented in sequence from Christ's entry into Gethsemane to the Entombment.[38] Each of the prayers is embedded in a systematically structured meditation, beginning with the prayer, called the 'theorema', followed by the 'articulus', which contains the relevant passion narrative, 'documenta' (with further subdivisions called 'puncti'), and then a 'conformatio', which states what the devotee must do in order to apply what has been learned to his own life. The text is structured according to the canonical hours. Although the *Meditationes de passione Christi* are first found as part of a sermon collection, they were often

---

[36] I have noted a copy of the *Hundert Betrachtungen* in a dated manuscript from 1348, München, Bayerische Staatsbibl., Cgm 717, fols 78ʳ–81ᵛ; not listed by Hofmann, 'Seuses Werke in deutschsprachigen Handschriften'.

[37] For a comprehensive account of Jordan, see Saak, *High Way to Heaven*, pp. 243–315.

[38] Jordan of Quedlinburg, *Opus postillarum*, Strasbourg edn, vol. 3, fols 209ᵛᵇ–233ᵛᵇ (*sermones* 189–254); conveniently available online from the Universitäts- und Landesbibl. Darmstadt (images 418–67). Cf. Baier, *Untersuchungen zu den Passionsbetrachtungen in der 'Vita Christi' des Ludolf von Sachsen*, vol. 2, pp. 309–25; Saak, *High Way to Heaven*, pp. 354 with n. 26 and 476–505; Hamburger and Palmer, *The Prayer Book of Ursula Begerin*, vol. 1, pp. 450–52.

presented on their own as an excerpt; there are translations into German and Dutch, and there are manuscripts which contain just the prayers excerpted, as a passion cycle, without the elaborate context devised by Jordan, sometimes in Latin, sometimes in the vernacular.[39] Occasionally they are illustrated. The Dutch transmission has been studied rather more than the Latin and the German, and the text is better known to art historians than to literary scholars.

The first of Jordan's sixty-five articles refers to Christ's sadness and fear on entering Gethsemane, picking up on his words 'Tristis est anima mea usque ad mortem' (My soul is sorrowful, even unto death, Matthew 26. 38), followed by a plea that the devotee might be empowered to see any sorrow that he experiences in his own life in the context of Christ's sorrow in Gethsemane:

> Domine iesu christe fili dei uiui. qui hora matutinali pro me misero peccatore et pro totius mundi redemptione imminente hora passionis tue tristari. pauere. et mestus esse voluisti. doce me omnem tristiciam ad te deum cordis mei semper referre. atque in vnione tue tristicie in te eam vincere. et tecum amanter suffere. (fol. 211ra, *sermo* 190 [image no. 421])

> (Lord Jesus Christ, Son of the living God, you who at the morning hour, as the hour of your passion approached, were filled on my behalf, a wretched sinner, and for the redemption of all the world with sadness, fear, and sorrow, teach me always to relate all sadness of my heart to you, God, and to overcome it in union with your sadness in you, and to endure it lovingly with you.)

This same structure, calling to mind a moment from the passion, followed by a petition, underlies almost all of the sixty-five prayers. Article 60, for example, refers to the vinegar and wine mingled with gall offered to Christ on the cross (Matthew 27. 34) and requests, in the petition, that he should display true devotion (wine) and be empowered to show penitence (myrrh/spice) and remorse (gall) for his sins and never be guilty of duplicity or causing offence (vinegar):

> Jesu qui nostram salutem sitiens aceto et vino mirrato cum felle potari voluisti. fac me vinum deuotionis cum mirra carnis mortificationis ac felle penitentialis compunctionis tibi digne offerre. acetum autem infidelitatis vel scandali nequaquam bibere sed tecum gustare *quam suauis es domine mi*. (fol. 230va, *sermo* 249 [image no. 460])[40]

---

[39] Saak, *High Way to Heaven*, p. 354 n. 26; Hamburger and Palmer, *The Prayer Book of Ursula Begerin*, vol. I, p. 451 n. 150. For a German text, see the Prayer Book for Duke Albrecht V of Austria, Wien, Österreichische Nationalbibl., Cod. 2722, fols 62r–87r; cf. Pirker-Aurenhammer, *Das Gebetbuch für Herzog Albrecht V. von Österreich*, p. 82, with further references.

[40] Emended from the *c.* 1498/1500 Magdeburg incunable edition of Jordan of Quedlinburg, *Meditationes Iordani*, sig. liv recto (the Schweinfurt copy online from the Bayerische Staatsbibl.,

(You, Jesus, who, thirsting for our salvation, were willing to be given vinegar and wine spiced with gall to drink, cause me to offer you, in a worthy manner, the wine of devotion seasoned with the spice of mortification of the flesh and the gall of penitence and remorse, and in no way ever to drink the vinegar of duplicity or offence, but rather to taste *how sweet you are, my Lord*.)

In article 61 the words 'Consummatum est' (It is finished, John 19. 30) are interpreted not with immediate reference to the death of Christ, but rather the devotee pleads for divine assistance in bringing to an appropriate conclusion ('consummation') the good things he has done in praise of God:

> Jesu qui consummationem totius passionis tue in summa deo patri offerens dixisti. consummatum est. da mihi omnia per me te operante bene acta et passa ad tuam laudem consummare et consummata per te deo patri offerre. (fol. 231ra, *sermo* 250 [image no. 461])

> (You, Jesus, who, finally offering up to God the Father the consummation of all your suffering, spoke the words 'It is finished', grant me that through your offices I might bring to consummation all the good things I have done or experienced in your praise, and that through you I might offer up to God the Father those things that have been brought to consummation.)

In the following prayers, which call to memory Christ's commendation of his soul to the Father, the side-wound, and the Deposition, the petitions express a desire to experience spiritual death in this life in the hope of a good death at the end, a request to undergo suffering for love's sake, and a request for worthy reception of the Eucharist on the basis of virtue and purity of heart.[41] In this way each petition is formulated as a request to be empowered by the Lord to apply the idea extracted from the list of moments in Christ's passion to some aspect of the Christian life. These are tropological interpretations far removed from the complex *Leidenstheologie* that we find in Bonaventure or Suso, and Jordan's passion devotion may for this reason be called a didactic reading of the passion. Eric L. Saak has rightly stressed the Augustinian epistemology that underlies Jordan's meditations and the lack of any specific focus on mystical union or the ascetic imitation of Christ's suffering.[42]

---

image no. 171); *ISTC* ij00475000; GW M15105. The reading of the last words remains uncertain. For manuscripts and the textual tradition of the *Opus postillarum*, see the introduction by Nadia Bray in Jordanus of Quedlinburg, *Opus postillarum et sermonum De nativitate domini. Opus Ior*, pp. 3–12.

[41] Jordan of Quedlinburg, *Opus postillarum*, Strasbourg edn, vol. 3, fol. 231rb–232vb, *sermones* 251–253 [images nos. 461–64].

[42] Saak, *High Way to Heaven* (as cited in note 37), who also suggests that the approach adopted in the *Meditationes de passione Christi* is conditioned by the needs of the wider, non-

Jordan provides a preface to the *Meditationes de passione Christi*, setting out the basic principles of his meditational system, in which he quite explicitly addresses the issue of how meditations on Christ's passion relate to meditation on the life of Christ. Imitation of Christ does not simply consist of visualizing the passion, but the devotee should follow in Christ's footsteps and imitate him in his actions efficaciously, he must learn how to act in his own life in order to follow his exemplar in Christ. He explains how the whole of Christ's life consisted of suffering hardships, documenting this in detail by explaining how he was born in unworthy conditions, how he shed blood at the circumcision, how he suffered from having to flee the persecution by Herod, and other experiences that entailed suffering, thoughout the whole of his life. As formulated here, therefore, *Vita Christi* meditation was for Jordan meditation on the life of Christ conceived more broadly, and his sixty-five articles simply focus, as a devotional practice that he wished to promote, on the culmination of this life of suffering, on the passion from Gethsemane onwards.

The final text for consideration is the *Vita Christi* of the Strasbourg Carthusian Ludolph of Saxony, also a work dating from the third quarter of the fourteenth century and first attested by mention in a will dated 1375, three years before Ludolph's death.[43] The text is datable to 1365/75, and thus only a few years after Suso's *Exemplar*.[44] The 1865 edition of the *Vita Christi*, which Baier has shown to follow the majority of manuscripts, presents the text as consisting of two books covering the whole of the life of Christ, if not in strictly chronological order, and contains 181 chapters in all. Each chapter is concluded by a prayer that relates back to the content of what precedes, and these prayers were sometimes excerpted and put together into collections, not necessarily following Ludolph's chapter order, as a prayer book, or as part of a prayer book. The Latin text was widely circulated, there is extensive reception in German vernacular versions, in particular four translations of just the section devoted to the passion, one of which is illustrated, an early printed edition in German that covers the whole in

monastic audience that Jordan had in mind for this particular text.

[43] Ludolph of Saxony, *Vita Jesu Christi*, ed. by Bolard and others (1865). Later printings omit the valuable marginal annotations. For Ludolph and his *Vita Christi*, see Baier, *Untersuchungen zu den Passionsbetrachtungen in der 'Vita Christi' des Ludolf von Sachsen*, and for further bibliography and the vernacular reception Hamburger and Palmer, *The Prayer Book of Ursula Begerin*, vol. 1, pp. 439–52.

[44] For Ludolph's quotations from Suso, for which he used the *Horologium* (*c.* 1334), not the *Büchlein der ewigen Weisheit* or the *Exemplar*, see Baier, *Untersuchungen zu den Passionsbetrachtungen in der 'Vita Christi' des Ludolf von Sachsen*, vol. 2, 300–02; Baier, 'Michael von Massa', p. 514.

abbreviated form, and two rather freer adaptations. There is evidence that the whole work may have been rendered into Dutch, although only one volume of this translation has been preserved.

The prayers are only one element in Ludolph's work, which is a huge assembly of materials relating to the life and passion of Christ, drawing on a variety of literary genres. There is evidence, however, that there was special focus on the prayers in the reception, for example in the German translations, where in one case just one hundred prayers are selected and highlighted in the manuscript, by the marking up of the Lucerne translation by Nikolaus Schulmeister by 'oratio' in red in the margins throughout, and by prayer cycles such as the *Begerin Picture Cycle and Prayers*, where Ludolph's prayers form the basis of more than half the material in an extensive text, often translated literally.[45]

How does Ludolph respond to the tension between life of Christ meditation and passion meditation? His writing method is to compile an enormous quantity of material from well-known sources, such that works like the *Speculum humanae salvationis*, the *Vita Christi* attributed in more recent literature on the basis of the attribution in a single manuscript to Michael de Massa (which was itself in good measure a compilation),[46] and Ekbert's *Meditatio de humanitate Christi* were broken up and then integrated, in sections, into Ludolph's text in their entirety. His work presents us with a multiplicity of voices, and to understand just where it stands in the literary history of this period we would need better information on how he chose what to include, how the voices in the different source texts relate to one another, and on the specifics of the material which we can identify as his own.[47] Whereas the *Vita Christi* covers the whole life of Christ, particular emphasis is given to the passion in the section devoted to Easter, Chapters 51–67 of Book II, which is presented as a self-contained

---

[45] Zurich, Zentralbibl., Cod. C10f (with a hundred *orationes*); Engelberg, Stiftsbibl., Cod. 339, fols 2ʳ–173ᵛ (the Lucerne text, dated 1396/1403). Cf. Hamburger and Palmer, *The Prayer Book of Ursula Begerin*, vol. I, pp. 442–44 et passim.

[46] For this not unproblematic attribution of the *Vita Christi* to the author of the *Angeli pacis* and *Extendit manum* treatises, which is too uncertain to be used as evidence for dating, see in particular the strong case against made by Willeumier-Schalij in 1980: 'Is Michael de Massa de auteur?'. Cf. Baier, *Untersuchungen zu den Passionsbetrachtungen in der 'Vita Christi' des Ludolf von Sachsen*, vol. 1, p. 134, and vol. 2, pp. 344–51; Baier, 'Michael von Massa'; Kemper, *Die Kreuzigung Christi*, pp. 116–33; Hamburger and Palmer, *The Prayer Book of Ursula Begerin*, vol. 1, pp. 436–39; McNamer, *Meditations on the Life of Christ*, p. cxxxvi.

[47] The three-volume study by Baier, *Untersuchungen zu den Passionsbetrachtungen in der 'Vita Christi' des Ludolf von Sachsen*, collects all the basic data, but an additional functional analysis would be needed to show how the numerous sources are employed by Ludolph.

unit. Much of the passion literature available in northern Europe in the mid-fourteenth century is assembled here, but restructured and set out according to the canonical hours.

Each chapter of the *Vita Christi* is concluded with a prayer, as a rule an original composition by Ludolph drawing on the material of the preceding chapter. In addition, the author appears to have interpolated into the text of the chapters devoted to the passion a complete set of the sixty-five prayers from the *Meditationes* of Jordan of Quedlinburg, a work that may well not have been finished much more than a year or two before Ludolph completed the *Vita Christi*. In many cases Ludolph augments Jordan's prayers with extra material, not just rhetorical elaboration, employing rhyme, word repetitions, and matching phrases, but sometimes quite significant additions in terms of content. His project was to create a body of material for meditation on the whole life of Christ, underpinned by salvation history. But like Bonaventure, whose *Lignum vitae* he knew and quoted (but does not seem to have used extensively), he gave the passion and crucifixion a central and privileged position, and includes in some of the prefatory passages material specifically relating to passion devotion, structured more in the manner of Suso, if not with the same ascetic/mystical focus.

In Ludolph's prayers for the ninth hour and for Passion Sunday, Book II Chapters 64 and 67, we find a combination of participation in Christ's suffering with a broader conception of the benefits of passion devotion:

> Domine Jesu Christe, qui hora diei nona pendens in patibula, et clamans voce magna, in manus Patris spiritum commendasti; et inclinato capite eumdem spiritum emisisti; et jam mortuus vulnus lateris, de lancea militis suscepisti; dignare, quaeso, nunc et semper, spiritum meum tibi commendatum habere, et gladio charitatis cor meum transverberare, eique vulnera tui corporis imprimere; et per haec, cogitationes illicitas ab ipso repellere, ac tandem in fine vitae meae, spiritum meum in manus tuas commendatum, cum beatis spiritibus collocare. Amen.[48]

> (Lord Jesus Christ, you who at the ninth hour, hanging on the cross and calling out with a loud voice, commended your spirit into the hands of the Father, and bowing your head gave up your spirit; and after your death received a wound in the side from the soldier's lance; deign, I beseech you, to take care of my spirit that I have commended to you now and for evermore, to strike through my heart with the sword of love, imprinting on it the wounds of your body; and by so doing to repel improper thoughts from my heart, and finally at the end of my life to place my spirit, commended into your hands, in among with the heavenly host. Amen.)

[48] Ludolph of Saxony, *Vita Jesu Christi*, II. 64, ed. by Bolard and others, p. 677.

Domine Jesu Christe, qui pro redemptione mundi miserias et angustias, opprobria et convitia, calumnias et injurias, poenas et afflictiones, passionem et mortem patienter ferre voluisti: tu per haec omnia quae propter peccata nostra pertulisti, a peccatis omnibus et vitiis, ab omnibus hujus saeculi periculis, et infernalibus poenis, a subitanea et aeterna morte, me libera; et da mihi, obsecro te, omnia quae pro me tolerasti non fugere vel oblivisci, sed prae oculis semper habere, et ardenter amplecti, ut laboris et doloris participem, etiam requiei et consolationis tuae me velis esse consortem. Amen.[49]

(Lord Jesus Christ, you who for the redemption of the world willingly and patiently endured miseries and fears, taunts and clamouring, slander and insults, torments and afflictions, suffering and death: by virtue of all those things which you underwent for our sins, free me from all sins and vices, from all the dangers of this world, from the infernal torments, and from sudden and eternal death; and grant, I beseech you, that I do not flee or forget all those things you underwent on my behalf, but rather that I might keep them for ever before my eyes, embrace them ardently, that you might willingly allow me to be not just a participator in your suffering and sorrow, but also a partner in your rest and consolation.)

The prayer for the ninth hour, at the end of Chapter II. 64, rehearses the material from the passion narrative in the preceding chapter, and then uses it as the basis for a plea to experience love of God and protection from improper thoughts, and finally for salvation. The idea of one's heart being cut through with the sword of love and Christ's wounds being imprinted on the heart, taken together, are powerful expressions of interaction with Christ, but they do not amount to imitation of Christ crucified in the manner of Suso or Bonaventure, for whom these ideas go beyond just being metaphors for a life devoted to the Lord. In the second prayer cited, that from Chapter 67, individual elements of Christ's suffering are listed, based on the passion narrative, as the basis for a plea for protection from sin, temptation, hellfire, and damnation, but combined with a plea that the devotee should be empowered to visualize and experience continually all those things that Christ suffered, not just in order to be a participator in Christ's suffering and sorrow, but also in his tranquillity and consolation, which implies rest in peace in the afterlife. What this amounts to is in fact a life of meditation on Christ, but without Suso's stress on bitter suffering in this life as the only gateway to heaven, total identification with Christ, or suffering again for Christ's sake what he suffered and thus experiencing the redemptive process in one's own body. In a prayer towards the end of the chapter for the ninth hour on Good Friday, which is an expansion of Jordan's prayer no. 63 from the *Meditationes*, Ludolph declares

---

[49] Ludolph of Saxony, *Vita Jesu Christi*, II. 67, ed. by Bolard and others, p. 691.

the side-wound to be the gateway to life from Psalm 117, rather than presenting it, with Suso, as the gateway of Christ's suffering through which the devotee must pass in the course of his ascent to God in his divinity:

> *Jesu, qui latus corporis tui mortui, lancea aperiri, et exinde sanguinem et aquam exire voluisti: vulnera, quaeso, cor meum lancea charitatis, ut tuis dignus efficiar sacramentis, quae de eodem sacratissimo latere profluxerunt.* In apertura lateris tui, Domine, aperuisti electis tuis januam vitae. Haec porta tua, Domine, justi intrabunt in eam. Noli, Domine, quaeso, iniquitatum mearum recordari, ut propter eas mihi claudas aditum istum, quem peccatoribus et poenitentibus providisti.[50]

> (*Jesus, you who desired that the side of your dead body be opened up by the lance and that blood and water should flow from it, I beseech you, wound my heart with the lance of love, so that I might be made worthy of your sacraments that flowed out from your most holy side.* In the aperture of your side, O Lord, you opened up for your chosen ones the gateway of life. Through this your gate, O Lord, the righteous shall enter (Psalms 117. 20). O Lord, I beg you, remember not my misdeeds, on account of which you might bar me from the entrance that you have provided for penitent sinners.)

There are similar shifts of emphasis in the other reworkings of Jordan's prayers. The bitterness of the vinegar and wine mixed with gall points paradoxically to its opposite, the joy and love the passion inspires; Christ's consummation of his mission with the words 'Consummatum est' (It is finished, John 19. 30) is matched by the devotee's joyous hope to achieve his goal of salvation; the devotee prays for salvation commending himself to the outstretched arms of Christ on the cross; his response to the Deposition is the plea that he might be empowered to hold back from being deposed, metaphorically, from the cross that he took up at his profession as a monk until the hour of his death.[51] This is a different model for a cycle of prayers on the passion and crucifixion of Christ from what we have found with either Suso or Jordan, the reception of whose meditational cycles also begins in the 1360s.

---

[50] Ludolph of Saxony, *Vita Jesu Christi*, II. 64, ed. by Bolard and others, p. 676. The italicized text is taken verbatim from Jordan's prayer no. 63: Jordan of Quedlinburg, *Opus postillarum*, Strasbourg edn, vol. 3, fol. 232ʳᵃ, *sermo* 252 [image no. 463].

[51] See the four prayers 'Jesu qui nostram salutem', 'Jesus Salvator noster', 'Jesus qui in cruce moriens', and 'Jesus qui de cruce non vivus', cited in the body of the text in Ludolph's *Vita Jesu Christi*, ed. by Bolard and others, II. 63 (p. 668), II. 63 (pp. 669–70), II. 64 (pp. 671–72), II. 65 (p. 679), which quote verbatim from articles 60, 61, 62, and 64 of Jordan's *Meditationes*, but also adapt and add to their source.

From now on, the different types of meditational prayer cycles were to coexist, sometimes even copied side-by-side, or mixed with one another, and they form the basis for a whole set of new developments that begin at the end of the fourteenth century and extend right through to the sixteenth century and beyond. It may be helpful to think of them as 'Antiseusiana', in order to stress how the literary presentation of meditation on 'Christ in his humanity' in this period did not simply focus on the bitterness and pain, which is so central to Suso's soteriological and mystical programme, but encompassed a range of rather different interpretations of what it meant to be an 'imitator of Christ'. Bonaventura is a significant precursor. And whereas it is important to note that Suso's *Hundert Betrachtungen* were formulated shortly before 1330, it was not until the early 1360s that he put together his *Exemplar* (which contains the *Hundert Betrachtungen* as Part III of the *Büchlein der Ewigen Weisheit*), thereby initiating a new phase in the circulation of his writings, on which Jordan's *Meditationes de passione Christi* (datable *c.* 1365) and the *Vita Christi* of Ludolph of Saxony (1365/75) were soon to follow.[52] These Franciscan, Dominican, Augustinian and Carthusian authors had by 1370 established a major body of differently nuanced devotional materials that not only went into wide circulation, but also established a set of practical devotional rituals that although based on monastic traditions would soon be taken up by very much wider audiences of recipients and devotees. This is the tradition in which the meditational practices of the *Devotio Moderna* were in turn to take their place.

---

[52] For the dates, which are important for my argument, but not universally accepted in earlier scholarship, see my discussion in Hamburger and Palmer, *The Prayer Book of Ursula Begerin*, vol. 1, pp. 419 (Bonaventure), 432 (Suso), 440 (Ludolf), and 451–52 (Jordan).

Works Cited

Manuscripts

Engelberg, Stiftsbibliothek, Cod. 339
München, Bayerische Staatsbibliothek, Cgm 717
St. Gallen, Stiftsbibliothek, Cod. Sang. 479
Sarnen, Benediktinerkollegium, Cod. chart. 208
Utrecht, Museum Catharijneconvent, BMH h 53
Zurich, Zentralbibliothek, Cod. C10f

Primary Sources

Bernard of Clairvaux. S. *Bernardi Opera*, ed. by Jean Leclercq and others, 8 vols (Roma: Editiones Cistercienses, 1957–1977)

Bonaventura, *Lignum vitae*, in *Decem opuscula ad theologiam mysticam spectantia in textu correcta et notis illustrata*, ed. by the fathers of the Collegium S. Bonaventurae (Quaracchi: Collegium S. Bonaventurae, 1896), pp. 168–223

——, *Opera omnia*, 10 vols, ed. by the fathers of the Collegium S. Bonaventurae (Quaracchi: Collegium S. Bonaventurae, 1882–1902)

David of Augsburg. David ab Augusta, *De exterioris et interioris hominis compositione secundum triplicem statum incipientium, proficientium et perfectorum libri tres*, ed. by the fathers of the Collegium S. Bonaventurae (Quaracchi: Collegium S. Bonaventurae, 1899)

Das Hermetschwiler Gebetbuch. Studien zur deutschsprachigen Gebetbuchliteratur der Nord- und Zentralschweiz im Spätmittelalter. Mit einer Edition, ed. by Ruth Wiederkehr, Kulturtopographie des alemannischen Raums, 5 (Berlin: De Gruyter, 2013)

Jordan of Quedlinburg, *Opus postillarum et sermonum Jordani de tempore* (Strasbourg: Husner, 1483)

——, *Meditationes Iordani de vita et passione Jesu Christi* (Magdeburg: Moritz Brandis, 1498/1500)

——, *Opus postillarum et sermonum de evangeliis dominicalibus. De nativitate domini. Opus Ior. Sermones selecti de filiatione divina*, ed. by Nadia Bray, Corpus philosophorum teutonicorum medii aevi, VII, 3 (Hamburg: Meiner, 2008)

Liber precum. Vollständige Faksimile-Ausgabe der Handschrift Ms. Lat.O.v.I.206 der Russischen Nationalbibliothek in St. Petersburg, ed. by Margarita Logutova and James H. Marrow, 2 vols, Codices selecti, 108 (Graz: ADEVA, 2003)

Ludolph of Saxony. *Vita Jesu Christi e quatuor evangeliis et scriptoribus orthodoxis concinnata per Ludolphum de Saxonia ex ordine Carthusianorum*, ed. by A.-Clovis Bolard and others (Paris: Palmé, 1865)

McNamer, Sarah, *Meditations on the Life of Christ: The Short Italian Text* (Notre Dame: University of Notre Dame Press, 2018)

Suso, Henry. Heinrich Seuse, *Deutsche Schriften*, ed. by Karl Bihlmeyer (Stuttgart: Kohlhammer, 1907; repr. Frankfurt am Main: Minerva, 1961)

——, *Heinrich Seuses Horologium sapientiae. Erste kritische Ausgabe unter Benützung der Vorarbeiten von Dominikus Planzer OP*, ed. by Pius Künzle, Spicilegium Friburgense, 23 (Freiburg Schweiz: Universitätsverlag, 1977)

——, *The Exemplar, with Two German Sermons*, trans. by Frank Tobin (New York: Paulist Press, 1989)

——, Bl. Henry Suso, *Wisdom's Watch upon the Hours*, trans. by Edmund Colledge, The Fathers of the Church, Continuation, 4 (Washington, DC: Catholic University of America Press, 1994)

Secondary Sources

Achten, Gerard, 'Die Meditationes und Orationes des Arnoldi von Alfeld wiederentdeckt', in *Historia et spiritualitas Cartusiensis. Colloquii quarti internationalis Gandavi – Antverpiae – Brugis, 16–19 Sept. 1982*, ed. by Jan de Grauwe (Destelbergen: de Grauwe, 1983), pp. 15–20

Aelst, José van, *Passie voor het lijden. De 'Hundert Betrachtungen und Begehrungen' van Henricus Suso en de oudste drie bewerkingen uit de Nederlanden* (Leuven: Peeters, 2005)

——, *Vruchten van de passie. De laatmiddeleeuwse passieliteratur verkend aan de hand van Suso's 'Honderd artikelen'* (Hilversum: Verloren, 2011)

Baier, Walter, 'Michael von Massa († 1337) – Autor einer "Vita Christi": Kritik der Diskussion über ihre Zuordnung zur "Vita Christi" des Kartäusers Ludolf von Sachsen († 1378)', in *Traditio Augustiniana. Studien über Augustinus und seine Rezeption. Festgabe für Willigis Eckermann OSA zum 60. Geburtstag*, ed. by Adolar Zumkeller and Achim Krümmel, Cassiciacum, 46 (Würzburg: Augustinus, 1994), pp. 495–524

——, *Untersuchungen zu den Passionsbetrachtungen in der 'Vita Christi' des Ludolf von Sachsen. Ein quellenkritischer Beitrag zu Leben und Werk Ludolfs und zur Geschichte der Passionstheologie*, 3 vols, Analecta Cartusiana, 44, 1–3 (Salzburg: Institut für englische Sprache und Literatur, 1977)

Blumrich, Rüdiger, 'Die Überlieferung der deutschen Schriften Seuses', in *Heinrich Seuses Philosophia spiritualis. Quellen, Konzept, Formen und Rezeption. Tagung Eichstätt 2.–4. Oktober 1991*, ed. by Rüdiger Blumrich and Philipp Kaiser (Wiesbaden: Reichert, 1994), pp. 189–201

Blumrich, Rüdiger, and Philipp Kaiser, eds, *Heinrich Seuses Philosophia spiritualis. Quellen, Konzept, Formen und Rezeption. Tagung Eichstätt 2.–4.Oktober 1991* (Wiesbaden: Reichert, 1994)

Cermann, Regina, *Katalog der deutschsprachigen illustrierten Handschriften des Mittelalters*. vol. 5, fasc. 1/2: *43. Gebetbücher* (München: Beck, 2002)

Constable, Giles, 'The Ideal of the Imitation of Christ', in Giles Constable, *Three Studies in Medieval Religious and Social Thought* (Cambridge: Cambridge University Press, 1995, repr. 1998), pp. 143–248

Deschamps, Jan, 'De Middelnederlandse vertalingen en bewerkingen van de *Hundert Betrachtungen und Begehrungen* van Henricus Suso', *Ons Geestelijk Erf*, 63 (1989), 309–69

Enders, Markus, *Das mystische Wissen bei Heinrich Seuse*, Veröffentlichungen des Grabmann-Institutes zur Erforschung der Mittelalterlichen Theologie und Philosophie, n. F. 37 (Paderborn: Schöningh, 1992)

Falque, Ingrid, '*Daz man bild mit bilden us tribe*: Imagery and Knowledge of God in Henry Suso's *Exemplar*', *Speculum. Journal of Medieval Studies*, 92 (2017), 447–92

Haas, Alois Maria, *Kunst rechter Gelassenheit. Themen und Schwerpunkte von Heinrich Seuses Mystik* (Bern: Peter Lang, ²1996)

Haas, Alois Maria, and Kurt Ruh, 'Seuse, Heinrich', in *Verfasserlexikon*, 2nd edn, vol. 8 (1992), cols 1109–24

Hamburger, Jeffrey F., *The Visual and the Visionary, Art and Female Spirituality in Late Medieval Germany* (New York: Zone, 1998)

Hamburger, Jeffrey F., and Nigel F. Palmer, *The Prayer Book of Ursula Begerin*, vol. 1, *Art-Historical and Literary Introduction*, with a conservation report by Ulrike Bürger; vol. 2, *Reproductions and Critical Edition* (Dietikon–Zurich: Urs Graf, 2015)

Haug, Walter, and Burghart Wachinger, eds, *Die Passion Christi in Literatur und Kunst des Spätmittelalters*, Fortuna vitrea, 12 (Tübingen: Niemeyer, 1993)

Hindman, Sandra, and James H. Marrow, eds, *Books of Hours Reconsidered* (Turnhout: Brepols, 2013)

Hoffmann, Werner J., 'Die volkssprachliche Rezeption des "Horologium sapientiae" in der Devotio moderna', in *Heinrich Seuses Philosophia spiritualis. Quellen, Konzept, Formen und Rezeption. Tagung Eichstätt 2.–4.Oktober 1991*, ed. by Rüdiger Blumrich and Philipp Kaiser (Wiesbaden: Reichert, 1994), pp. 202–54

Hofmann, Georg, 'Seuses Werke in deutschsprachigen Handschriften des späten Mittelalters', *Fuldaer Geschichtsblätter*, 45 (1969), 113–208

Hogg, James, 'Arnoldi, Heinrich, von Alfeld', in *Biographisch-Bibliographisches Kirchenlexikon*, vol. 16 (1999), cols 55–59

Jahn, Bruno, 'Seuse, Heinrich', in *Deutsches Literatur-Lexikon. Das Mittelalter*, Vol. 2, *Das geistliche Schrifttum des Spätmittelalters*, ed. by Wolfgang Achnitz (Berlin: De Gruyter, 2011), pp. 180–89

Karnes, Michelle, *Imagination, Meditation, and Cognition in the Middle Ages* (Chicago: University of Chicago Press, 2011)

Kemper, Tobias A., *Die Kreuzigung Christi: Motivgeschichtliche Studien zu lateinischen und deutschen Passionstraktaten des Spätmittelalters*, Münchener Texte und Untersuchungen zur deutschen Literatur des Mittelalters, 131 (Tübingen: Niemeyer, 2006)

McGinn, Bernard, *The Harvest of Mysticism in Medieval Germany*, The Presence of God: A History of Western Christian Mysticism, 4 (New York: Crossroad, 1998)

McNamer, Sarah, *Meditations on the Life of Christ: The Short Italian Text* (Notre Dame: University of Notre Dame Press, 2018)

Michel, Paul, 'Seuse als Diener des göttlichen Wortes', in *Das "einig Ein". Studien zu Theorie und Sprache der deutschen Mystik*, ed. by Alois Haas and others (Freiburg Schweiz: Universitätsverlag, 1980), pp. 281–367

Ochsenbein, Peter, 'Deutschsprachige Privatgebetbücher vor 1400', in *Deutsche Handschriften 1100–1400. Oxforder Kolloquium 1985*, ed. by Volker Honemann and Nigel F. Palmer (Tübingen: Niemeyer, 1988), pp. 379–98

O'Connell, Patrick F., 'The "Lignum vitae" of Saint Bonaventure and the Medieval Devotional Tradition' (PhD dissertation, Fordham University, 1985)

——, 'Aelred of Rievaulx and the "Lignum vitae" of Bonaventure: A Reappraisal', *Franciscan Studies*, 48 (1988), 53–80

——, 'Eckbert of Schönau and the "Lignum vitae" of St Bonaventure', *Revue Bénédictine*, 101 (1991), 341–82

Palmer, Nigel F., 'Allegory and Prayer. The House of the Heart and the Ark of the Virtues in the "Gebetbuch der Ursula Begerin"', in *Auf den Schwingen des Pelikans. Gedenkschrift für Christoph Gerhardt*, ed. by Ralph Plate, Niels Bohnert, Christian Griesinger, and Michael Traut (Trier: Verlag für Geschichte und Kultur, in press)

Pirker-Aurenhammer, Veronika, *Das Gebetbuch für Herzog Albrecht V. von Österreich (Wien, ÖNB, Cod. 2722)*, Codices illuminati, 3 (Graz: ADEVA, 2002)

Preisinger, Raphaèle, *Lignum vitae. Zum Verhältnis materieller Bilder und mentaler Bildpraxis im Mittelalter* (München: Fink, 2014)

Reinburg, Virginia, *French Books of Hours: Making an Archive of Prayer, c. 1400–1600* (Cambridge: Cambridge University Press, 2012)

Ruh, Kurt, *Geschichte der abendländischen Mystik*, vol. 3, *Die Mystik des deutschen Predigerordens und ihre Grundlegung durch die Hochscholastik* (München: Beck, 1996)

Saak, Eric L., *High Way to Heaven: The Augustinian Platform between Reform and Reformation, 1292-1524*, Studies in Medieval and Reformation Thought, 89 (Leiden: Brill, 2002)

Schuppisser, Fritz Oskar, 'Schauen mit den Augen des Herzens. Zur Methodik der spätmittelalterlichen Passionsmeditation, besonders in der Devotio Moderna und bei den Augustinern', in *Die Passion Christi in Literatur und Kunst des Spätmittelalters*, ed. by Walter Haug and Burghart Wachinger, Fortuna vitrea, 12 (Tübingen: Niemeyer, 1993), pp. 169–210

Steer, Georg, 'Die Passion Christi bei den deutschen Bettelorden im 13. Jahrhundert. David von Augsburg, "Baumgarten geistlicher Herzen", Hugo Ripelin von Straßburg, Meister Eckharts "Reden der Unterscheidung"', in *Die Passion Christi in Literatur und Kunst des Spätmittelalters*, ed. by Walter Haug and Burghart Wachinger, Fortuna vitrea, 12 (Tübingen: Niemeyer, 1993), pp. 52–75

Ulrich, Peter, 'Zur Bedeutung des Leidens in der Konzeption der *philosophia spiritualis* Heinrich Seuses', in *Heinrich Seuses Philosophia spiritualis. Quellen, Konzept, Formen und Rezeption. Tagung Eichstätt 2.–4.Oktober 1991*, ed. by Rüdiger Blumrich and Philipp Kaiser (Wiesbaden: Reichert, 1994), pp. 124–38

Willeumier-Schalij, J. M., 'Is Michael de Massa de auteur van de Latijnse grondtekst van het zgn. Pseudo-Bonaventura-Ludolphiaanse Leven van Jezus?', *Nederlands Archief voor Kerkgeschiedenis*, 60 (1980), 1–10

Modern Devotion and Arrangements for Commemoration: Some Observations

Koen Goudriaan

At her death in 1419 Bartraet Costijn's widow left a sum of money to the 'sisters of St Pancratius at the Kercgraft' in the town of Leiden, which enabled them to buy fuel (peat or turf). In return each of them was expected to participate in Bartraet's perpetual commemoration, which was to take place quarterly on the third day of March, June, September, and December, by attending vigil and high Mass, and by sitting on her tomb until its 'beganghenisse' (visitation) was over.[1] We know this from a short list of benefactions to this community, dating from the early fifteenth century and inserted in a manuscript which also contains a memorial register. This register is arranged according to the liturgical year, but it starts on 3 September, i.e., on one of the dates of Bartraet's *memoria*. The list was written down approximately a century later, but it still contains several entries going back to Bartraet's generation. The small community of the sisters of St Pancratius belonged to the type categorized by Madelon van Luijk as a 'House of Devout Sisters'.[2] When it received Bartraet's

[1] Leiden, ELO, Kloosters inv. 518, fol. 20ʳ.

[2] Van Luijk, *Bruiden van Christus*, pp. 46–50. Cf. the Census of Medieval Monasteries in the Netherlands, http://www2.fgw.vu.nl/oz/monasteries/kdetails.php?ID = L12 [accessed 21 November 2018]. A new version of the Census will be launched shortly which will include all the monasteries in the Netherlands until 1800. The new database's name will be 'Monasteries in the Netherlands until 1800: a Census'.

Koen Goudriaan (goudriaan50@gmail.com) is Emeritus Professor of Medieval History at the Vrije Universiteit Amsterdam. His main fields of interest are the late medieval religious culture of the Low Countries in general and the *Devotio Moderna* in particular.

Inwardness, Individualization, and Religious Agency in the Late Medieval Low Countries, ed. by Rijcklof Hofman, Charles Caspers, Peter Nissen, Mathilde van Dijk, and Johan Oosterman, MCS 43 (Turnhout: Brepols, 2020), pp. 121–136   BREPOLS 🖳 PUBLISHERS   10.1484/M.MCS-EB.5.119392

legacy it had only just started, as one of the many communities which arose in those days in the Low Countries under the impact of the religious revival we are accustomed to call the *Devotio Moderna*. Characteristically, this community undertook commemorative duties right from the beginning. The sisters had to fulfil them in the nearby parish and collegiate church of St Pancratius: they lacked a chapel of their own and would never acquire one.

Memoria, prayers for the deceased, is of course a key religious activity. 'Death and commemoration' are central concepts in any kind of religious consciousness. Medieval commemorative practices rest on the deep-seated belief that solidarity is possible between the living and the dead whose souls are sojourning in purgatory. Memorial arrangements reflecting this conviction have a wide potential for providing insight into the diversity of religious life, the individualization of religious practices, and possible long-term trends to be observed in this area. My contribution to the present volume will focus on commemoration within the sphere of the *Devotio Moderna*. This great religious revival that originated in the northern Low Countries experienced its heyday in the fifteenth century. Its institutions continued into the sixteenth century, until the Revolt as far as the northern Low Countries are concerned; in neighbouring countries they lasted longer and eventually petered out. The Modern Devotion has been well studied, not least because of its extensive written heritage that has come down to us. However, commemoration practices in the sphere of the *Devotio Moderna* have not received a great deal of attention, despite the ample availability of source material for this topic. A general explanation for this may be the habit of interpreting the *Devotio Moderna* as a herald of the early modern period rather than as a continuation of the Middle Ages.[3] In contrast, my approach will be that the Modern Devout linked up with a long line of medieval monastic movements in attaching much value to *memoria*.[4] And the central element in commemorative practices, the maintenance of the communion between the living and the dead, the individual and the community, survived right into the sixteenth century.

The example at the beginning of this article was tracked down using the MeMO (Medieval Memoria Online) website which was launched a couple of years ago.[5] MeMO 'contains inventories and descriptions of objects and texts

---

[3] In Goudriaan, 'Grundmann and the Devotio Moderna' (in preparation), I discuss the longstanding effects of the interest taken in particular by scholars of a protestant conviction on the way we view the *Devotio Moderna*.

[4] I have introduced this topic in a detailed case study: Goudriaan, 'The *Devotio Moderna* and Commemoration. The Case of St Margaret's Convent in Gouda'.

[5] http://memodatabase.hum.uu.nl/memo-is/detail/index?detailId = 122&detailType = TextCarrier [accessed 21 November 2018].

that had a function in the commemoration of the dead in the area that is currently the Netherlands, until 1580'.[6] The database is the result of a collaborative effort of art and general historians based at three universities: Utrecht, Groningen, and VU Amsterdam. The best represented category is that of works of art, which consists of 3677 objects, including no fewer than 3074 tombstones (Table 1). A second category is made up of manuscripts, which can be further subdivided into two main branches: chronicles (188), and manuscripts with memorial registers proper (239). In addition, the website contains short descriptions of the approximately 800 ecclesiastical institutions from which the objects and the texts originate.

Table 1. Items entered in MeMO.

Types of items	Number	Specification
Memorial Objects	3677	including 3074 tombstones and tomb monuments
Text Carriers	427	188 chronicles
		239 manuscripts with memorial registers
Institutions	838	including 170 monasteries and convents

A textual category which could not be included was that of wills; these had to be omitted due to the lack of preliminary work. In 1994 Hans Mol investigated the 200-odd surviving medieval wills from the province of Friesland with regard to their relevance to the issue of arrangements for the afterlife, applying the approach of well-known historians from the French school such as Michel Vovelle and Jacques Chiffoleau.[7] He was able to assess the relative importance for commemoration of monastic institutions, many of which were related in one way or another to the *Devotio Moderna*. But so far there has been no follow up.[8] This is a drawback: details of memorial arrangements not registered in the memorial registers are often to be found in wills. The foundation of chantries, for example — an individual type of memorial arrangement which was the prerogative of the rich and famous — is not signalled systematically in MeMO.[9] Nevertheless, the considerable amount of source material MeMO does contain furnishes a

---

[6] Medieval Memoria Online: http://memo.hum.uu.nl/database/index.html: Introductory Page.

[7] Vovelle, *Mourir autrefois*; Chiffoleau, *La comptabilité de l'au-delà*.

[8] Mol, 'Friezen en het hiernamaals', pp. 199–203.

[9] Speetjens, 'The Founder, the Chaplain and the Ecclesiastical Authorities'.

convenient starting point for the analysis of diversification and individualization, which — if approached as diachronic processes — imply a quantitative as well as a qualitative dimension.

The reigning paradigm in *memoria* research is the interpretation of commemoration as a 'total social phenomenon', as formulated by Otto Gerhard Oexle.[10] Arrangements to perpetuate the community of the living and the dead involved not only the religious dimension, but also the social, the economic, and the political dimension. The *do ut des* rule is the central organizing principle: gifts in land, kind, and money in return for intercessory prayers during vigil and Mass, and if possible a visit to the tomb.[11] This was conspicuous to a certain degree, depending of course on the notability of the person concerned. As a general rule, *memoria* incorporated the aspect of self-presentation, and in this way reflected the structures of real life. For that reason alone, *memoria* studies have to allow for a certain amount of individualization, commemoration being a natural vehicle for the expression of rank and distinction which makes up its social aspect. Variety may occur in the intentions with which gifts were given and in their exact destinations, e.g., the repair of a church or the outfit of the liturgy.[12] Individuality is implied in the inscription of one's name in a memorial register and in reading it aloud during acts of commemoration. All these aspects of differentiation, however, do not impinge on the central element of *memoria*: the binding of the individual into a communal liturgical framework which transcends even the border between the living and the dead.

In his programmatic article on *memoria* in the Carolingian era, published in 1976, Oexle took as his point of departure the 'Essai sur le don' by sociologist Marcel Mauss.[13] It was precisely Mauss who had pinpointed the centrality of the *do ut des* rule as the organizing principle of social life. Oexle's step forward consisted in highlighting liturgical prayer as the gift *par excellence* that dominated social relationships in the period he was studying. In practice, in *memoria* studies as carried out nowadays, the emphasis is more on the social mechanisms at work in commemoration than on the potential of this theme for the history of religious belief. Combining *memoria* research with the work done by literary and general historians in the field of the *Devotio Moderna* might

[10] Oexle, 'Memoria und Memorialbild', p. 395.

[11] Oexle, 'Memoria und Memorialüberliefering', pp. 87–95. Cf. the studies reassembled in Bijsterveld, *Do ut des*.

[12] Van Bueren, 'Care for the Here and the Hereafter', p. 28; Biemans and Van Bueren, 'A Veritable Treasure Trove', p. 260.

[13] Mauss, 'Essai sur le don'.

be fruitful for both sides. On the one hand, it reminds us of the potentialities of *memoria* studies for illuminating the more strictly religious aspects of commemoration. In reverse, insofar as the *Devotio Moderna* is often associated with 'individualization' and 'privatization' of religious life, it is useful to offset this approach against a type of research which assigns to the 'community of the living and the dead' a central place in religious life and concentrates on quantifiable source material.

Modern Devout communities are well represented in MeMO. The database makes available information from 239 text carriers containing one or more memorial registers. These belonged to religious institutions in several categories: parishes, collegiate churches, chapels, confraternities, hospitals, and monasteries and comparable religious communities (Table 2).

Table 2. Memorial Text Carriers.

	Institutions	Text Carriers
Total	146	239
Monastic	55	78
Devotio Moderna c.s.	35	48

The category of religious communities is well represented, with 78 items: slightly less than one third of the total. More than half of these manuscripts, 48 in total, originate from newly founded religious houses belonging — in the broad sense — to the *Devotio Moderna*: the Regular Canons of Windesheim and Sion, the Tertiaries of the Chapter of Utrecht, the Brethren and Sisters of the Common Life (together making up the institutional core of the *Devotio Moderna*), along with a few Charterhouses, convents of Crutched Friars, and new Cistercian houses belonging to the Sibculo Congregation. The 48 text carriers in this sample originate from thirty-five different religious communities; they contain a total of 121 memorial registers.

These registers show a high degree of diversity, which parallels the variety in memorial objects which have long attracted the attention of art historians. The objects belong to a wide variety of types and are often idiosyncratic in nature. Table 3 shows the categories into which they have been subdivided (sometimes with a certain amount of force) for the purposes of MeMO:

Table 3. *Devotio Moderna*: Memorial Texts.

Type	Number
Calendars	35
Lists of Pittances	9
Registers of Gifts	29
Lists of Names	39
Registers of Graves	11
Uncertain	1
Total	**121**

The most stable category appears to be that of calendars of memorial services, but even here we cannot be certain that all these calendars had the same function. Some are bound together with a martyrology and a commentary on the Rule of St Augustine, suggesting that they were used liturgically.[14] Others may have been purely administrative documents. The lists of names include series of prioresses, confessors, and ordinary members of a community. But the sources from the Utrecht Charterhouse and the Amersfoort Tertiary convent of St Agnes, for instance, also contain enumerations of benefactors, conveniently listed according to the size of their gifts. Examples of such variation could be multiplied.

Several of these registers have been the subject of monographs, a type of study which reached a climax in Rolf de Weijert's recent doctoral thesis on memorial practices in the Utrecht Charterhouse on behalf of laypeople.[15] There is as yet, however, no comprehensive study of memorial registers originating in monastic institutions; neither can it be presented here. Just to give an impression of the possibilities of these sources, some data will be analysed pertaining to two late examples of calendars originating in monastic institutions: the Canons Regular of the monastery of Stein near Gouda,[16] and the convent of Augustinian converses of

[14] I discuss the manuscript London, BL, Harley, MS 2939, an example of this type, in Goudriaan, 'The *Devotio Moderna* and Commemoration. The Case of St Margaret's Convent in Gouda', pp. 147–48. Cf. also Medieval Memoria Online: http://memodatabase.hum.uu.nl/memo-is/detail/index?detailId = 8&detailType = TextCarrier [accessed 21 November 2018].

[15] De Weijert-Gutman, 'Schenken, begraven, gedenken'. An English edition has been announced.

[16] Gouda, Streekarchief Midden Holland, MS Librije 932, fol. 129ʳ–138ᵛ. Medieval Memoria Online: http://memodatabase.hum.uu.nl/memo-is/detail/index?detailId = 9&detailType = TextCarrier [accessed 21 November 2018]. For the monastery see the Census:

St Agnes in Amsterdam.[17] Both of them can be associated with the small Chapter of Sion, which had its origin in a group of Tertiary convents changing over to the Rule of St Augustine and which competed with the much larger Chapter of Windesheim: Stein was a full member, while St Agnes's convent was subject to visitation by the Chapter (Table 4).[18]

Table 4. Entries in Two Memorial Calendars.

	Gouda: Stein, regular canons			Amsterdam, St Agnes, converses of St Augustine		
	Number	*Gifts*	*Liturgy*	*Number*	*Gifts*	*Liturgy*
Inmates	135	1	-	202	-	1
Confessors	-	-	-	15	5	-
Benefactors	122	84 (73)	15	108	79	4
Total	**257**	**85**	**15**	**325**	**84**	**5**

These two registers date from the sixteenth century, though they contain many entries taken over from earlier, now lost copies. Both registers offer ample scope for drawing up a social profile of the donors-benefactors. Sterck observed the presence in St Agnes's convent of daughters from prominent and wealthy Amsterdam families.[19] The present author identified the patriciate of Gouda in combination with the regional gentry as the main residents in and benefactors of Stein monastery, which itself was situated a couple of miles east of Gouda.[20] These registers are interesting also because of the insight they offer into the variety of gifts by which the benefactors secured the prayers of the religious. Most often these consisted of sums of money, but gifts in kind also occurred, as well as gifts of pieces of land (in the case of Stein), and in addition liturgical utensils and books, and in St Agnes's convent on one occasion even a painted portrait of

http://www2.fgw.vu.nl/oz/monasteries/kdetails.php?ID = H26 [accessed 21 November 2018].

[17] Amsterdam, Universiteitsbibliotheek, MS XXV C 77. Edition: Sterck, 'Van kloosterkerk tot Athenaeum', pp. 241–65. Medieval Memoria Online: http://memodatabase.hum.uu.nl/memo-is/detail/index?detailId = 281&detailType = TextCarrier [accessed 28 April 2017]. For the convent see the Census: http://www2.fgw.vu.nl/oz/monasteries/kdetails.php?ID = A26 [accessed 21 November 2018].

[18] Ypma, *Het Generaal Kapittel van Sion*; for the status of St Agnes's convent esp. p. 86.

[19] Sterck, 'Van kloosterkerk tot Athenaeum', pp. 224–25.

[20] Goudriaan, 'Stein bidt voor zijn weldoeners', pp. 211–15.

a sister and her family.[21] Memorial registers are also an attractive source for art historians, as is exemplified by Biemans and Van Bueren in their analysis of the memorial registers of the Utrecht Tertiaries of St Nicholas.[22] Nevertheless, the essential point remains that these gifts were an integral element of the rituals of commemoration.

What is interesting in the registers under scrutiny here, however, is the exceptionally small number of specific instructions regarding liturgical elaboration of the commemorations: only fifteen in Stein and just five in St Agnes. The vast majority of commemorations have no individual features at all, but conform to the standard pattern of what in Stein was called the *anniversarius communis*.[23] This was less elaborate than the commemoration of a member of the community and his parents, and consisted of a private Mass (as opposed to a conventual Mass), supplemented by an *oratio* in the convent's Mass and vigils of the same day. One could refer to this as the default *memoria*, for which regulations had been laid down in the decisions of the General Chapter and in the *Ordinarius*.[24] The rare instances of individual arrangements prove that there was indeed scope for negotiation. But in general the donors trusted the canons in their capacity as professionals in intercession and accepted the standard packages offered by the General Chapter.

The recognition of the important share Modern Devout communities had in offering memorial services for the laity corroborates the ongoing reinterpretation of this movement in terms of 'monastic observantism'.[25] The volume edited by Hildo van Engen and Gerrit Verhoeven in 2008 represents the interim state of the art of this trend in scholarship. A key observation is that people in search of a safe

[21] Sterck, 'Van kloosterkerk tot Athenaeum', p. 225; Goudriaan, 'Stein bidt voor zijn weldoeners', pp. 215–16.

[22] Biemans and Van Bueren, 'A Veritable Treasure Trove'. For the registers see Medieval Memoria Online: http://memodatabase.hum.uu.nl/memo-is/detail/index?detailId = 240&detailType = TextCarrier and http://memodatabase.hum.uu.nl/memo-is/detail/index?detailId = 242&detailType = TextCarrier [accessed 21 November 2018]. For the convent see the Census: http://www2.fgw.vu.nl/oz/monasteries/kdetails.php?ID = U17 [accessed 21 November 2018].

[23] Gouda, Streekarchief Midden Holland, MS Librije 932, memorial register passim. Goudriaan, 'Stein bidt voor zijn doden', pp. 204–05; Goudriaan, 'The *Devotio Moderna* and Commemoration', pp. 135–36.

[24] Amsterdam, Bibliotheek Vrije Universiteit, MS XV 0003. See *Beeldbank*: http://imagebase.ubvu.vu.nl/cdm/compoundobject/collection/mhs/id/6003/rec/8 [accessed 21 November 2018].

[25] Van Engen and Verhoeven, eds, *Monastiek observantisme en Moderne Devotie*.

arrangement for the care of their souls had a clear preference for entrusting it to newly founded convents which had made a fresh start with a rigorous observance of the rule.[26] The new convents one might adduce as evidence are exactly those within the sphere of the *Devotio Moderna*. And, of course, one of the elements implied in regular observance is the strict maintenance of congregational religious practices.

In undertaking tasks in the field of *memoria* and intercession for the living and the dead, the monasteries, convents, and houses belonging to the wave of new observant foundations triggered by the *Devotio Moderna* stand in a long tradition that reaches all the way back to the Carolingian era. The description given by Oexle for the working of *memoria* in that period is seamlessly applicable to the late medieval period. Even the great variety in the types of gifts in return for prayer, as observed above, was no new development, but can equally be found in the Carolingian period.[27] It is an epiphenomenon, however, when compared to the underlying principle of forging mutual solidarity between the monastery and its benefactors by the exchange of material for spiritual gifts. With regard to the non-monastic houses of the *Devotio Moderna*, awareness of this basic rule emerges in the words of the Dominican Grabow — on a negative note, though, since he opposed the right of such houses to participate in *memoria*:

> eis [...] pro animarum vivorum et mortuorum salute census, redditus, domus, mobilia et immobilia, anniversaria, legata, testamenta, prandia, cene et alia elemosinarum[28] genera a populo offeruntur.

> (to them are offered for the salvation of the souls of the living and the dead payments, rents, houses, movable and immovable goods, yearly allowances, legacies, testaments, meals, and other kinds of alms.)[29]

Not even this clear statement of what was going on was new, however. It was similarly formulated almost three centuries before by abbot Peter the Venerable:

> monachi [...] cuncta fidelium oblata sive in mobilibus sive in immobilibus suscipiunt atque orationum, ieiuniorum et ceterorum bonorum instantiam benefactoribus recompensant.

---

[26] Mol, 'Friezen en het hiernamaals', pp. 200–03.

[27] Oexle, 'Memoria und Memorialüberlieferung', p. 91.

[28] For the use of the term *elemosinarum* here cf. the quotation from the *Liber Memorialis* of Newminster in Oexle, 'Memoria und Memorialüberlieferung', p. 92.

[29] Staubach, 'Zwischen Kloster und Welt?', p. 412. I have discussed the passage in more detail in Goudriaan, 'The *Devotio Moderna* and Commemoration', pp. 122–26.

(monks accept all offerings by the faithful, whether in movable or in immovable goods, and they retribute their benefactors by the assiduity of their prayers, fasts and other goods.)[30]

It was on this exchange that *memoria* was based, an exchange which was vital for the community of those who held *memoria*, but was extended beyond this circle to those — the dead — whose names were mentioned during the ritual and who by this mentioning were in a sense really present in the community.[31]

To summarize the argument so far: the ritual perpetuation of the community of the living and the dead is quintessential for commemorative practices. And the *Devotio Moderna*, characterized by regular observance, was an important platform for such commemoration. This inevitably leads to the question: how does 'individualization' fit in?

In these observations so far it has been suggested that *memoria* as revealed by the registers which have come down to us from religious houses within the sphere of the *Devotio Moderna* exhibits two conspicuous characteristics: great variation in the structure and administration of memorial practices in these houses, but standardization of the memorial arrangements themselves, with only limited recourse to individuation. Of course, the conventionality of *memoria* does not exclude the possibility that for everybody who made such an arrangement this may have been a moment of great intimacy and high religious tension. The memorial sources naturally remain silent about the inner conviction with which such arrangements were made. In the last resort, however, the one conspicuous quality that emerges from the registers is the undiminished communal nature of commemoration.

In an ardent passage in the fourth book of *De imitatione Christi* Thomas a Kempis expresses the importance of having an intense, and personal, desire for God. Although he is aware of frequently being tepid himself, he continues to long for this desire:[32] 'Tamen de gratia tua illius magni inflammati desiderii desiderium habeo' (Yet by your grace I have a desire for this same great inflamed desire).

At first sight, these words could be taken as an accentuation of personal inwardness without regard for collective worship. In reality, however, the words in no way detach personal devotion from communal practice. They do represent

---

[30] Quoted by Oexle, 'Memoria und Memorialüberlieferung', p. 92.

[31] Oexle, 'Memoria und Memorialüberlieferung', p. 95.

[32] Thomas a Kempis, *De imitatione Christi*, 3 (4). 14. 8, ed. by Pohl, p. 129. 27–28, this and the following translations adapted from the English version published by the Bruce Publishing Company at Milwaukee in 1940, available as pdf on the internet. The words were quoted in the original Call for Papers for the conference in Nijmegen.

the reflections of a lonely individual, standing eye to eye with his God. But they are taken from a chapter in which Thomas reminds himself of the fervour with which devout people around him participate in the Eucharist, the shared religious practice *par excellence*: precisely at this moment 'Quando recordor devotorum aliquorum ad Sacramentum tuum, Domine, cum magna devotione, et affectu accedentium' (When I think how some devout persons come to your Sacrament with the greatest devotion and love), he finds that he must lament his own tepidity. His aim in wishing to be filled with a fitting desire for God is to be numbered among the saintly company of all true lovers of God:

> Etenim licet tanto desiderio tam specialium devotorum tuorum non ardeo; tamen de gratia tua illius magni inflammati desiderii desiderium habeo: orans et desiderans omnium talium fervidorum amatorum tuorum participem me fieri, ac eorum sancto consortio annumerari.

> (For although I am not now inflamed with as great desire as those who are singularly devoted to You, yet by Your grace I long for this same great flame, praying and seeking a place among all such ardent lovers that I may be numbered among their holy company).[33]

Pinpointing 'individualization' in late medieval religion, therefore, calls for a great degree of cautiousness, and this is particularly true where the *Devotio Moderna* is concerned. For one thing, we must be precise in defining what we mean, and must distinguish, for example, between diversity of inner beliefs and individualization of religious practices. At the same time, we must never lose sight of the fact that personal religiosity was firmly embedded in communal practices. Recent research has seen competition between several related but not identical judgements about late medieval religious life. One phenomenon that is often observed is an increase of participation in the life of the faith by the laity. With respect to the Netherlands, Judith Pollmann recently (2011) claimed that lay involvement and responsibility in ecclesiastical affairs was an important factor in what she calls the 'modernity of early sixteenth-century Christianity in the Low Countries'.[34] But how is this phenomenon related to the 'deepened interiority' in both cloistered and lay circles identified by John van Engen as characteristic for fifteenth-century

---

[33] Thomas a Kempis, *De imitatione Christi*, 3 (4). 14. 8, ed. by Pohl, p. 129. 24–31. The translation is from the English version published by the Bruce Publishing Company at Milwaukee in 1940, available as pdf on the Internet: http://faculty.gordon.edu/hu/bi/ted_hildebrandt/spiritualformation/Texts/ThomasAKempis_ImitationOfChrist/ThomasAKempis_ImitationOfChrist.pdf [accessed 21 November 2018]. The Latin text is available on-line at http://www.thelatinlibrary.com/kempis/kempis4.shtml.

[34] Pollmann, *Catholic Identity and the Revolt of the Netherlands*, pp. 14–43.

spirituality?[35] It is certainly true that we have at our disposal an abundant and rich heritage of textual material pointing to this interiority. This material is quite naturally the object of several articles in the present volume. But is it correct to infer from this category of material handed down to us that religious practice overall was in a process of being individualized in any meaningful sense?

In order to assess such practice, theory and history of culture have reached a considerable degree of sophistication. Pierre Bourdieu's 'Theory of practice' and his concept of *habitus* may be taken as a landmark in this respect.[36] *Habitus* represents a set of dispositions, acquired by the individual through socialization, which shape his patterns of thinking, feeling, and acting. This is not sheer determinism: on the contrary, *habitus* enables the individual to perform an infinite variety of actions. It conditions his agency, but also guarantees its unity. At the same time, it is the common denominator of the agency of all individuals socialized under the same conditions. This implies that the concept of *habitus* reconciles structure and agency, conditioning and freedom, the collective and the individual. However, this same concept causes considerable complications when it comes to any predictions about a linear development towards greater individuality. On the contrary, it implies a certain amount of contingency in long-term developments.

With a focus on the Middle Ages, Gert Melville has repeatedly drawn attention to the interweaving of the personal and the collective. In a 1992 article he defines the mutual relationship between 'institutions', both as standardized practices and as organizations devised to channel them, and the individuals participating in them. Institutions do not limit individual freedom; rather, by creating stable circumstances on the basis of shared notions about values, they enable individuals to acquire an amount of freedom precisely by playing their personal roles within these institutions.[37] In 2002 Melville applied this same basic approach to a penetrating analysis of the fundamentals of medieval monastic life. In this context he explicitly mentions commemoration: the 'choreography of the liturgy' connects the individual and the community especially in the face of death.[38] Melville here supplements the binary relationship between the individual and the collective with an indispensable third 'pole': God. The person

---

[35] Van Engen, 'Multiple Options', p. 282, where he contrasts this type of interiority with the 'ruthless "emptying of the self"' and the mystic extremism to be observed in monastic circles during preceding centuries.

[36] Bourdieu, *Outlines of a Theory of Practice*.

[37] Melville, 'Institutionen als geschichtwissenschaftliches Thema'.

[38] Melville, 'Einleitende Aspekte zur Aporie von Eigenem und Ganzem', pp. xxvi–xxvii; cf. also the Introduction to this volume.

and the group are closely bound together precisely by their common effort to conform the inner person to the image of God. It is with this general idea in mind that the passage from Thomas' *De imitatione Christi* quoted above receives its full relevance for the present topic.

Arrangements for commemoration after death cannot in any manner be taken as being exclusively representative of the full range of religious practices, but their ubiquity bears witness to the importance attached to them in the late medieval period. The overview given above suggests that, indeed, a fair amount of variety was allowed for shaping *memoria* in a manner that fitted individual wishes. It would be widely off the mark, however, to state that this went in a direction counter to shared religious practices. Religion was not a primarily private affair. On the basis of a collective belief in purgatory, *memoria* — despite its ample, but ultimately finite number of possible variations in individual elaboration — kept the community between the living and the dead intact through the continued maintenance of shared liturgy and ritual. I doubt whether it is possible to prove on the basis of the sources we have at our disposal that the individual element in religion was stronger at the end of the fifteenth century than at its beginning.

Change came about only when belief in purgatory became contested and the very sense of spending so much time on communal forms of liturgy was questioned. Within the sphere of the *Devotio Moderna*, but as a dissident voice, a harbinger of this development was the response given by Erasmus — a Canon Regular of Stein — to his prior, when the latter ordered him to return to his monastery. Erasmus refused, and one of the reasons he gave for not complying with his superior's orders was his reluctance to resume a life revolving around the time-consuming task of participating in the canonical hours. This would leave him no opportunity to do his work on the sacred texts, the one field in which — as he stated — his personal capacities really came to the fore.[39] In claiming priority for his individual engagement at the cost of monastic community life Erasmus ushered in a new era which really and fundamentally stressed the personal element of religious involvement.

---

[39] Summarized from Erasmus, *Opus epistolarum*, no. 296, 'To Servatius Rogerus', ed. by Allen, t. 1, pp. 564–73.

Works Cited

Manuscripts

Amsterdam, Universiteitsbibliotheek, MS XXV C 77
——, Bibliotheek Vrije Universiteit, MS XV 0003
Gouda, Streekarchief Midden Holland, MS Librije 932
Leiden, Erfgoed Leiden en Omstreken (ELO), Archieven van de Kloosters, inv. 518
London, British Library, Harley, MS 2939

Primary Sources

Erasmus Roterodamus, Desiderius, *Opus Epistolarum*, I, *1484–1514*, ed. by P. S. Allen (Oxford: Clarendon, 1906)
Thomas a Kempis, *De imitatione Christi*, in *Thomae Hemerken a Kempis canonici regularis ordinis S. Augustini Opera omnia*, 2, ed. by Michael Josephus Pohl (Freiburg im Breisgau: Herder, 1904), pp. 3–263

Secondary Sources

Ariès, Philippe, *L'homme devant la mort* (Paris: Éditions du Seuil, 1977), trans. by Helen Weaver as: *The Hour of our Death* (New York: Vintage, 1982)
Biemans, Bini, and Truus van Bueren, 'A Veritable Treasure Trove: the Memorial Book of St Nicholas' Convent in Utrecht and its Art Donations', in *Care for the Here and the Hereafter: Memoria, Art and Ritual in the Middle Ages*, ed. by Truus van Bueren with the help of Andrea van Leerdam (Turnhout: Brepols, 2005), pp. 249–65
Bijsterveld, Arnoud-Jan A., *Do ut des: Gift Giving,* Memoria, and *Conflict Management in the Medieval Low Countries* (Hilversum: Verloren, 2007)
Bourdieu, Pierre, *Outlines of a Theory of Practice*, trans. by Richard Nice, Cambridge Studies in Social Anthropology, 16 (Cambridge: Cambridge University Press, 1977)
Bueren, Truus van, 'Care for the Here and the Hereafter: A Multitude of Possibilities', in *Care for the Here and the Hereafter: Memoria, Art and Ritual in the Middle Ages*, ed. by Truus van Bueren with the help of Andrea van Leerdam (Turnhout: Brepols, 2005), pp. 13–34
Chiffoleau, Jacques, *La comptabilité de l'au-delà. Les hommes, la mort et la religion dans la région d'Avignon à la fin du Moyen Age (vers 1320 – vers 1480)* (Roma: École Française de Rome, 1980)
Engen, Hildo van, and Gerrit Verhoeven, eds, *Monastiek observantisme en Moderne Devotie in de Noordelijke Nederlanden* (Hilversum: Verloren, 2008)
Engen, John van, 'Multiple Options: The World of the Fifteenth-Century Church', *Church History*, 77 (2008), 257–84

Goudriaan, Koen, 'Stein bidt voor zijn weldoeners. Het dodenboek als bron van informatie over de betrekkingen van het klooster Stein met zijn omgeving', *Tidinge van die Goude*, 24 (2006), 200–20

——, 'The *Devotio* Moderna and Commemoration: The Case of St Margaret's Convent in Gouda', in *Memory in Religious Communities in the Medieval Low Countries*, ed. by Jeroen Deploige and Renée Nip. Special Issue *The Medieval Low Countries*, 2 (2015 [2016]), pp. 109–54

——, 'Grundmann and the Devotio Moderna', in *Between Orders and Heresy: Rethinking Medieval Religious Movements*, ed. by A. Lester and J. Kolpacoff Dean (in preparation)

Luijk, Madelon van, *Bruiden van Christus. De tweede religieuze vrouwenbeweging in Leiden en Zwolle, 1380–1580* (Zutphen: Walburg Pers, 2004)

Mauss, Marcel, 'Essai sur le don. Forme et raison de l'échange dans les sociétés archaïques', in *L'Année Sociologique*, seconde série, t. 1 (1923–1924 [1925]), 30–186. English trans. by I. Cunnison as *The Gift: Forms and Functions of Exchange in Archaic Societies* (London: Cohen & West, 1974)

Melville, Gert, 'Institutionen als geschichtswissenschaftliches Thema. Eine Einleitung', in *Institutionen und Geschichte. Theoretische Aspekte und mittelalterliche Befunde*, ed. by Gert Melville (Köln: Böhlau, 1992), pp. 1–24

——, 'Einleitende Aspekte zur Aporie von Eigenem und Ganzem im mittelalterlichen Religiosentum', in *Das Eigene und das Ganze*, ed. by Gert Melville and Markus Schurer (Münster: LIT, 2002), pp. xi–xli

Mol, J. A. (Hans), 'Friezen en het hiernamaals. Zieleheilsbeschikkingen ten gunste van kerken, kloosters en armen in testamenten uit Friesland tot 1580', in *Zorgen voor zekerheid. Studies over Friese testamenten in de vijftiende en zestiende eeuw*, ed. by J. A. (Hans) Mol (Leeuwarden: Fryske Akademy, 1996), pp. 175–214

Oexle, Otto Gerhard, 'Memoria und Memorialüberlieferung im früheren Mittelalter', *Frühmittelalterliche Studien*, 10 (1976), 70–95

——, 'Memoria und Memorialbild', in *Memoria. Der geschichtliche Zeugniswert des liturgischen Gedenkens im Mittelalter*, ed. by Karl Schmid and Joachim Wollasch, Münstersche Mittelalter-Schriften, 48 (München: Fink, 1984), pp. 384–440

Pollmann, Judith, *Catholic Identity and the Revolt of the Netherlands, 1520–1635* (Oxford: Oxford University Press, 2011)

Speetjens, Annemarie, 'The Founder, the Chaplain and the Ecclesiastical Authorities: Chantries in the Low Countries', in *Living Memoria: Studies in Medieval and Early Modern Memorial Culture*, ed. by Rolf de Weijert and others (Hilversum: Verloren, 2011), pp. 195–206

Staubach, Nikolaus, 'Zwischen Kloster und Welt? Die Stellung der Brüder vom gemeinsamen Leben in der spätmittelalterlichen Gesellschaft. Mit einem Anhang: Neue Quellen zum Grabow-Konflikt', in *Kirchenreform von unten. Gerhard Zerbolt von Zutphen und die Brüder vom gemeinsamen Leben*, ed. by Nikolaus Staubach (Frankfurt am Main: Peter Lang, 2004), pp. 368–426

Sterck, J. F. M., 'Van kloosterkerk tot Athenaeum. Uit de geschiedenis der S. Agnes-kapel te Amsterdam', *Bijdragen Bisdom Haarlem*, 40 (1921), 216–81

Vovelle, Michel, *Mourir autrefois. Attitudes collectives devant la mort aux XVIIe et XVIIIe siècles* (Paris: Gallimard, 1974)

Weijert-Gutman, Rolf de, 'Schenken, begraven, gedenken. Lekenmemoria in het Utrechtse kartuizerklooster Nieuwlicht (1391–1580)' (unpublished doctoral thesis, Utrecht University, 2015)

Ypma, Eelco, *Het Generaal Kapittel van Sion. Zijn oorsprong, ontwikkeling en inrichting* (Nijmegen : Dekker & Van de Vegt, 1949)

Close Enough to Touch:
Tension between Inner Devotion and Communal Piety in the Congregations of Sisters of the *Devotio Moderna*

Anne Bollmann †

T raditionally, the establishment of normative rulebooks for Sisters of the Common Life was the task of the male representatives within the movement of the Modern Devout.[1] However, the responsible heads of the chapters, rectors and confessors of the congregations played only a limited part in the daily life of the sisters under their guidance. The official statutes that are still extant give only a general impression of the structure of the sisters' communal life. Existing codes of conduct for individual communities are more likely to reveal what should have been rather than what actually was the case.

Salome Sticken's (1369–† 1449) *Vivendi formula* ('Spiritual Guide of Common Life') is therefore an absolute exception in the corpus of rules of conduct for congregations of Devout women, and a godsend for those of us who want to learn more about their lives, as it is the only surviving document of its kind written by a woman for women. The text had originally been conceived as a guide

---

[1] I am most grateful to Nigel F. Palmer and Rijcklof Hofman for their help in seeing this essay through the press. Also, I would like to thank Robert Olsen for translating this article from German. For the *Devotio Moderna*, see the recent overview by Van Engen, *Sisters and Brothers of the Common Life*; Krauß, *Devotio moderna in Deventer*.

Anne Bollmann was Assistant Professor in the Department of European Languages and Cultures of the Faculty of Arts at the University of Groningen, The Netherlands.

Inwardness, Individualization, and Religious Agency in the Late Medieval Low Countries, ed. by Rijcklof Hofman, Charles Caspers, Peter Nissen, Mathilde van Dijk, and Johan Oosterman, MCS 43 (Turnhout: Brepols, 2020), pp. 137–158   BREPOLS 🔖 PUBLISHERS   10.1484/M.MCS-EB.5.119393

to communal life written in the vernacular, but it is preserved only in a Latin translation, which was accorded the Latin title *Vivendi formula* by its first editor, derived from its Prologue.[2]

Already during her lifetime, Salome Sticken was considered to be a female role model for the *Devotio Moderna* in and beyond the area of the Low Countries. She began her spiritual career in 1390 as a sister in the Meester Geerts House in Deventer, the mother-house of the female branch of this late medieval religious reform movement.[3] She was chosen as *mater* (Mother) of the community of sisters as early as 1392/1393. More than fifty-five years later, in 1446, she relinquished her position as the successful prioress of the Diepenveen convent of Windesheim regular canonesses for health reasons, her renown then extending far beyond the IJssel region.[4] Salome devoted her final years of life to documenting her experiences as a spiritual leader and teacher and during this period she wrote her *Vivendi formula* for newly established communities of Sisters of the *Devotio Moderna*.[5]

Written by this 'personification of the Devout life ideal', these regulations give us the perspective of a highly adored Devout female leader with many years of experience in the common life and as superior in charge of the first community of Sisters of the Common Life in the Meester Geerts House, and, afterwards, the community of Windesheim canonesses under the Augustinian monastic rule with its stricter cloister practices. Her work therefore provides us with a view of

---

[2] The text survives in the manuscript Brussels, Koninklijke Bibliotheek, MS 8849–59, fols 169ʳ–176ᵛ, originating from the Heer Florens House in Deventer. This place of origin underlines the importance attributed to it by the Modern Devout. On the manuscript cf. Schoengen, *Jacobus Traiecti alias De Voecht, 'Narratio'*, pp. lxxxi–cvii. Kühler edited the Latin version in the appendix to Kühler, *Johannes Brinckerinck en zijn klooster te Diepenveen*, pp. 360–80; for an annotated Dutch translation, see Van Dijk, *Salome Sticken*, pp. 385–419 (Supplement 4), for a partial English translation, see Van Engen, *Devotio Moderna*, pp. 176–86; for a discussion of the text see Bollmann, *Frauenleben und Frauenliteratur in der Devotio moderna*, pp. 164–72; Van Dijk, *Salome Sticken*, pp. 236–67, offers new insights into the spiritual content of the text. As there is no further information about the presentation of the text in the original manuscript and because of the fact that, in the meantime, the Latin title '*Vivendi formula*' is well established in research literature it will also be used in this article.

[3] On the history of the Meester Geerts House, see Van Engen, *Sisters and Brothers of the Common Life*, pp. 125–37; Bollmann, *Frauenleben und Frauenliteratur in der Devotio moderna*, pp. 43–96.

[4] Van Dijk, *Salome Sticken*, offers the most up-to-date research on this remarkable woman, and examines her achievements and career on the basis of biographies and other sources.

[5] On the female branch of the *Devotio Moderna*, see Rehm, *Die Schwestern vom gemeinsamen Leben*, Bollmann, *Frauenleben und Frauenliteratur in der Devotio moderna*; Scheepsma, *Medieval Religious Women*.

the common life whose authority is underpinned by multiple and clear references to its prominent authoress.[6] In her *Vivendi formula*, Salome Sticken devotes much attention to the communal day of the community of sisters. She recapitulates the daily rhythm of the conventuals from rising in the morning to going to sleep at night. She frequently describes how a sister should use her time during the few moments of the day that she has to herself and in the many situations where she spends time with others.

For example, the sisters should consciously and emotionally dedicate the short periods of time which they have for themselves immediately after rising and just before falling asleep to their prayers, kneeling before their bed, concentrating on the Lord's passion. While at work and during the communal meal in the refectory, the sisters should silently devote themselves to their activities while listening to mealtime readings or mentally dealing with a text describing the passion of Christ. Above all, however, they should also endeavour to maintain silence in the group by speaking as little as possible, refraining from walking around or from causing other disturbing noises.

Salome describes the central importance of manual labour for the social relations of the sisters in a highly moral and didactic account of the day's events:

> Est eciam in omnibus bonis congregacionibus consuetudo, quod a mane usque ad vesperam ferialibus diebus fideliter et alacriter operentur opus suum, excepto eo quod missam audiant. [...] Videretur eciam sororibus nostris, quod magnum ipsis dispendium inferret in amore diuino, si non fideliter et alacriter operi manuum suarum insisterent [...] Hec nempe institucio nostra primaria fuit ut alacriter propter Deum operi manuum intenderemus. Quicumque ergo putauerit graciam Dei et internam dulcedinem in sola vacacione aut ocio inueniendam, penitus errat.

> (In all good communities, it is a convention that, on week days, the sisters work faithfully and diligently from morning to night, except when they are hearing Mass. [...] Our sisters believe that they would suffer a great loss of divine love if they were

---

[6] The importance of the *Vivendi formula* is further confirmed by the fact that Heinrich Loder (1416–† 1439), prior of the male Windesheim convent Frenswegen, near Nordhorn, is called the initiator. He was the one who asked Salome to write this guide. In the first half of the fifteenth century, he was responsible for the establishment and/or reform of communities of religious women, and he wanted to use this Spiritual Rule of Life to provide a general guide to daily life for the many houses of sisters that he founded in Westphalia. On Heinrich Loder, see 'Liber de fundatione', chaps 45–52, ed. by Löffler, *Quellen*, pp. 90–105; Alberts and Hulshoff, eds, *Frensweger Handschrift*, pp. 172–86; Johannes Busch, *Chronicon Windeshemense*, ed. by Grube, pp. 164–86. On his reform activities, see the overview in Rehm, *Die Schwestern vom gemeinsamen Leben*, pp. 74–78, 83; Kohl, *Die Schwesternhäuser nach der Augustinusregel*, pp. 35–129, as well as the discussion in Van Dijk, *Salome Sticken*, pp. 236–38; 242–45.

not faithfully and diligently devoted to manual labour. [...] For our basic tenet is to concentrate diligently and in God's name on manual work. Anyone thinking that God's grace and inner sweetness can only be found during moments of detachment or relaxation is greatly mistaken.)[7]

The intertwining of the *uita activa* and *uita contemplativa* that arises during work or other group activities should strengthen the spiritual feeling shared by the sisters. The last admonishment particularly evokes the impression that Salome thought it necessary to warn sisters who wanted to avoid communal activities.[8]

Unlike these ongoing efforts to implement individual devotional practices both in private and in the midst of the social community, the meetings on Sundays and feast days are the occasion where the sisters, together with the mother superior, were supposed to discuss issues concerning daily life in a community on a spiritual basis, in which occasional irritation about other members in the group was bound to arise. However, this *collatio* was also intended to focus on the passion of Christ and on the concrete possibilities for the sisters to follow the Lord in the sense of *Imitatio Christi*.[9]

Pious discussions about their spiritual models (Christ, Mary, the saints) were meant to encourage the sisters to practice humility, voluntary self-abasement, and abandonment of their own will, and to focus instead on the ideals of common life. On the occasion of these congregations under the direction of the mother superior, their chapter of faults, with public discussion of personal failings and weaknesses, was intended to be a group exercise to strengthen love among the sisters.

Salome Sticken regularly addresses prospective sisters as her immediate audience in her *Vivendi formula*, and she uses empathic expressions such as 'Oh, dearly beloved sisters' and 'dearest one', while also offering them standardized expressions to allow them to exhort each other. In this manner they can at the same time take care that their statements in the chapter of faults function within the bounds of constructive criticism and not cross-over into severe reproaches. Abusive language or accusations cause unrest in communities and would only foster antipathies in the group. Instead, it is the prerogative of the mother superior alone to discipline, criticize and punish individual sisters without restriction, and to take them aside and castigate them at all times. Salome Sticken hereby stresses the

---

[7] Salome Sticken, *Vivendi formula*, pp. 375–76; cf. Van Dijk, *Salome Sticken*, pp. 406–08.

[8] For the interweaving of work and prayer in the communities of sisters, see Bollmann, 'Mijt dijt spynnen soe suldi den hemel gewinnen'.

[9] Salome Sticken, *Vivendi formula*, pp. 372–73; 380; Van Dijk, *Salome Sticken*, pp. 400–04; 414–17.

high value placed on openness and obedience to the Mother.[10] It is furthermore interesting to note the various perspectives that she takes when discussing the subject of 'obedience'.

The focus on imitating or reliving the passion of Christ throughout one's daily life is by no means a great surprise, as there was generally a special predilection for Passion devotion during this period. The *Imitatio Christi* of the Windesheim regular canon Thomas a Kempis (1379/80–† 1471)[11] is only one example of the literature on this topic, which was disseminated either in texts produced by the scriptorium of the house or as copies and adaptations of older and comparable spiritual texts that served as reading and meditation material in the communities of the *Devotio Moderna*.[12]

All the same, the prominence which is given to notions and reflections concerning Passion Devotion in a text that should serve as a spiritual and practical regimen for newly founded communities of Sisters of the Common Life still remains quite astonishing. It is obvious that the *Vivendi formula* is not conceived as an official house rule in the sense of *consuetudines* or even statutes. Rather, we have a spiritual and pedagogical manual giving instructions for a way of life that should help female Devout and their spiritual leader to deal with the tension between the pursuit of a close personal relationship with God while at the same time fulfilling the obligations of communal living. The passion of Christ was the focal point that was supposed to interconnect both.

Toward the end of the first section, which deals with the mode of life to be practised by the community of sisters, Salome also explicitly addresses a desire for the spiritual connection with the Lord which every sister should seek as a reward for her tireless pursuit of Devout virtues.

However, in order to achieve this our own desires and human inclinations must first be abandoned, and we must completely submit to the will of God:

> Sorores carissime, dulcedinem et saporem sentire in Domino Deo multum delectabile est. Sed fundamentum tocius sanctitatis in hoc consistit, ut integraliter abnegemus nosmetipsas et mortificemus malas affectiones nature nostre corrupte, insuper et voluntatem nostram conuertamus ad Dominum et eam toto conatu conformemus voluntati illius.

---

[10] Salome Sticken, *Vivendi formula*, p. 374; Van Dijk, *Salome Sticken*, pp. 404–05.

[11] Bodemann and Staubach, eds, *Aus dem Winkel in die Welt. Die Bücher des Thomas von Kempen*. The Latin text edition is available online: http://www.thelatinlibrary.com/kempis.html.

[12] On the writing culture of the Modern Devout, see Mertens, 'Lezen met de pen'; Staubach, 'Pragmatische Schriftlichkeit im Bereich der Devotio moderna'; Kock, *Buchkultur der Devotio moderna*; the contribution by N. F. Palmer to this volume.

(Dearest sisters, to taste the sweetness and savour of our Lord God is most
delectable. However, the foundation of all holiness is that we should completely
abandon our personal concerns and suppress the sinful inclinations of our corrupt
nature, and also direct our will to the Lord and transform that will with all our
might in order to conform to His will.)[13]

After a detailed description how each individual should serve the community by
striving for obedience, performing manual work and participating in communal
prayer, and as if to reassure those who have extremely high expectations about
attaining intimacy with God, Salome Sticken refers here to the occasions in
which, regardless of the zeal displayed, a feeling of abandonment by God might
nevertheless be experienced. Geert Grote (1340–† 1384), the founding father of
the Devout movement, had already pointed out this possibility:

> Quia cum Dominus tribuit nobis dulcedinem et solacium, tunc ministrat nobis.
> Sed quando nos in multis tribulacionibus et temptacionibus fideliter illi adheremus,
> tunc illi seruimus, quod est multo maioris meriti [...] Si autem consolacio et
> interna dulcedo prestetur nobis a Domino, hanc cum magna graciarum actione
> suscipiemus. Si autem illam quam dedit, aliquando subtrahat, eque ut antea in omni
> loco et tempore conabimur adherere Domino deuotis desideriis et piis affectibus.

> (For when the Lord gives us sweet savour and consolation, he is serving us. When,
> however, we cling to him in many torments and trials, we are serving him, which is
> a much higher merit. [...] If, however, we obtain consolation and inner sweetness
> from God, we must receive it with great gratitude. But if he sometimes withdraws
> the grace which he has given us, we must endeavour everywhere and always to
> remain close to the Lord just as before, with devout longing and pious affection.)[14]

Parallel to such emphatic comforting words, Salome nevertheless addresses the
personal responsibility of each of the Devout sisters. They should seek and rely
on the help of the Lord, but they must also make sure that they are not too much
attracted to everyday and earthly things. She specifically speaks to the head of the
community, based on her own experience as *mater* or mother superior and prioress:

> Dilectissima soror, cui cura domus imposita est, humiliter peto, ut solicite caueas
> inutiles confabulaciones et crebrius hinc inde circuire sine necessitate, sed magis
> tempus, quod ab occupacionibus vacuum est, expendere cures in recollectione
> tue ipsius et postulacione a pio Domino, ut tibi concedat sic sibi vniri, ut nec

---

[13] Salome Sticken, *Vivendi formula*, p. 377; cf. Van Dijk, *Salome Sticken*, p. 410.

[14] Salome Sticken, *Vivendi formula*, p. 377; cf. Van Dijk, *Salome Sticken*, pp. 410–13.
Salome uses the word 'affectio', cf. on this concept the contribution by Mertens and Van de Poel
elsewhere in this volume, p. 162–64, esp. n. 15, below.

exterioribus occupata separeris ab illo, quia facile retrocedit homo et aridus corde efficitur, nisi cautissime prouideat sibi exterioribus et temporalibus occupatus.

(Dearly beloved sister who is in charge of the house, I humbly ask you to carefully guard against useless small talk and frequent walking around for no reason. Instead, take care to use the time when you are free from your duties for inward reflection and to ask the dear Lord to grant that you might be united with him, in such a way that you cannot be separated from him by your engagement with external things. For a person easily takes a step backwards so that her heart becomes unfeeling and — unless she takes care — preoccupied with external and worldly things.)[15]

Complete renunciation of personal volition and endeavour to obtain intimacy with God does not, in Salome's eyes, provide a solution for this dilemma, which arises from competing communal and personal commitments and desires. According to Salome, sisters cannot evade their personal responsibility, and must, though cautiously, stand up for their own interests.

Salome Sticken supplements these admonitions with a thematically organized section describing the behaviour recommended to the sisters for the most important everyday situations in the community. The text is written in prose, and the sisters are directly addressed as 'dearest sisters', suggesting an epistolary style. Above all, the tone adopted derives from the explanations associated with the rules of conduct and the illustrative examples from the author's wealth of experience.

In fact, the narrative technique used in this text is clearly reminiscent of the style of the *Collationes* by Johannes Brinckerinck († 1419), Dirk van Herxen (1409–† 1457), and other confessors and rectors of communities of Sisters of the Common Life, which have often been transmitted to us in copies written by individual sisters belonging to these communities. Salome's text similarly contains pious anecdotes and proverbs from the *Vitae Patrum* and other classics of moral didactic writing, as well as excerpts from well-known religious authors, such as Bernard of Clairvaux.[16] These are supplemented by citations from authors belonging to the Devout movement, such as Geert Grote and Johannes Brinckerinck. In the *Vivendi formula*, Salome repeatedly interweaves herself and

[15] Salome Sticken, *Vivendi formula*, pp. 379–80; cf. Van Dijk, *Salome Sticken*, p. 416.

[16] Salome Sticken, *Vivendi formula*, pp. 374 ff. Van Woerkum, *Het libellus 'Omnes, inquit, artes', een rapiarium van Florentius Radewijns*, p. 24 (nos. 8, 30–35), has already pointed out that the corpus of citations in the *Vivendi formula* is strongly reminiscent of the *Libellus 'Omnes, inquit, artes'* of Radewijns. A copy of this rapiarium was available in the Diepenveen monastery library [MS Deventer, SAB, I, 61 (11 L 1)], cf. Van Woerkum, *Het libellus 'Omnes, inquit, artes', een rapiarium van Florentius Radewijns*, pp. 7–9.

'her' sisters into the succession of these founding fathers, and endeavours to give the newly established communities of sisters the feeling that they are following in those footsteps that she herself had followed.

Not the least, the *Vivendi formula* also reminds us of the narrative style found in the *Sister Books* of the *Devotio Moderna*. Five complete manuscripts of *Sister Books* have survived today, as well as a few other fragmentary ones. Two manuscripts come from the Meester Geerts House in Deventer (MSS *G* and *D*), the founding institution of the female branch of the Devout movement, and three from houses directly dependent on this institution. These are the Lammenhuis in Deventer (MS *L*), the convent of the Windesheim regular canonesses in neighbouring Diepenveen (MS *DV*), and the community of St Agnes in Emmerich (MS *E*). These five *Sister Books* of the Devout movement resemble each other in their textual form and also reflect the long-lasting interrelationships between the communities.[17]

The surviving manuscripts with their biographies date to the last third of the fifteenth century and the first third of the sixteenth century, and therefore post-date the *Vivendi formula*. However, they are the result of an intergenerational tradition of *vita* writing, which must have begun no later than the middle of the fifteenth century, and thus be roughly concurrent with Salome Sticken's 'Spiritual Guide of Common Life', the *Vivendi formula*.

When we now turn to the biographies of Devout sisters as narrated in these *Sister Books*, we find that here also the search for a balance between a sister's virtuous lifestyle in the midst of the community and the need to withdraw in

---

[17] Bibliographical details about the five surviving *Sister Books* are as follows: 1) MS *G*, compiled in the Meester Geerts House in Deventer, containing biographies of sisters who lived in that house, ed. by De Man, *Hier beginnen sommige stichtige punten van onsen oelden zusteren*; 2) MS *D*, also originating from the Meester Geerts House, containing biographies of members of the convent of Windesheim regular canonesses in Diepenveen, ed. by Brinkerink, *Van den doechden*; 3) MS *DV*, compiled in the convent in Diepenveen, a convolute containing an enlarged collection of *vitae* of Diepenveen canonesses as well as the *vita* of its first male rector Johannes Brinckerinck, unedited, but edition announced by Wybren Scheepsma and Ingrid Biesheuvel; 4) MS *E*, originating from the Windesheim convent St Agnes in Emmerich (Lower Rhine region), ed. by Bollmann and Staubach, *Schwesternbuch und Statuten des St Agnes-Konvents in Emmerich*; 5) MS *L*, containing biographies from the Lamme-van-Diesehuis in Deventer, long lost, but recently recovered, see Mulder, 'Het zusterboek van het Lamme van Diesehuis te Deventer'; Bollmann, 'Das Schwesternbuch aus dem Lamme van Diesehuis'; 'Het leven der eerwaardige moeder Andries Yserens', ed. by Spitzen. Finally, abbreviated biographies of both sisters and brothers from Deventer have been included in the Latin compilation originating from the Deventer Heer Florens House, transmitted in Brussels, Koninklijke Bibliotheek, MS 8849–59, partially ed. by Kühler, 'Levensbeschrijvingen van devote zusters te Deventer'.

order to internalize spiritual thought apart from the community is a topic regularly addressed. Devout virtue, prayer, and the exercise of piety are discussed in the biographies (*vitae*) in more anecdotally narrated episodes from the lives of the deceased members of the congregation.

Salome Sticken is the only sister who is included in all three collections of biographies of women in the Meester Geerts House and Diepenveen. Her biographies show how she herself also, in her life as a sister, nun and mother superior, tried to implement the behavioural norms propagated in the *Vivendi formula*.[18] In the late manuscript miscellany *D*, which has, as its core, a collection of biographies of women from the Meester Geerts House who moved as co-founders to Diepenveen, Salome Sticken's biography is found at the beginning of the series of *vitae*, indicating her special role in both communities (see Fig. 1).[19] Salome's period of office as head of the community is described in the *Sister Books* containing *vitae* of the Diepenveen Sisters as 'the' glorious age.[20]

According to the matching statements in her *vitae*, which survive from both communities, Salome Sticken remained throughout her life a disciple of the original spiritual ideals of common life from the founding phase of the Devout movement, this despite her stellar career, starting as a sister in the Meester Geerts House and becoming prioress of the Windesheim convent.[21] Her *vitae* state that

---

[18] Cf. *Van den doechden*, ed. by Brinkerink, pp. 23–25 (fols 12ᵈ–13ᵈ) and MS *DV*, fols 211ʳ–212ʳ, on social cohesion and the common gatherings where sisters could reproach each other, as well as *Van den doechden*, pp. 29–31 (fols 16ᵈ–17ᵇ) and MS *DV*, fols 217ʳ⁻ᵛ, on the observance of the vow of silence.

[19] Various of Salome's fellow sisters in the Meester Geerts House as well as in the Diepenveen monastery repeatedly excelled in reform activities at other convents in this phase of the blossoming Devout movement during the first half of the fifteenth century and, in this way, established the glory of the Meester Geerts House as well as the Diepenveen Augustinian convent as mother house for the female branch of the Windesheim Congregation. However, none of these women has enjoyed as wide-ranging a degree of recognition or fame as that accorded to Salome Sticken, and their successful reforms are often only known through the accounts in the *Sister Books*.

[20] Cf. *Hier beginnen sommige stichtige punten van onsen oelden zusteren*, ed. by De Man, pp. 210–13 (fols 119ᵃ–120ᵈ), *Van den doechden*, ed. by Brinkerink, pp. 3–36; MS *DV*, fols 190ʳ–225ᵛ, and the Latin version in MS Brussels, KB, 8849–59, fols 149ʳ and 164ᵛ; for more on her life and work, see Van Dijk, *Salome Sticken*; Kühler, *Johannes Brinckerinck en zijn klooster te Diepenveen*, pp. 202–28.

[21] Cf. the account in her *vita* in the *Sister Book* of the Meester Geerts House, ed. by De Man, *Hier beginnen sommige stichtige punten van onsen oelden zusteren*, pp. 212 ff.: 'Mer van oetmodicheit en wolde si giene nonne worden, al wasset dat sijt nochtan daernae tegen oeren willen moste doen, [...] soe wart si overmids gehorsomheit, doe dat cloester ten Diepen-vene

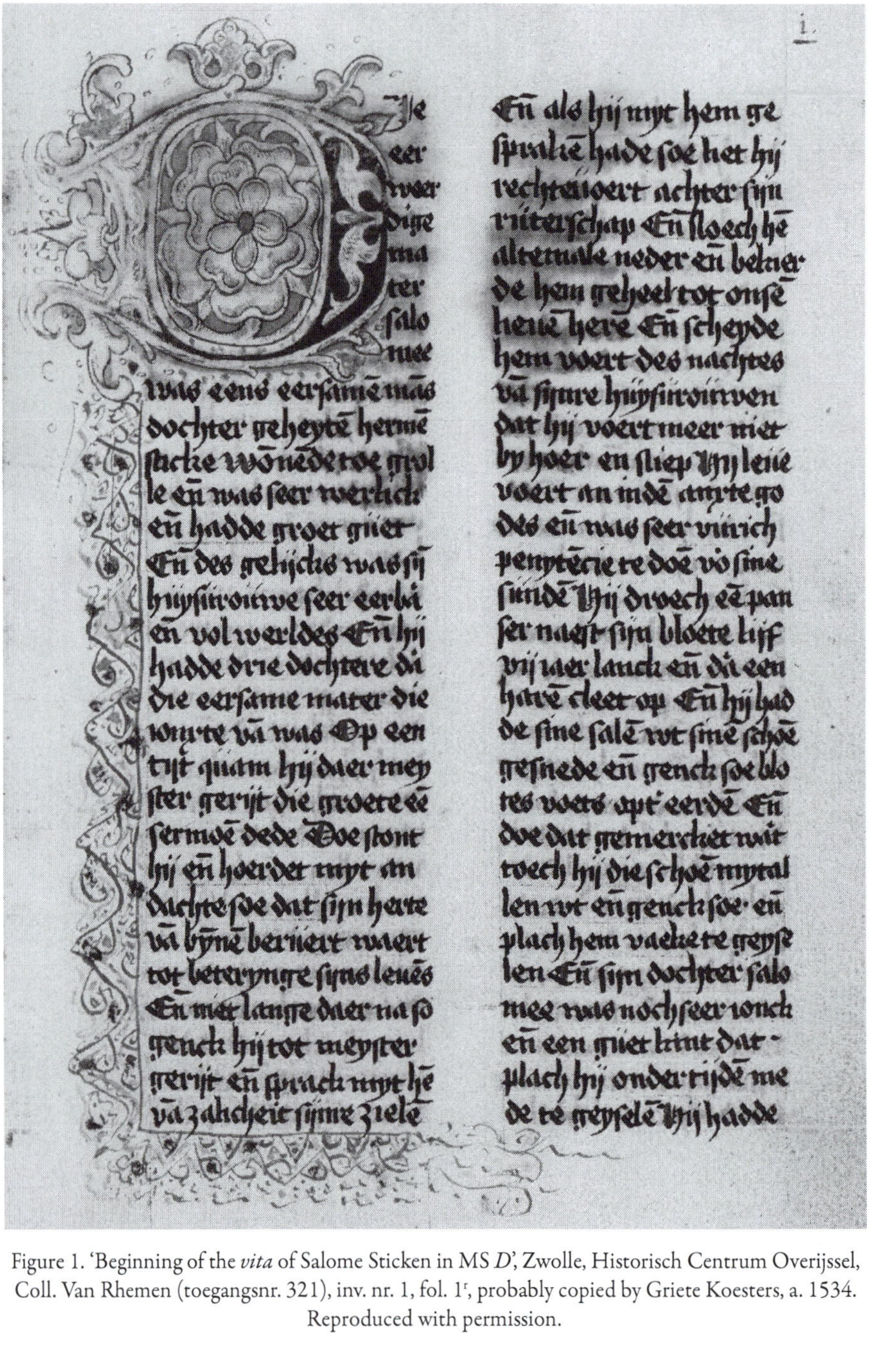

1.

Die
eer
weer
dige
ma
ter
salo
mee
was eens eersamē mās
dochter geheytē hermē
sticke wōnede toe swol
le eñ was seer werlick
eñ hadde groet gůet
Eñ des gelijcks was sij
huysvrouwe seer eerbā
eñ vol werldes Eñ hij
hadde drie dochtere dā
die eersame mater die
ionxte vā was Op een
tijt quam hij daer mey
ster gerijt die groete eē
sermoē dede Doe stont
hij eñ hoerdet uuyt an
dachte soe dat sijn herte
vā bynē berůert waert
tot beteryngē sijns levēs
Eñ niet lange daer na so
genck hij tot meyster
gerijt eñ sprack myt hē
vā zalicheit sijnre ziele

Eñ als hij myt hem ge
sprakē hade soe het hij
rechtevoert achter sijn
ritterschap Eñ sloech hē
altemale neder eñ bekier
de hem geheel tot onsē
heuē here Eñ scheyde
hem voert des nachtes
vā sijnre huysvrouwen
dat hij voert meer niet
by hoer en sliep Hij leve
voert an indē angte go
des eñ was seer vurich
penytēcie te doē vā sine
sundē Hij dwech eē pan
ser naest sijn bloete lijff
vij iaer lanck eñ dā een
harē cleet op Eñ hij had
de sine salē vut sine schoē
gesnede eñ genck soe blo
tes voets opt eerdē Eñ
doe dat gemerchet wart
toech hij die schoē myt al
len vut eñ genck soe eñ
plach hem vaeke te geyse
len Eñ sijn dochter salo
mee was noch seer ionck
eñ een gůet kint dat
plach hij onder tijdē me
de te geyselē Hij hadde

Figure 1. 'Beginning of the *vita* of Salome Sticken in MS *D*', Zwolle, Historisch Centrum Overijssel, Coll. Van Rhemen (toegangsnr. 321), inv. nr. 1, fol. 1r, probably copied by Griete Koesters, a. 1534. Reproduced with permission.

Salome succeeded in performing intensive devout exercises, even while engaging in manual labour. The luminous halo around her head witnessed by a fellow sister during reading in the spinning house is an example that can stand for many:

> Sie [Salome Sticken, A. B.] plach vake ten Diepenven toe comen, doe sie noch toe meister Gherdes huus wonde. [...] Op een tijt was sie hier ene wieltides. Doe vielt op ene margenstont, dat die susteren die metten lesen vander Wiesheit. Ende het was suster Elsebe Hasenbroecks weke in die coeken toe ghaen [...] Doe had sie wat marckelicks int bedehuus toe done, ende als sie daer quam, soe lesen die susteren soe rechte vuoerrichlick, ende sonderlinghe suster Salame die las soe andachtelick ende goddienstelick, dat suster Elsebe een luttick opten dorpel bleef staen ende sach op suster Salame. Soe sach sie dat hoer vuorrighe stralen wtten monde ghenghen, hent totten spynrocken toe, gheliek der sonnen van mannigherhande warwen, telken dat hoer die woerde wtten monde ghenghen. Daer toende onse lieue Here hoe andachtich dat hoer harte tot hem was.

> (She [Salome Sticken, A. B.] often used to come to Diepenveen when she was still living in the Meester Geerts House. [...] On one occasion she stayed here for a while. One morning it happened that the sisters were reading the Hours of Divine Wisdom [from their Book of Hours in the translation by Geert Grote, A. B.] during matins. And it was Sister Elsebe Hasebroeck's week to work in the kitchen [...] Now she had something important to do in the prayer room. And when she arrived, the sisters were reading filled with such zeal and Sister Salome in particular read so devoutly and in fear of God that Sister Elsebe remained a while standing in the doorway, staring at Sister Salome. Then she saw that rays of light would come out of her mouth, stretching right to the spindle, with many colours just like the sun, every time her words left her mouth. This is how the dear Lord showed how devoutly her heart was focused on him.)[22]

Her fellow sisters interpreted this miraculous event, that was being experienced by the *mater* of a community of sisters while she was engaged in manual work, as a sign of Salome's suitability for contemplation and as proof of her closeness to God.

In a parallel passage the Emmerich *Sister Book* describes how Mother Ide Prumers († 1487) was immersed in a comparable contemplative state of mind while working, in this case reading a spiritual book while spinning:

begonnen waert, daer gesat, opdat si dat solde helpen stichten ende fondieren inden rechten doechden, als si oeck trouwelike gedaen heeft' (However, she did not want to become a nun due to her humility, although she was later to become one against her will. [...] When the monastery was founded in Diepenveen (deep marshland), she obediently went there so that she could help to found and organise it according to the proper virtues, a task that she reliably carried out).

[22] MS *DV*, fols 196ᵛ–197ʳ; cf. for a Dutch translation of the parallel account in MS *D* Van Dijk, *Salome Sticken*, pp. 346–47, with explanatory notes.

Als si sat ende span, soe hadde si een boeck bij hoer, daer dat leuen ons lieuen
Heren in stont. Ende wanner sie ijet aen quam, soe socht si hoeren troest ende hulp
daer in, ja sie hadde sulke gracie ontfaen van onsen lieuen Here, dat si altemael in
hem getaghen was.

(While she was sitting and spinning, she had a book with her, which contained an
account of the life of our dear Lord. And if ever anything troubled her, she would
seek consolation and help from it; indeed, she had received such grace from our
dear Lord that she became completely immersed in him.)[23]

Earlier on we have seen that Salome Sticken repeatedly stresses in her *Vivendi
formula*, written for recently founded communities of sisters, that it was quite
possible to succeed in combining the daily duties of community life with
private devotion. The biographies of the sisters indeed provide proof that
such a combination is not merely a theoretical issue, and the external signs of
the experience of grace visible to fellow sisters are taken as proof that genuine
internalization of the passion of Christ is indeed possible for individual sisters.

Conversely, we also find passages in the *vitae* with references to sisters who were
plagued with doubts on this point, and who became torn between demands based
on communal principles and their own need for spiritual closeness to God. The
following passage from the biography of Mother Ide Prumers in Emmerich
documents the fact that sisters sometimes actually avoided participating in the
gatherings of the whole community on Sundays and feast days:

Des heiligen dages als die susteren bij een quamen, om wat guedes toe verkallen,
daer was si altoes bij, ende soe was si alsoe vuerich ende leerden ons vol guedes, ende
hadde oec gern dat wij malckanderen toeharden ende tochgen tot den gueden, si
plage toe seggen: 'Die vuerige mijnlicke aensprack hulpet duc beet dan groete
boecken toe leesen, ia hi sal oc wake al die heel weke toe wackerlicker wesen tot
allen gueden werken te doen', ende hier om soe hadde si oec gern dat wij daer dan
semelick bij een quamen. Ende mercten si dat daer iemant hen bleef sonder oerlof,
den plach si daer om toe straffen ende toe schelden ende seide: 'Het is een quaet
teiken, dat een noede comt, daer men guet doet. Mer et behaget God ende den
menschen, dat een gern ende vlittelicke comt bij der gemeijnten, daer men guede
ende goddienstichge kallinge heuet'.

(On feast days, when the sisters came together to discuss good things, she [Ide,
A. B.] was always there, and then she was so eager and taught us so much good.
And she was also pleased when we encouraged and motivated each other to do
good. She used to say: 'Fiery and loving encouragement often does more good than

---

[23] *Schwesternbuch und Statuten des St Agnes-Konvents in Emmerich*, ed. by Bollmann and
Staubach, p. 89.

reading great tomes, indeed, someone will often take care throughout the week to busy himself to carry out all sorts of good works', and for this reason she also liked us to gather together there. And when she noticed that someone remained away without permission, she would berate and criticize her. And she would say: 'It's a bad sign that someone is reluctant to go where good is being done. But it is pleasing to God and to men that somebody should come gladly and motivated to a gathering, where people engage in good and reverent conversations'.)[24]

One example that describes a sister's individual mental journey into faith, undertaken without reference to her community, is provided by the life of Sister Alijt Plagen from Deventer († 1428).[25] Her biography describes how it took Alijt all of her life to struggle against her failure to participate successfully in the daily life of her community. She was, and remained, a solitary person. At the end, the in-house biographer explains her reasons for including this *vita* of her fellow sister:

Dit gebreck ende dese apenbaeringe hebbe wi daeromme geschreven, opdat wi hieruut weten ende mercken moegen, hoe seer schadelick dat dese sonderlincheit is dengenen, die in cloesteren of in vergaderinge een gemyene leven heeft aengenomen te leyden; ende mede daeromme, opdat wi weten moegen, waervoer dat wi ons hueden sullen.

(We have therefore included her failure and this report so that we may learn from them and note how harmful such aloofness is to those who have decided to live together in monasteries or convents. And also in order that we may thereby learn, in this manner, what we must guard ourselves against.)[26]

The Diepenveen biographies also discuss internal doubts concerning the usefulness of the monastic teaching about inward devotion. The biography of Griete Koetkens († 1452), a member of the Diepenveen convent, contains a passage in which this issue is addressed with regard to the inner conflict of the still young Griete:

Meer zuster Griete Koetkens lerde hie hastelicke inwendelicke mit hem wanderen in groter ghenochten ende danckberheit [...] Suster Griete Koetkens, doe sie toe scolen solde ghaen, om toe leren dat hoer noet was totter orden, dat was hoer zeer py[n]lick, om dat hoer dochte dattet hoer hynderde an hore inwendiger devocien.

[24] *Schwesternbuch und Statuten des St Agnes-Konvents in Emmerich*, ed. by Bollmann and Staubach, p. 97.

[25] *Hier beginnen sommige stichtige punten van onsen oelden zusteren*, ed. by De Man, pp. 91–93.

[26] *Hier beginnen sommige stichtige punten van onsen oelden zusteren*, ed. by De Man, pp. 91–93.

Sie was nochtant ghehorsam ende gaf hoer vlitelick daer toe die tijt dat sie in die
scole was. Ende als sie uter scolen was, soe nam sie die tijt soe nauwe waer ende was
dan hastelicke mitten harten by onsen lieven Heren, dat hoer dochte, of hoer die
hemel op ghedaen waert, soe wonderlike ende wal waert hoer toe mode vander
gracien Gades.

(But soon he [the dear Lord, A. B.] taught Griete Koetkens to keep company with
him inwardly with great pleasure and gratitude. [...] When Sister Griete Koetkens
had to go to school to learn what the order required of her, this caused her great
suffering, as it seemed to her that it would hinder her in her inward devotion. Still,
she was obedient and devoted herself diligently to her duties as long as she was in
class. And when she was out of school, she was very conscious of her time, and she
would quickly turn her heart toward our dear Lord, so that it seemed to her as if
Heaven were opening to her — so wonderful and agreeable were her sensations
through the grace of God.)[27]

After this account the biography quickly focuses on Griete's unconditional
obedience, which is emphasized in great detail. She was always obedient,
despite her personal doubts about the advantages of compulsory education.
Consequently, this episode provides a model of behaviour for sisters who, like
Griete, longed to retreat from wearisome day-to-day living, but could not give
way to their wish because of the strictly regulated monastic day.

Superiors, such as Salome Sticken, always emphasised that the observance of
the house rules did not involve mechanical observance of regulations but, in fact,
required upright and faithful compliance with and adherence to them. Anyone
lacking inner conviction and serious commitment could experiencee neither real
love for the communal life nor true devotion. This applied both to Sisters of the
Common Life, whose handiwork, such as spinning and weaving or administrative
duties, contributed to the livelihood of the community, and to nuns living as
Windesheim regular canonesses under the strict Rule of St Augustine and whose
daily life consisted for a large part just of praying. Both groups endeavoured
to unite the outer and inner realm of experience into the greatest possible
harmonious unity of a consecrated life, no matter if their everyday life was
primarily concerned with for instance spinning or the performance of the liturgy.
They combined these tasks carried out in the community or group with inward
prayer during the moments which they had for themselves. Salome Sticken spent
many years in the Devout sisters' house before transferring to Diepenveen, and
she knew both forms of devotional life. Essentially, her message came down to
convincing the sisters that their own attitude was ultimately decisive.

---

[27] MS *DV*, fols 348[r-v]; *Van den doechden*, ed. by Brinkerink, p. 288.

The conflicts that such stringent requirements could instigate in prospective young candidates for religious life come to the fore in the autobiography of a woman in another Devout convent, Alijt Bake (1415?–† 1455), towards the end of her life as canoness prioress of the Windesheim convent of regular canonesses Galilee in Ghent.[28] Alijt had decided to enter this convent precisely because she believed that this religious community would enable her to deepen her experience of the pious contemplative life that she had already longed for in her youth in Utrecht. When Alijt underwent her profession, the prioress of the convent Galilee was Hille (Hilde) Sonderlants († 1445), a fellow sister of Salome Sticken, who had moved with her from the Meester Geerts House to the newly established convent of regular canonesses in Diepenveen. Unlike Salome, who never left Diepenveen after she had entered the community, Hille was later sent on to various other monastic communities by the (male) governing body of the Chapter of Windesheim, in order to reform them in accordance with the Devout ideal of monastic observance. She was appointed to increasingly higher offices, until she finally became the prioress of the Galilee convent.[29] The experienced Windesheim prioress expected nothing else from Alijt than what Salome Sticken had formulated in her *Vivendi formula*: to adhere with humility, obedience, and diligence to the communal regimen. Since Alijt found it hard to follow the rules, and her inner resistance to her superiors could not be overlooked, she was often criticised by her superiors, and humiliated and punished in the presence of the whole community. Much later, Alijt looked back at these events in her autobiography, describing her situation and inner conflicts as follows:

> Ende omdat ick mij tot dien dingen qualijck keeren cost die sij voor setten, soo ghecreghen sij mishagen ende misnoeghen hier op mij, om dat [ick] soo inghetrocken was in die dinghen die mij Godt van binnen leerde, ende veroordeelden mij seer eijghenwijs [sijnde] ende goetdunckelijck in mij selven, ende mijns self ghevoelen ende mij selven beter gheloovende dan imant anders, ende aldus in mijn selven blijvende ende mij selven levende ende niet anders, een vrauwe te sijn op mijn selfs handt. Dit soude al tot een quaet eijnde wtcommen, ende ten lesten soude

---

[28] Alijt's date of birth is disputed; in his new English translation, John van Engen proposes 1413 rather than 1415 as date of birth. On Alijt Bake's life and writings, see further Bollmann, 'Being a woman on my own', and the introduction to Van Engen, *The Writings of Alijt Bake*.

[29] Hille Sonderlants obtained the office of prioress in Diepenveen in 1408. In 1412 Salome Sticken was selected to be prioress, while Hille in that year moved to Amsterdam for a position as prioress of Mariënkloster, a convent of Windesheim canonesses, which she held until 1424, and finally – after further reforms in the convent Klaarwater near Hattem (Gelderland) and Nijeklooster in Scharnegoutum (Friesland) – to the convent of regular canonesses Galilee in Ghent in 1439, see *Van den doechden*, ed. by Brinkerink, p. 243 ff.

ick hierinne bedroghen worden. Deser ghelijcke seijden sij veel, end dat ick noijnt ghemaeckt en was om in een ghemeinte to comen oft te wesen.

(Since I could turn to the things they set before me only badly, they got quite displeased and dissatisfied with me because I was so drawn inwards to the things God was teaching me from within. They condemned me as very stubborn and as thinking well of myself, and as believing myself and my feelings better than anyone else's, and so remaining inside myself and living in myself, and thus nothing but a self willed woman. This would all come to a bad end, and I would finally be deceived in it. Things of this sort they said often. Also that I was never made to enter or be part of a community.)[30]

According to Alijt, looking back on her initial period in the monastery, the other part of personal responsibility, namely the cautious awareness of the 'self', had been missing from the postulant's education programme. Alijt, however, wanted to devote herself to her own contemplative exercises, and the ongoing criticism by her superiors of her behaviour during that phase pushed her into deep doubt:

Want al dochte hunlieden dat dit aldus in mij was omdat ick tot hun niet en quaem om hulpe ende raet, recht oft ick dat versmaet hadde ende dat ick mij selven soo groot achte ende liet mij voorstaen dat ick dies niet en behoefde, [maer] dit en was in mij alsoo niet, want mijn herte was alsoo cleijn in mij selven dat het hun al onderworpen was sonder onderscheet, al en docht hun dit en niet omdat ick soo eenvoudich door ghinck in mij selven. [...] Ende dat en dochte mij niet, maer mij dochte datter gheen sijmbelder, onnoseldder, noch [noch] slechtteren mensch en was.

(For although it seemed to them that I looked so [self-conscious, A. B.] to them because I did not come to them for help and advice, as if I had scorned them, and that I regarded myself so highly and behaved as if I did not need their help, [but] I did not look like that, as my heart was so small that it was completely and unconditionally subordinate to them, even if it did not seem so to them because I was and simply remained so introverted. [...] And that did not seem to me to be so, but it seemed to me that there was no simpler, meeker or even more unassuming person.)[31]

Alijt gives extensive accounts of her violent clashes with her superiors, ultimately bringing her to the point of leaving the monastery. To avoid these constant nerve-racking conflicts, she retrospectively relates that she adhered to the requirements of the monastic daily routine in order to avoid wasting any more energy in these discussions:

[30] Spaapen, 'Autobiografie van Alijt Bake', pp. 219–20. 31–56; text and translation of all passages quoted form Alijt's work taken over from John van Engen's forthcoming annotated translation, *The Writings of Alijt Bake*, with slight adaptations.

[31] Spaapen, 'Autobiografie van Alijt Bake', pp. 220–21. 62–73.

Ende dan en wiste ick, aerm mensche, wat doen ende veroodtmoedichde mij aldus, dat ick sweech ende en sprack niet meer, maer sloech mijn hooft ende ooghen met groote bescaemtheijt ende banghicheijt nederwaert, naer dat exempel ons liefs Heeren Jesu Christi [...] ende viel op mijn knijen en badt hun dat sijt mij verghehen wilden om Godt: 'Het was mijn schult, ick wilde mij gheerren beteren'. [...] Ick thoonde simpelijck die ghemeijne oodtmoedicheijt ende hadde ghemeent dat ghenoech hadde gheweest. Maer al was dit ghenoecht voor Godt in mijn consciencie, het en was niet ghenoech voor hunlieden, want sij wilden dat ick al met blijtschappen ontfanghen hadde ende mede gheconsenteert met soeter, blijder herten, ende hun ghebeden, dat zij mij gheholpen hadden, dat ick verwoonen hadde alsoo blijdelijck opelijck. Ende dat conste ick niet ghedoen, soo seere ick altoes inghetrocken tot Godt mijnen vriendt. Ick en peijse om gheen ander vrienden.

(And then I, poor woman, did not know what to do, and I humbled myself to the extent that I remained silent, said nothing and lowered my head and my eyes with great shame and fear, following the example of our dear Lord Jesus Christ [...], and fell on my knees and asked them to forgive me for God's sake: 'It was my fault, I wanted to improve myself'. [...] I simply showed the usual humility and thought that it would be enough. But even if, according to my conscience, this was enough before God, it was not enough for them [the superiors, A. B.], for they wanted me to receive everything with joy and accept it with a sweet and joyful heart, and to publicly celebrate their prayers that had helped me to defeat [the weaknesses, A. B.]. And I could not do that, so strongly was I always drawn to God, my friend. I did not long for other friends.)[32]

The ritual expression of confession ('It was my fault, I want to improve myself') was not sufficient for Alijt's superiors. They did not perceive any signs of joy and gratitude, which Alijt could also not exhibit to them. Instead, she remained drawn to God, whom she described as 'her friend', which made any desire for assistance from other 'friends' superfluous. He ultimately showed Alijt how much further she was on the way to 'letting go and suffering' than her superiors and fellow-conventuals were. As a result, it was understandable why these backward-looking women could not comprehend Alijt.

In the end, the death of prioress Hille Sonderlants brings a change. Surprisingly to the reader and without real explanation of any of the underlying developments, Alijt Bake is appointed as the new prioress of the convent and begins to show her sisters the new, more contemplative path, which she believes she can teach them.

We do not know exactly how, nine years later, a dismissal, exile, and institution of proceedings against Alijt came before the annual general assembly of the Windesheim Chapter. The ban on writing about philosophical teachings

---

[32] Spaapen, 'Autobiografie van Alijt Bake', pp. 229–30. 257–87.

or mystical experiences by spiritual women enacted in 1455 has generally been regarded as proof that the dissemination of Alijt's teachings, propagating her spiritual, mystical doctrine, was a thorn in the eyes of the Windesheim fathers.[33]

Alijt's openly stated refusal to obey her superiors in the monastery may, after she obtained the office of prioress, have been extended to outside the convent walls. The exile from her monastery and the corresponding separation from her 'beloved sisters' suggests a desire to deprive her of any influence in the community and among others. In her *Letter from Exile*, Alijt still insists that her path of spiritual internalization is the only correct one, and in it she encourages her community to hold to this path.[34] Vague references in her letter to her physical weakness and her early death in 1455 suggest that this Windesheim judgement impacted on her more strongly than she wanted to admit. The fact that at least some of her writings have survived, despite an explicit prohibition issued by the Windesheim authorities, shows that the spirit of self-determined piety propagated by the Ghent prioress was supported by her community, albeit more cautiously and less blatantly than the temperament and self-assurance of Alijt Bake had allowed.

The question whether Alijt Bake might have had more freedom to perform her contemplative exercises if she had entered the convent of Windesheim regular canonesses in Diepenveen than she attained when she entered the convent of Galilee in Ghent, is an interesting intellectual exercise, but there is no clear answer. If Salome Stickens's *Vivendi formula* is to be regarded as representative of the manner in which she executed the office of prioress in Diepenveen, then the self-confident manner of Alijt Bake that brought her into difficulty as a postulant at Galilee would probably have led to similar bickering with Salome Sticken, who would have been prioress of the Diepenveen convent at the time. In her *Vivendi*

---

[33] *Acta Capituli Windeshemensis*, ed. by Van der Woude, p. 53 (interpunction modified): 'Nulla monialis aut soror, cuiuscunque status fuerit, conscribat aliquos libros doctrinas philosophicas aut revelationes continentes, per se interpositamve personam ex sua propria mente vel aliarum sororum compositas sub poena carceris; si qui in posterum reperti fuerint, praecipitur omnibus quod statim illi ad quorum conspectum vel aures pervenerit, eos igni tradere curent, similiter nec aliquem transferre praesumant de latino in theutonicum' (No nun or sister, whatever status [= religious or lay, A.B.] she may have, is permitted to copy books containing philosophical teachings or revelations, irrespective of whether they were composed by the scribe herself or another person, either reflecting her own thoughts or those of other sisters, under pain of imprisonment; and if any [= such writings, A.B.] are found in the future, it is mandatory that all those to whose eyes and ears their existence comes, ensure that they are committed to the flames; nor may they venture to make translations from Latin into the vernacular).

[34] Bake, *Brief*, ed. by Spaapen, pp. 351–67.

formula, Salome ultimately emphasizes the prime importance of observing the vow of obedience and the communal pursuit of virtues among fellow sisters. The abandonment of one's own will and the castigation of 'the wicked inclinations of our depraved nature',[35] as formulated in Salome's vernacular original of the *Vivendi formula*, were part of her teaching programme for young women in communities of sisters. Even if we are uncertain about the extent to which this regimen devised for sisters would be applied to (future) novices in the strictly cloistered convent of Windesheim regular canonesses in Diepenveen, indications in the biographies of Diepenveen canonesses transmitted in MS *DV* certainly suggest that, towards the middle of the fifteenth century, there was also a desire to seek the mystical encounter with God in that convent. It would be an exciting and rewarding task to pursue these parallels with the situation in the convent of Galilee in Ghent, especially against the background of the ban on writing by Devout women authors issued by the male Windesheim canons.

---

[35] Sticken, *Vivendi formula*, p. 379 f.: 'Vt mali mores et consuetudines praue corrigantur et emendentur'; Van Dijk, *Salome Sticken*, pp. 418 f.

Works Cited

Manuscripts and Other Unedited Sources

Belgium, Private property (H. Mulder) (MS *L*)

Brussels, Koninklijke Bibliotheek, MS 8849-59 (MS *B*)

Deventer, Stads- en Athenaeumbibliotheek (SAB), MS I, 61 (11 L 1)

——, MS Suppl. 198 (101 E 26) (MS *DV*)

——, MS Suppl. 208 (101 F 25) (MS *G*)

Emmerich, Stadtarchiv, MS "R" [= St A. De 44] (transcription made in the early twentieth century by W. Richter) (MS *E*, lost)

Zwolle, Historisch Centrum Overijssel (HCO), Collectie van Rhemen, MS inv. no. 1 (MS *D*)

Primary Sources

Acta Capituli Windeshemensis. Acta van de kapittelvergaderingen der Congregatie van Windesheim, ed. by Sape van der Woude, Kerkhistorische studiën, 4 (Den Haag: Martinus Nijhoff, 1953)

Alijt Bake, 'Autobiografie' (*Mijn Beghin ende Voortghanck*), see 'Middeleeuwse passiemystiek III. De autobiografie van Alijt Bake', ed. by Bernhard Spaapen, in *Ons Geestelijk Erf*, 41 (1967), 209–301, 321–50

——, 'De brief uit de ballingschap' (*Brief*), see 'Middeleeuwse passiemystiek IV. De brief uit de ballingschap', ed. by Bernhard Spaapen, in *Ons Geestelijk Erf*, 41 (1967), 351–67

——, *The Writings of Alijt Bake: Teacher, Preacher, Prioress, and Spiritual Autobiographer*, ed. by John van Engen (forthcoming)

Busch, Johannes, *Chronicon Windeshemense*, ed. by Karl Grube, *Des Augustinerpropstes Iohannes Busch Chronicon Windeshemense und Liber de reformatione monasteriorum* (Halle: Otto Hendel, 1886), pp. 1–375

Florens Radewijns, see M. T. P. van Woerkum, ed., *Het libellus 'Omnes, inquit, artes', een rapiarium van Florentius Radewijns*, 3 vols (doctoral thesis, University of Leuven, 1950)

Het Frensweger handschrift betreffende de geschiedenis van de moderne devotie, ed. by Wybe J. Jappe Alberts and Adam L. Hulshoff (Groningen: Wolters, 1958)

Hier beginnen sommige stichtige punten van onsen oelden zusteren. Naar het te Arnhem berustende handschrift, ed. by Dirk de Man (Den Haag: Martinus Nijhoff, 1919)

'Het leven der eerwaardige moeder Andries Yserens, overste in het Lammenhuis te Deventer, overleden in den jare 1502', ed. by Otto Antonius Spitzen, *Archief voor de Geschiedenis van het Aartsbisdom Utrecht*, 2 (1875), 178–216

'Levensbeschrijvingen van devote zusters te Deventer', ed. by Willem J. Kühler, *Archief voor de Geschiedenis van het Aartsbisdom Utrecht*, 36 (1910), 1–65

Salome Sticken, *Vivendi formula*, ed. by Wilhelmus J. Kühler, *Johannes Brinckerinck en zijn klooster te Diepenveen* (Rotterdam, 1908; 2nd edn Leiden: Van Leeuwen, 1914), pp. 360–80

Schwesternbuch und Statuten des St Agnes-Konvents in Emmerich, ed. by Anne Bollmann and Nikolaus Staubach (Emmericher Forschungen; 17), (Emmerich: Emmericher Geschichtsverein, 1998)

Van den doechden der vuriger ende stichtiger susteren van Diepen Veen ("Manuscript D"). Eerste gedeelte. De tekst van het handschrift, ed. by Dirk A. Brinkerink (Leiden: A.W. Sijthoff, 1904)

Secondary Sources

Bodemann, Ulrike, and Nikolaus Staubach, eds, *Aus dem Winkel in die Welt. Die Bücher des Thomas von Kempen und ihre Schicksale* (Frankfurt am Main: Peter Lang, 2006)

Bollmann, Anne, "Being a woman on my own': Alijt Bake (1415–1455) as reformer of the inner self', in *Seeing and Knowing: Women and Learning in Medieval Europe 1200–1550*, ed. by Anneke B. Mulder-Bakker (Turnhout: Brepols, 2004), pp. 67–96

——, 'Frauenleben und Frauenliteratur in der Devotio moderna. Volkssprachige Schwesternbücher in literarhistorischer Perspektive' (unpublished PhD dissertation, Groningen University, 2004)

——, "Mijt dijt spynnen soe suldi den hemel gewinnen'. Die Arbeit als normierender und frömmigkeitszentrierender Einfluß in den Frauengemeinschaften der Devotio moderna', in *Normative Zentrierung = Normative Centering*, ed. by Rudolf Suntrup and Jan Veenstra (Frankfurt am Main: Peter Lang, 2002), pp. 85–124

——, 'Das Schwesternbuch aus dem Lamme van Diesehuis in Deventer im Kontext der Schwesternbiographik der Devotio moderna', *Queeste*, 16. 2 (2009), 141–73

Dijk, Mathilde van, 'Salome Sticken, een vrouw uit de kring der moderne devoten', *Ora et Labora. Twaalf opstellen over christelijke spiritualiteit in de praktijk*, ed. by J. van Amersfoort, P. van Beek and G. Schutte (Hilversum: Verloren, 2014), pp. 29–44

Dijk, Rudolf Th. M. van, *Salome Sticken (1369–1449) en de oorsprong van de Moderne Devotie* (Hilversum: Verloren, 2015)

Engen, John van, *Devotio Moderna: Basic Writings* (New York: Paulist Press, 1988)

——, *Sisters and Brothers of the Common Life: The Devotio Moderna and the World of the Later Middle Ages* (Philadelphia: University of Pennsylvania Press, 2008)

——, *The Writings of Alijt Bake: Teacher, Preacher, Prioress, and Spiritual Autobiographer* (forthcoming)

Kock, Thomas, *Buchkultur der Devotio moderna. Handschriftenproduktion, Literaturversorgung und Bibliotheksaufbau im Zeitalter des Medienwechsels* (Frankfurt am Main: Peter Lang, ²2002)

Kohl, Wilhelm, *Die Schwesternhäuser nach der Augustinusregel* (Berlin: De Gruyter, 1968)

Krauß, Susanne, *Die Devotio moderna in Deventer. Anatomie eines Zentrums der Reformbewegung* (Berlin: LIT, 2007)

Kühler, Wilhelmus J., *Johannes Brinckerinck en zijn klooster te Diepenveen* (Rotterdam, 1908; 2nd ed. Leiden: Van Leeuwen, 1914)

Löffler, Klemens, ed., *Quellen zur Geschichte des Augustinerchorherrenstifts Frenswegen* (Soest: Jahn, 1930)

Mertens, Thom, 'Lezen met de pen. Ontwikkelingen in het laatmiddeleeuws geestelijk proza', in *De studie van de Middelnederlandse letterkunde. Stand en toekomst*, ed. by Frits van Oostrom and Frank Willaert (Hilversum: Verloren, 1989), pp. 187–200

Mulder, Herman, 'Het zusterboek van het Lamme van Diesehuis te Deventer', *Queeste*, 16. 2 (2009), 112–40

Rehm, Gerhard, *Die Schwestern vom gemeinsamen Leben im nordwestlichen Deutschland* (Berlin: Duncker und Humblot, 1985)

Scheepsma, Wybren, *Medieval Religious Women in the Low Countries: The Modern Devotion, the Canonesses of Windesheim, and their Writings* (Woodbridge: Boydell, 2004)

Schoengen, Michiel, ed., *Jacobus Traiecti alias De Voecht, 'Narratio de inchoatione Domus Clericorum in Zwollis', met akten en bescheiden betreffende dit Fraterhuis* (Amsterdam: Müller, 1908)

Staubach, Nikolaus, 'Pragmatische Schriftlichkeit im Bereich der Devotio moderna', *Frühmittelalterliche Studien*, 25 (1991), 408–61

Woerkum, Martin van, 'Het 'Libellus Omnes, inquit, artes'. Een rapiarium van Florentius Radewijns', *Ons Geestelijk Erf*, 25 (1951), 113–58, 225–68

Individuality and Scripted Role in Devout Song and Prayer

Thom Mertens and Dieuwke van der Poel*

In late medieval religious practice, one of the text genres reflecting the individualization of that practice is vernacular devout song. In many song texts a lyrical 'I'-persona expresses her feelings and experiences. The person singing the song takes on the role of this 'I'-persona and vicariously relives her or his experiences and feelings. This can be regarded as a specific instance of the individualization of a general religious practice: in the moment of singing, the individual takes on the identity of a scripted role. In this respect devout songs are similar to prayers, as both genres use the first-person singular or plural as well as the present tense to invite the supplicant to apply the words of the text to his or her personal devotion.[1]

Late medieval religious treatises contain few theoretical observations on devout songs and even fewer on the way in which such songs act as roles for their

* The research for this article was done as part of the project *In Tune with Eternity: Song and the Spirituality of the Modern Devotion* (The Netherlands: NWO; Flanders: FWO). The authors would like to thank Hermina Joldersma for her comments on an earlier version of this article and her language advices.

[1] McNamer, *Affective Meditation and the Invention of Medieval Compassion*, pp. 67–80.

Thom Mertens (thom.mertens@uantwerpen.be) is Emeritus Professor at the Ruusbroec Institute, University of Antwerp. His research and teaching are focused on late medieval spiritual literature of the Low Countries.

Dieuwke van der Poel (D.E.vanderPoel@uu.nl) is Associate Professor at the University of Utrecht. She is a specialist in medieval Dutch literature and has written many articles on secular and religious songs.

Inwardness, Individualization, and Religious Agency in the Late Medieval Low Countries, ed. by Rijcklof Hofman, Charles Caspers, Peter Nissen, Mathilde van Dijk, and Johan Oosterman, MCS 43 (Turnhout: Brepols, 2020), pp. 159–179   BREPOLS 📖 PUBLISHERS   10.1484/M.MCS-EB.5.119394

singers and listeners. However, some writers devote considerable attention to the technique of praying, especially to the question of the relationship between the feelings of the one who prays and such feelings as they are worded in the prayer at hand.[2] In this article we argue that late medieval theories about prayer provide a framework for a better understanding of the way in which devout songs 'work', i.e. the intention and function of such songs.

While meditation was originally an independent activity of low-voice repetition of words or phrases, in the early Middle Ages it became part of the coherent series *lectio – meditatio – oratio* (spiritual reading, meditation, prayer). This development reflected the increasingly complex, intellectual, and reflexive character of meditation.[3] Particularly the coherence between meditation and prayer became so strong that the theories on them merged, and what one treatise writes about meditation, another writes about prayer.

In modern scholarship medieval meditation is often described as an intense, receptive method of appropriating texts and images. More recently, however, scholars have called attention to a different aspect, namely the major role of meditation in the creation of texts and images. In her overview of medieval discourses on the nature of religious visions, the medieval techniques that facilitated the occurrence of visions, and the harsh clerical response to lay appropriations of such techniques, Barbara Newman develops the idea of 'visionary scripts'.[4] Citing a wide array of medieval sources, she argues that while visions could occur spontaneously, they could also result from spiritual discipline and meditation.[5] Monastic writers developed meditational techniques that encouraged the visualization of the supernatural, and the cultivation of those techniques could, indeed, induce visions. The visions could be literarily elaborated through the composition of poetry or visionary texts in prose.[6] From the mid-twelfth century onward, this phenomenon was not limited to monastic culture, as clerical writers began to write visionary scripts for lay people with a

---

[2] For example Hugh of Saint-Victor's *De virtute orandi*, and partially inspired by that: Gerard Zerbolt of Zutphen's *De libris teutonicalibus et de precibus vernaculis*. Both texts pay special attention to the praying of the Psalms.

[3] Von Severus and Solignac, 'Méditation', esp. cols 907–11.

[4] Newman, 'What did it mean to say "I saw"?'.

[5] One of these sources is the *Scala claustralium* by Guigo II the Carthusian (twelfth century), an important treatise in the tradition of texts about the techniques of praying and meditation, which mentions *lectio, meditatio, oratio, contemplatio* as the rungs of a ladder that the devotee must ascend.

[6] Newman, 'What did it mean to say "I saw"?', pp. 17–25.

less intensive religious training; these texts visualized sacred scenes in great detail in order to assist practitioners in performing meditations that could shade into visionary experiences.[7] While Newman focuses on visions, it is clear that her insights are valid for meditation in general.

A similar view, arguing that prayer is first and foremost the art of arousing affects and emotions, is developed by Niklaus Largier. The very basis of meditation, according to him, is the combination of rhetorical practices of figuration and amplification, the configuration of tropes drawn from the scriptures, from life experience, from lives of saints, from memory and, indeed, from any other available sources. To deploy their affective forces, these rhetorical practices are staged in a moment of exteriorization and spatial arrangement.[8]

This interpretation of meditation as a means of producing images and texts is valid for all imaginative, i.e. narrative and lyrical, religious texts, and therefore also for prayer and song. It is all the more valid for those texts in which an 'I'-persona is actualised during performance and functions as a scripted role for the performer.[9]

Newman and Largier base their insights on a thorough knowledge of medieval writings about meditation and prayer. For our discussion of Middle Dutch devout song specifically, we turn to the writings about meditation by the most important contemporary authority in this field for the Middle Dutch-speaking regions, Gerard Zerbolt of Zutphen. His work is not mentioned explicitly by Newman and Largier, but his writings are in line with the tradition they describe. In spite of his short life (1367–1398) he was the most influential theoretician of the *Devotio Moderna*,[10] which epitomized a broader observant movement in the Low Countries during the long fifteenth century (1375–1525).[11] We concentrate on Zerbolt's *De spiritualibus ascensionibus* (The Spiritual Ascents), arguably the most influential representative of the late medieval observant spirit in the Low Countries (after Thomas a Kempis's *De imitatione Christi*, less relevant for our subject).[12]

---

[7] Newman, 'What did it mean to say "I saw"?', pp. 25–33.

[8] Largier, 'The Art of Prayer', esp. pp. 62–63.

[9] McNamer, *Affective Meditation and the Invention of Medieval Compassion*, pp. 67–68, coins the term 'Impassionate I' for this scripted role, to be distinguished from the 'Autobiographical I'.

[10] Staubach, *Kirchenreform von unten*; Van Engen, *Sisters and Brothers of the Common Life*; in some respects superseded: Post, *The Modern Devotion*.

[11] Van Engen and Verhoeven, eds, *Monastiek observantisme en Moderne Devotie*; Van Engen, 'Multiple options'.

[12] Modern, critical edition: Gérard Zerbolt de Zutphen, *La montée du coeur / De spiritualibus*

Zerbolt's point of departure is the triple fall of man: through original sin he fell from the state of rectitude, through his concupiscent desire he falls to impurity of heart, and through mortal sin he falls into the region of dissimilitude. Each individual must rise from these three falls by means of spiritual ascents. The second fall into the concupiscent desire must be counteracted by three steps: fear of the Lord, hope, and love.[13] The ascent from the second fall, from concupiscent desire to a regained purity of heart, is achieved through the coherent exercise of *lectio – meditatio – oratio*.[14]

In Chapter 46, on prayer and the manner of praying, Zerbolt first and foremost points to the importance of the affect (*affectus*):[15]

> De primo igitur, scias quod vigor oracionis et virtus surgit ex affectu orantis: magis enim audit Deus desiderium cordis quam clamorem oris. Ideo, semper affectum aliquem et desiderium tibi assumes et indues secundum modum exercicii vel meditacionum quibus pro tempore occuparis, ut semper oracio tua procedat de radice cordis, non tantum ex labiis oris procedat, semper vel ex affectu timoris, meroris, dilectionis, admiracionis, congratulacionis, etc.

> (First, the vigor and virtue of prayer proceeds from the affect of the person praying: God hears the desire of the heart more than the noise of the voice. Therefore always assume an affect and desire like that of the exercises or meditations with which you are occupied, so that your prayer may proceed from the roots of your heart, and not

ascensionibus, ed. and trans. (in French) by Legrand; a recent profound commentary: Gerard Zerbolt of Zutphen, *Geestelijke opklimmingen*, trans., intr. and comm. by Van Dijk; an almost complete English translation: *Devotio Moderna: Basic Writings*, trans. and intr. by Van Engen, pp. 243–315. In this article we use Van Engen's translation, but sometimes adapt it when a more literal translation is needed for our purposes. Florens Radewijns's *Tractatulus devotus* and Gerard Zerbolt's *De reformatione virium animae* are also relevant, but the views of these two works are integrated in the later *De spiritualibus ascensionibus*. Zerbolt also discusses the relationship between individual feelings of the praying person and prescribed prayer texts like the Psalms of the Divine Office in his treatise *De libris teutonicalibus et de precibus vernaculis* (On [reading] Dutch texts and prayers in the vernacular), but this is less relevant for the way in which we discuss our subject in this article.

[13] Zerbolt, *De spiritualibus ascensionibus*, chap. 15, ed. by Legrand, p. 152. 46–55, trans. by Van Engen, p. 260.

[14] Zerbolt, *De spiritualibus ascensionibus*, chaps 43–46, ed. by Legrand, pp. 274–97; cf. also Florens Radewijns's *Tractatulus devotus*, chaps 6–8, ed. by Legrand, pp. 74–83, and Goossens, *De meditatie*, pp. 95–120.

[15] On the medieval meaning of *affectus* in religious contexts as being 'affected' and changed by God's love, see Hollywood, 'Song, Experience, and Book', pp. 66–68. Any modern translation of Latin *affectus* risks anachronism. Cf. Hugh of St Victor, *On the Power of Praying*, intr. and tr. by Hugh Feiss, p. 344 n. 6.

just from the lips of your mouth, always from a feeling of fear or sadness or love or wonder or gratitude, and so on.)[16]

Zerbolt advises enacting the feeling, assuming a role:

> Unde breviter ut modum habeas secundum predicta: si te in prima examinacione discusseris et inveneris peccata tua multiplicata super numerus arene maris, forma in te affectum humilitatis vel meroris et assume personam servi qui dominum suum offendit. Et ex tali affectu, forma oracionem dicens: 'Secundum multitudinem miseracionum tuarum, dele iniquitatem meam'.

> (For instance, in order that you have a disposition in accordance with what I said before, if in your first examination [of your conscience] you discover your sins multiplied beyond the sands of the sea, assume the affect of humility or grief and take on the person of the servant who offended his Lord. In such a frame of mind, shape a prayer, saying: 'According to the multitude of your mercies wipe away my iniquity' [Psalms 50. 3].)[17]

Against evil lust and depraved desire one should assume the feeling of humility and take on the role of a sick person calling upon a doctor for healing. During meditation on death one should take on the role of someone standing before a judge with the fear and trembling of one convicted:

> Si te in secundo ascensu in timore per meditaciones mortis vel iudicij vel inferni exercueris, assume affectum timoris et assume personam rei astantis coram iudice cum timore et tremore, quasi iam convictus, contra quem de iure proferenda est sentencia et dic: 'Noli me condemnare', 'Non intres in iudicium cum servo tuo', vel 'Domine, ne in furore', etc.

> (If in the second ascent you exercise yourself in fear through meditation on death, the judgment, or hell, assume an attitude of fear and take on the person of someone standing before a judge with fear and trembling, as if you are convicted already, against whom by law a sentence must be handed down, and say: 'Do not condemn me' [Job 10. 2], 'Enter not into judgment with thy servant' [Psalms 143 (142). 2], or 'Lord, in thy indignation...' [Psalms 6. 2], and so on.)[18]

---

[16] Zerbolt, *De spiritualibus ascensionibus*, chap. 46, ed. by Legrand, p. 290. 11–18; English trans. by Van Engen (adapted), p. 290. Cf. also Hugh of St Victor, *De virtute orandi*, chap. 11, ed. by Feiss and Sicard, p. 144. 251–54; *On the Power of Prayer*, trans. by Feiss, § 11. 1–2, pp. 337–38.

[17] Zerbolt, *De spiritualibus ascensionibus*, chap. 46, ed. by Legrand, p. 290. 19–25, trans. by van Engen (adapted), p. 290.

[18] Zerbolt, *De spiritualibus ascensionibus*, chap. 46, ed. by Legrand, p. 292. 33–37 (punctuation adapted), trans. by Van Engen (adapted), p. 290. Similarly, chap. 19, 'Generalis

After more such analogies Zerbolt concludes with the general advice: 'Et sic de aliis affectibus quos ex istis formare poteris et assumere debes sicut exercicium tuum exigit et meditacio tua requirit' (Do the same with all the other affections, which you can style in accordance with these as examples, and which you must perform, just as your exercises and meditations require.).[19]

The Middle Dutch song cycle *Die gheestelicke melody* (The Spiritual Melody) offers a fascinating example of how late medieval theories on meditation might be executed in devotional song. Of this cycle three manuscripts are extant, all dating from the last three decades of the fifteenth century: *H* (Den Haag, Koninklijke Bibliotheek, MS 75 H 42), *L* (Leiden, Universiteitsbibliotheek, MS Ltk. 2058), and *W* (Wien, Österreichische Nationalbibliothek, MS s.n. 12875). In addition, the texts of some individual songs are preserved in a number of other manuscripts.[20] Manuscripts *H*, *L*, and *W* offer different versions of the song cycle.[21] Manuscript *L* is the only one with illustrations, most of them showing a nun (in three cases several nuns) kneeling in devotion before a depiction of the situation that is described in the corresponding song, for example Jesus carrying the cross (see Fig. 3). Thus the miniatures provide a model for the devotional use of the songs. The occurrence of nuns in these miniatures argues in favour

---

modus ad formandum meditaciones de morte' (A General Way of Preparing Meditations on Death) discusses the inescapability of death (chap. 19, ed. and trans. by Legrand, pp. 160–63. 1–23) and the necessity to give account before the Judge (chap. 19, ed. by Legrand, pp. 164–65. 64–67). Zerbolt seems to quote David ab Augusta, *De extorioris et interioris hominis compositione*, L. 3. 54. 2, ed. Quaracchi, 1899, p. 301.

[19] Zerbolt, *De spiritualibus ascensionibus*, chap. 46, ed. by Legrand, p. 292. 41–44, trans. by Van Engen (adapted). On quotations from Scripture as expression of one's feelings (with many examples), cf. Hugh of St Victor, *De virtute orandi*, chaps 12–14.

[20] Cf. the diagram in Mertens, 'Die Gheestelicke Melody', pp. 140–41, and www. liederenbank.nl for the preservation of the individual songs.

[21] MS *L* presents two cycles of songs, arranged in two Books; in MS *W* the songs of Book One are presented less obvious as a coherent whole, while the general prologue and the introductions to Song # 2 and 6 are absent; also the songs of Book 2 are included elsewhere in the manuscript as independent songs, without any indication that they are meant as a cycle at all. For a discussion of the different versions in the manuscripts, see Mertens, 'Die Gheestlicke Melody' (esp. pp. 139–41) and De Morrée, *Voor de tijd van het jaar*, chap. 6. In addition, a manuscript in private ownership has excerpts of Songs #5 and #6, cf. Mulder 'Een nog onbekend gebedenboek'. The songs of MS *H* are edited in the Nederlandse liederenbank (www. liederenbank.nl); we use our own transcription of the prologue and the prose passages. MS *L* is available in a facsimile edition (*Die gheestelicke melody*, intr. by Obbema) and a critical edition (*Die gheestelicke melody*, ed. by Oosterman, Willaert and others). The songs of MS *W* are edited in *Het geestelijk lied van Noord-Nederland*, ed. by Bruning and others.

of a public of Devout Sisters for this manuscript. Manuscript *W* is the only one with musical notation, indicating that the songs were in fact meant to be sung.[22] In this article, we base our argument on manuscript *H* (dated 1473), which most likely represents an older version than those in *L* or *W*.[23] Manuscript *H*, a miscellany with different types of devotional texts, such as treatises, sermons, and poems, offers the *Die gheestelicke melody* cycle on fols 217ʳ–255ʳ; it was intended for Devout Brothers.[24] After a short introductory prayer song (Song # 1), a prologue mentions the title of the cycle and introduces the following coherent series of eight songs (# 2–# 9), each of them with its own introduction in prose. This alternation of devout songs and prose introductions is unique in Middle Dutch literature.

In the next part of our article we will first summarize how the general prologue instructs singers and readers to use these songs in their own devotional practice. That the songs of *Die gheestelicke melody* are related to a weekly cycle for meditation, was already noted by previous scholars,[25] but in our discussion of the songs themselves and their prose introductions, we intend to extend this discussion in two ways: first we will discuss the cycle of songs of *Die gheestelicke melody* (# 2–# 9) from the perspective of the ideas about the technique of praying as articulated by Zerbolt and his predecessors; this will lead to a more precise description of the relation between meditation and devout song. In line with this, we will also argue that the songs visualize the exciting of affect by dramatization

---

[22] The provenance of this manuscript is unknown, the earlier attribution to the Convent of Saint Margaret in Amsterdam by Bruning and Wagenaar-Nolthenius *Het geestelijk lied van Noord-Nederland in de vijftiende eeuw* was proved wrong by Obbema 'Het einde van de Zuster van Gansoirde'.

[23] MS *H* offers Book One, which was conceived as an autonomous whole (Mertens, 'Die Gheestlicke Melody', pp. 132–34). Book 2 in MS *L* can be regarded as a consolation text as it thematizes the importance of patience for the soul who suffers because of the absence of God, so the subject is slightly different from Book One (Mertens, 'Die Gheestlicke Melody', p. 127). That MS *H* transmits the oldest of the extant versions is not our only reason for choosing this witness: Book One bears the closest resemblance to the writings of Zerbolt, because of its structure according to the three 'cords' fear, hope and love. The date is based on a note on fol. 286ʳ: 'int jaer ons heeren MCCCC ende LXXIII'.

[24] That the texts in the manuscripts were possibly intended for female or male users is suggested by the different forms of address: *H* addresses only brothers ('broeders'), *W* has sisters as well as brothers ('susterkijns', 'bruederkijns'), while *L* only mentions sisters ('susterkyn'), cf. Van Buuren, 'Soe wie dit lietdkyn sinct of leest', pp. 245–46.

[25] Van Buuren, 'Soe wie dit lietdkyn sinct of leest'; Hascher-Burger, *Singen für die Seligkeit*; Mertens, 'Die Gheestlicke Melody'.

of scriptural tropes.[26] In this respect, they are patterned after the manuals on meditation and prayer and offer a script to awaken the singer-reader's affect.[27]

According to the main prologue, *Die gheestelicke melody* was fashioned to combat idle thoughts or temptation. In such circumstances, 'we' should turn toward spiritual joyfulness and sing in honour of Jesus and his beloved mother Mary to chase away those idle thoughts and temptations. The songs are arranged according to the days of the week: every day a song can be used to perform a spiritual exercise (*te oeffene*), because each one is all the more full of taste (*alte vele smakeliker*) if the words are carefully considered (*wel overdinckes*).[28] Subsequently the prologue explains that God uses three cords to draw the soul away from the idle world toward the sweet land of eternal glory: first, fear of God, which is the beginning of all virtue, secondly hope, which is exercising virtue, and thirdly love, that is perfection in virtues. This triad of fear, hope and love corresponds exactly to the teachings of Zerbolt, who, as we have seen earlier, mentions them as the three steps required in the second ascent to return to pureness of heart.[29] In addition, the songs of the cycle are connected to the three cords: fear to song # 2–6, hope to song # 7, love to song # 8, while song # 9 is a visualization of heaven.

The idea of the three cords is introduced as an amplification of John 6. 44: 'Niement en comt tot my dan die van minen hemelschen vader ghetoghe<n> wort' (No man can come to me, unless my heavenly Father draws him). Also, the idea that the soul longs to be drawn by the third cord of love is underpinned by a reference to Song of Songs 1. 3: 'Trecket my na dij ende wij sullen lopen in den roke dijnre welrikender zalven' (Draw me to you, and we will run in the odour of your ointments). This is entirely in accordance with Zerbolt, who advises to cry out these words, if the ascent seems too difficult to accomplish (*De spiritualibus ascensionibus*, chap. 1, ed. by Legrand, p. 102. 63–66).

In the light of Zerbolt's teachings on the technique of praying, two aspects of the prologue deserve special attention. First, the prologue stresses the importance of the affect. Each of the songs of the cord of fear (with the exception of # 4) is

---

[26] Cf. Largier, 'The Art of Prayer', p. 66.

[27] Cf. Newman, 'What did it mean to say "I saw"?', pp. 14–33.

[28] The days of the week are mentioned in headings: Song # 2 is connected to Sundays, Song # 3 has no heading which indicates that it should be used on Sundays as well, Song # 4 is linked to Mondays, et cetera; cf. Mertens, 'Die Gheestelicke Melody', esp. the diagram on pp. 140–41.

[29] Zerbolt, *De spiritualibus ascensionibus*, chap. 15, ed. by Legrand, p. 152. 46–55, trans. by Van Engen, p. 260. The similarity was already noticed by Van Buuren, 'Soe wie dit lietdkyn sinct of leest', p. 243, and discussed in more detail by Hascher-Burger, *Singen für die Seligkeit*, pp. 119–24 and Mertens, 'Die Gheestlicke Melody'.

connected to the notion of affect (*begheren*): in song # 2 the soul longs to leave the world, in # 3 she wishes for help and consolation from Jesus, in # 5 she asks Mary for consolation against temptation, in # 6 she wishes for Mary's help to fulfil her advice. In these four songs, then, the soul obtains help and consolation in answer to the affect (*begheren*) which is performed and voiced in the text.[30] Secondly, the general prologue stresses the involvement of the senses in the manner in which the songs incite a range of feelings connected to fear, hope and love. In particular the sense of taste (and also smell) is addressed in the frequent use of the adjective *zoet* (sweet), most frequently as a quality of heaven: the sweet land of eternity. In addition, the prologue says that the each song will be much more full of taste (*alte vele smakeliker*) if the user considers and exercises the songs one by one on a daily basis. The wording ('taste', 'consider') corresponds to the idea that experiential wisdom can be obtained via meditation.[31] Thus the general prologue instructs each singer-reader of *Die gheestelicke melody* to take on the role that is scripted in the song by putting oneself in the position of the soul (the 'I'-persona), and thus experience the *begheerte* which is a prerequisite for successful prayer.[32]

The introductions to the individual songs # 2–9 repeat and elaborate the most important points of the general prologue and explain the particular phase of the spiritual ascent of the soul and the affect that is essential in that phase.[33] Remarkable is the use of the present tense to reinforce the immediacy of the experience: the soul longs to leave the world, advises others, sees the land of eternal glory. Moreover, each of the introductions ends with one or two short Bible quote(s) in Latin. We argue that song # 2–9 elaborate the preceding Bible quotes, in accordance with Zerbolt's advice on the manner of praying which says that one should assume the desired affect and take on a certain role, with the assistance of a scriptural quote appropriate to the situation. Indeed, the enactment of the emotions expressed in the biblical words often results during the song in a request or indeed a direct contact with Mary or Jesus in the form of a dialogue. In other

---

[30] *Begeerte* seems to be the Middle Dutch word for *affectus*, as is evident from the Middle Dutch translation of Zerbolt's *De spiritualibus ascensionibus* (edition of the Middle Dutch text in modernized spelling: Gerard van Zutphen, *Van geestelijke opklimmingen*, ed. by Mahieu, pp. 235–45). In the translation of chap. 46 (pp. 236–44), we mostly find *begeerte*, *begeerlijke gevoellijkheid*, and *gevoellijke begeerte* as Middle Dutch renderings of *affectus*.

[31] Cf. Largier, 'Inner Senses – Outer Senses', pp. 5–9.

[32] The human soul is the protagonist in *Die gheestelicke melody* and the introductions use the pronoun 'she' to refer to 'the soul'. The 'I'-persona in the songs refers to the soul, and therefore to each human being.

[33] Mertens, 'Die Gheestlicke Melody', offers a more detailed analysis of the phases of this spiritual ascent.

words, the songs seem to be the result of meditation, that is a process in which Bible quotes are evoked and amplified in order to arouse the sensitivity that is needed to communicate with God, the *lectio*, *meditatio* and *oratio* as discussed in the medieval ideas about contemplation.[34] Also, the importance of the *affectus* is often articulated directly in words, as 'desire' (*begheeren*, *verlangen*) is a recurrent motif in these songs.

The introduction to song # 2 describes the aspired affect of the soul: she is in a state of longing and she wants to part from the world — i.e. to convert —, but fears to have to give account of her offences before Jesus. This is very similar to what Zerbolt advises in Chapter 46, ll. 33–37, that is to assume the attitude of someone standing before a judge, trembling with fear.[35] The Bible quote in question is Psalms 111 (110). 10, 'Initium sapientie timor Domini' (The fear of the Lord is the beginning of wisdom). The song itself, *Der weerels minne es al verloren* (Wordly love is completely in vain — eleven stanzas of four lines) stages the role of an 'I'-persona who expresses fear of judgement: she works out in detail her anxiety (the *timor domini*) that on a certain day she will have to give account for her reluctance to part from the idleness of the world. The last part of the song expresses the desire (*mijn begheeren*, 9.3) to leave all worldly pleasure behind, and the fervent wish that Jesus will receive her prayer and that her soul will be translated into heaven (stanza 10), where she will always sing the praise of Jesus! In short, the 'I'-persona dramatizes the 'fear' mentioned in the Bible, which leads to a state of longing and the wish to be heard by Jesus. This is very much in accordance with Zerbolt, who also mentions this very Psalm quote while treating the second ascent, particularly the fear that is essential to purify the heart.[36]

The introduction to song # 3 imagines what the soul does next: she still wishes (*begheert*) to leave the world, which is difficult for her, therefore she prays to Jesus to be delivered from fear, upon which he offers consolation. In addition, the introduction refers to two verses from the Psalms, Psalms 34 (33). 19, 'Iuxta est Dominus hiis qui tribulato sunt corde' (The Lord is nigh unto them that are of a contrite heart), and Psalms 145 (144). 18, 'Prope est Dominus omnibus invocantibus eum' (The Lord is nigh unto all them that call upon him). The song itself, *O Jhesus, heere, keert u tot my* (O Jesus Lord, turn thyself unto me — eleven stanzas of four lines), is a dialogue between the 'I'-persona, the loving soul, and

---

[34] Cf. Largier, 'Inner senses – Outer Senses'.

[35] Zerbolt, *De spiritualibus ascensionibus*, chap. 46, ed. by Legrand, p. 290. 33–37; quoted earlier in this article.

[36] Psalms 111 (110). 10 is quoted in Zerbolt, *De spiritualibus ascensionibus*, chap. 21, ed. by Legrand, pp. 174–76. 56–73.

Jesus. It stages the next step that results from song # 2: Jesus is now willing to hear her prayer (stanza 1) and to free her from fear; he reassures her that though her anxiety and struggle are ineluctable, they will result eventually in a state of rejoicing and illumination. He also emphasizes the importance of prayer: the soul should call upon him in her need (stanza 7). Then the soul is indeed inspired to leave the world and to focus solely on Jesus. In all, the dialogue is based on the Bible quotes as it shows in great detail that Jesus is indeed nigh unto the fearful believer and further moves him from fear to (future) heavenly delight.

The introduction to song # 4 mentions Matthew 5. 12: 'Gaudete et exultate quoniam merces vestra copiosa est in celis' (Be glad and rejoice, for your reward is great in heaven). The introduction states that the soul now gives consolation. The song, *Verblijdt u, lieve broeders mijn* (Rejoice, dear fellow brothers of mine) has twenty stanzas of four lines. In a new role, the soul brings the words of the quote into practice and spurs 'brothers' to be glad, because everyone who despises the world will be rewarded. Thus, the 'I'-persona acts as a teacher who admonishes fellow believers. Stanzas 3–8 then picture in detail the fate of one who does serve the world, that fate being the tortures of hell. By contrast, a person who detests the world will be rewarded in heaven. Stanzas 11–16 offer an invitation to give careful thought (*O dincket*, 12. 1) to the sweetness of heaven that awaits the true servant. The evocation of heaven is full of sensory notions: everything is sweet (*zuet*, 13. 1) and beautiful (*scoen*, 13. 1), as is the heavenly groom (14. 1); the blessed wear crowns more radiant than the sun and the stars, and the groom's face is similarly described as 'radiant' (*claer*, 13. 3, 15. 1); also the sounds of heaven are very pleasant (stanza 16). Additionally, the experience of time is entirely different: while in hell every day seems to last more than thousand years, in heaven being near the heavenly groom for ten thousand years seems to take less than a moment (stanza 7. 15). This extensive evocation of the pangs of hell and the joys of heaven leads to a call to prayer (stanza 17), and the song then does end in a prayer to Jesus (stanzas 18–20) which expresses the wish (*begheeren*, 18. 4) to be heard by him, and to be able to serve him gladly. In short, the song elaborates on considerations for the reasons for rejoicing mentioned in the Bible quote, and the detailed imagining of hell and heaven stimulate the longing of the singer/reader to be heard by Jesus in prayer.

The introduction to song # 5 has two quotes, both from Sirach: 'Fili, accedens ad servitutem Dei prepara animam tuam <ad> temptationem (Son, when thou comest to the service of God, [stand in justice and in fear, and] prepare thy soul for temptation', Sirach 2. 1), and 'Qui edunt me adhuc esurient' (They that eat me, shall yet hunger, Sirach 24. 29). The song begins with *Ave Maria, maghet reyn* (Hail Mary, pure maiden), and its twelve stanzas of thirteen lines (by a good margin the most extensive song in the cycle) are both a prayer to Mary and a dialogue with her, as she responds in stanzas 9–10. The 'I'-persona takes on the role of someone who laments being separated from Mary (stanza 1), but then she nourishes her longing (*verlangen*, 2. 1) by recounting in detail the Holy Virgin's excellent qualities. This leads to a direct address to Mary, asking for help so that she will be led to heaven (stanzas 5–6). However, the 'I'-persona is afraid that her prayer will not be heard (stanza 7). Then Mary confronts the soul with her main fault, her idle thoughts, which should be countered by reflecting in her heart on Jesus's passion (*ghedenct*, 9. 2; *draecht zijn liden in u hert*, 9. 4). In other words, the temptation mentioned by Sirach is fleshed out as 'idleness'. When the 'I'-persona finally understands that she must leave all idleness, she praises Mary and stresses that everyone should do this. The description of Jesus and Mary again involves several senses: the crown of the groom will radiate beautifully, Mary as the rose of paradise is called *Scoen, edel, claer, frisch, zuet en wijs* (Beautiful, noble, radiant, youthful, sweet and wise) and both the smell and the sound of the virgin are experienced as *zoet* (sweet). In short, a detailed evocation of the heavenly rewards is offered as an alternative for idleness, the temptation mentioned in Sirach.

The introduction to song # 6 again describes the function of the affect: here, the soul feels that she cannot follow Mary's advice without help, therefore she desires (*begheert*) Mary's grace, who indeed listens to this desire. Again the quote is from Sirach: 'Ecci.[37] Ego mater pulcre dilectionis, etc'. (I am the mother of fair love [and of fear, and of knowledge, and of holy hope], Sirach 24. 24). With its twenty-eight stanzas of four lines, this is again a lengthy song, and a dialogue between the soul (stanzas 1–8, 13, 28) and Mary (stanzas 9–12, 14–27). The song elaborates extensively on the Sirach quote, strongly stressing the fact that Mary is the mother of Jesus. The 'I'-persona enters fully into the awareness that she does not serve Jesus sufficiently, due to the sin of acedia or sloth (*traecheit*, 4. 4) and she desires to be worthy of the love of Jesus (stanzas 1–8). Thereupon Mary answers and promises to act as a mediator (stanzas 11–12). The notions of fear, knowledge, and holy hope (to be filled in for the etc. in the quote) also feature in the song: the 'I'-persona calls upon Mary out of fear, and acclaims in the end that Mary always comes to her aid when she is frightened (stanza 28). In stanzas 14–27 Mary explains in detail that the 'I'-persona should be well aware that the Lord gained everything for her: she should not be slow in praying and also ponder that Mary's Child has suffered for her. Mary is also the one who offers hope and the 'I'-persona should cherish a hope in her Child's wounds. Thus the song elaborates the words of the quote in detail. The song thematizes the importance of meditation: the soul wants her heart

---

[37] *Ecci* in *H* is a scribal error; *leg. Eccl.*, a designation for *Ecclesiasticus Iesu filii Sirach*.

to enflame (*Helpt mi int herte barnen*, 5. 3) and is urged to consider Christ's passion (*dinct*, 20. 3, 24. 3, also: stanza 20 and 23–26). Mary emphasizes the importance of *affectus*: she answers the longing of the soul (*begheeren*, stanza 10) and argues that her prayer will be heard if the soul expresses her desires (stanzas 16–18). In short, when the 'I'-persona gives careful thought to her faults, Mary answers her, and affirms the importance of longing and praying.

Song # 7 is preceded by Psalms 34 (33). 5, 'Exquisivi Dominum, et exaudivit me et ex omnibus tribulationibus meis eripuit me' (I sought the Lord, and he heard me, and he delivered me from all my troubles). The song *Hi trore die troren wille* (Let him grieve who wants to) is not only the shortest of the collection (eight stanzas of four lines) but also differs in being remarkably cheerful in tenor. In it, the 'I'-persona acts out her joy now that she is relieved from troubles and fear, because she knows she is chosen by the Lord. She expounds on the fact that she is delivered thanks to the passion (stanzas 3–7 all refer to Jesus's death) and ends with giving thanks to Mary.

The introduction to song # 8 says that the soul is drawn by the burning love of Jesus and that she is obliged to love him with all her heart because of his passion. For her it is now sweet and pleasant to carry his passion in her heart. The relevant Psalm verse is: 'Quemadmodum desiderat servus ad fontes, etc'. (As the hart panteth after the fountains of water, [so my soul panteth after thee, O God], Psalms 42 (41). 2). In his treatise on praying, Zerbolt says that when someone wants to exercise himself in hope through the recollection of the Kingdom of Heaven, he must assume an attitude of love (*affectum amoris*) and pray from a fervent heart. Then he suggests praying precisely this psalm.[38] The song *O Jhesu, uutvercoren Heer* (O Jesus, chosen Lord — eleven stanzas of six lines) thematizes the desire of the heart mentioned in the Psalm, and can indeed be regarded as the expression of the assumption of an attitude of love (Fig. 2).

It opens with an elaboration on the image of the believer panting after Jesus and the soul's desire to receive him (stanza 1–2). Then the 'I'-persona considers that only Jesus's suffering has made it possible for her to come to God's kingdom. In stanzas 4–7 the 'I'-persona addresses Jesus again and visualizes his suffering in detail (*ic dincke*, 5. 3, 6. 3): 'you were mocked, scourged, had to carry the cross barefooted, bleeding and severely wounded'. She connects his suffering with herself: 'for my sake (7. 1) you had yourself caught, and your feet and hands nailed down on the cross'. Stanza 8 emphasizes the proper reaction of the heart: 'Truly full of stones is the heart of someone who considers your death and sorrow and does not weep out of love' (8. 1–3). The next stanza refers to the sense of

---

[38] Zerbolt, *De spiritualibus ascensionibus*, chap. 46, ed. by Legrand, p. 292. 37–41.

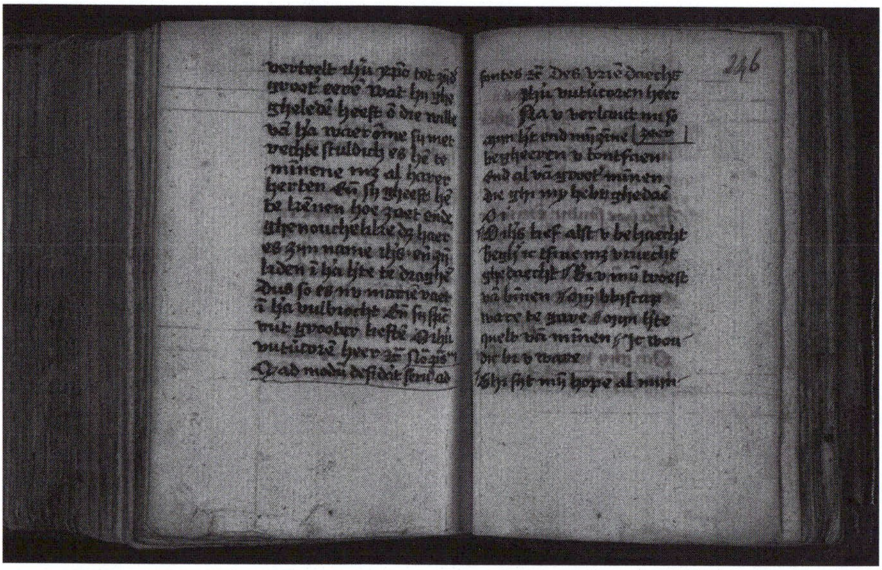

Figure 2. 'The beginning of song # 8 in MS *H*', Den Haag, Koninklijke Bibliotheek,
MS 75 H 42, fols 245ᵛ–246ʳ, *c*. 1475–1500. Reproduced with permission.

taste in the mentioning of the 'sweet' name of Jesus, that is 'sweet' to hear (9. 3–4)
and his name is so pleasant to the heart that there is no better medicine against
the devil's venom (stanza 10). The last stanza is a prayer: the 'I'-persona prays to
Jesus that he will put his name and love, his death and passion constantly in her
mind (*zin*). The song follows exactly the prescriptions for prayer and meditation,
which consist of the *lectio* of the psalm, the amplification of the longing and the
painting of a detailed picture of the passion (*meditatio*), and which results in the
arousal of affect in the heart, when it is no longer rock-hard, but weeps out of
love. Then the heart is in the appropriate condition to pray, and the concluding
stanza is indeed a prayer.

The introduction to song # 9 connects affect, contemplation and meditation
very explicitly: because the soul longs to be with Jesus, she is drawn by this great
love and affect into a contemplation and meditation of the sweet land of eternal
glory. With this sweetness which she sees in her contemplation, she now consoles
all Jesus's servants (with the following song).[39] Before song # 9 a Psalm quote is

---

[39] The entire text of prose # 9 in Middle Dutch is: 'Want die ziele ghecomen es tot grooter
minnen Jhesu Cristi ende zeer begheert bi hem te zine, zo wert sij nu ghetrocken met deser
grooter lieften ende begheerten in eene contemplacie ende overdinckene des zoeten lants der
eewigher glorien, daermen eewelijc Jhesum Cristum aenscouwet sonder eewighe mutacie. Ende

given again: 'Plantati in domo Dei, etc'. (They that are planted in the house of the Lord [shall flourish in the courts of the house of our God]', Psalms 92 (91). 14).[40] The song itself is very much in line with Zerbolt's recommendations in Chapter 24, which discusses the way of shaping meditations on the Kingdom of Heaven. Zerbolt advises the reader to make images of the celestial homeland that can be observed with the senses (*similitudines sensibiles*, chap. 24, ed. by Legrand, p. 182. 3–4) and then enumerates one by one all the details that one can imagine, which is very much in line with all the beauties as visualized in the song *O ghij die Jhesus wijngaert plant* (Oh thou who cultivateth Jesus's vineyard). As this song has no fewer than forty-four stanzas of three lines each, it certainly offers the scope for imagining in great detail the rewards that await the intended audience (addressed as plural *ghi* (you)): those who cultivate Jesus's vineyard (1. 1, 6. 1, 37. 2), have love for Jesus in their hearts (stanza 5) and long to be with him (stanza 6) in the courts of God (*dat soete lant* (the sweet land), 1. 2; or *Jherusalem*, 4. 1). All senses are engaged in the many pleasures of heaven that are evoked: for example, heaven is more beautiful than gold with radiating and sweet flowers, it is paved with pure gold and sweet smelling roses (stanzas 7–9). The song testifies to sensory experience by frequently using qualifications such as *zoet* (sweet, which involves smell and hearing), *claer* (radiant) and *scoon* (beautiful) in descriptions of heaven, the Holy Spirit, Mary and the songs on the saints and the virgins.[41] This sweet land is characterized by cheerfulness and delight, it is marvellous and will last forever.[42] This song describes the final stage of the meditation: the contemplation of the beauties of heaven, which are to be considered one by one, while at the same time realizing that words cannot explain them.[43] The last stanza

---

met deser zoeticheit die sij [the manuscript reads: hij] verneemt in haren contemplacie ende overdinckene des lants der eewigher glorie, soe troest zij hier in dit laeste liedekin alle die ghene die Jhesu Cristo dienen ende sprect aldus: 'O ghij die Jhesus wijngaert', etc.'

[40] MS *L* has a longer quote: 'Plantati in domo Domini, in atrijs domus Dei nostri florebunt. etc'.

[41] Words related to sweet (*zoet*) smell: 8. 3; 9. 2; 23. 1; 29. 1, sweet hearing: 26. 2; 30. 1, sweet in a more general sense: 1. 2; 12. 1; 14. 1; 30. 2; 32. 2; 36. 2. Radiant sight (*claer*): in 3. 1; 8. 1; 20. 1; 28. 2, the same word *claer* is also used for hearing songs (and then means 'clear'): 26. 2. Beautiful to see (*scoen*) in: 4. 2; 7. 2; 13. 2; 20. 1; 25. 1; and again the heavenly songs are beautiful (26. 2). The songs of the virgins and angels also add greatly to the beauty of heaven (stanzas 24–25; 33–35).

[42] Words related to cheerfulness (*bliscap*): 1. 2; 2. 2; 15. 1; 17. 1; 33. 2; 40. 1. Delight (*vruecht*) 3. 1; 4. 3; 35. 3. Marvellous (*wonder*(*like*)): 10. 3 (twice), 13. 2; 21. 1; 26. 2. Eternal (*eewich*): 7. 1; 9. 3; 11. 1; 13. 1; 17. 1; 34. 2; 35. 1; 42. 2.

[43] Ineffability (*onsprekelijc*): 2. 1; 3. 3; 10. 1; 20. 3; stanza 39; incomprehensible (*En mach gheen mensche begripen*): 26. 3.

is an address to God, asking him to grant everybody the consideration of this (heavenly) land while being on earth, and living there afterwards.[44]

These eight songs can be regarded as a result of the cultivation of the theories of meditation and prayer: on the basis of a Bible quote (*lectio*), an inner experience is constructed, usually in a way that exploits the senses (*meditatio*) involving a state of longing and desire (*affectus*), ending in a prayer to or a dialogue with Jesus or Mary (*oratio*). The songs furnish a lively script that enables the singer-reader to imagine and re-experience the entire process, using all senses.[45] The 'I'-persona offers a scripted role to be adopted, by which singers and readers are enabled to become a participant in this experience in order to engage in the meditation on the scriptures and the production of the affect in which this results.[46] The illuminations in manuscript *L* support this process of imagination leading to participation: they depict one or more nuns showing the behaviour and emotions imagined in the song text. One drawing, for example (MS *L*, fol. 26ʳ), depicts the soul as a nun, who is present while Jesus carries his cross, barefoot, bleeding, and severely wounded, just as the accompanying song # 8 relates (Fig. 3). These drawings are visual aids that double the visualization already present in the song text, and they underscore the identification with the exemplary soul for each reader of MS *L*.

We are not the first to argue that devout songs might have had a function in meditation, as the introductions of *Die gheestelicke melody* are directly informative about this. However, by comparing this collection with medieval theories about prayer, we were able to show *how* they could have been used during meditation, and we point out striking resemblances with the entire process of *lectio*, *meditatio*, *oratio*, and *contemplatio* as well as the importance of the affect. This also leads to a new interpretation of the song texts as resulting from cultivating the prescriptions for prayer, in the larger sense of this word. The songs can be regarded as scripts that enable the singer-reader to assume a role and engage in meditation. Thus they aim at an individual devotional practice, although this does not entirely exclude the use by a group of likeminded believers. In this context, the bookmark in manuscript *L* offers interesting indications that the book went from private to common property, and maybe back again:

[44] In MS *H*, *Die gheestelicke melody* ends with one more reference to a Psalm, 'Gloriosa dicta sunt de te, etc.' (Glorious things are said of thee, [O city of God]), Psalms 87 (86). 3.

[45] Newman discusses the 'scripted visions', texts that were meant 'to help readers visualize the life of Christ so vividly that pious imagination shade into visionary experience'; Newman 'What did it mean to say "I saw"?', p. 25.

[46] McNamer, *Affective Meditation and the Invention of Medieval Compassion*, pp. 67–85.

Figure 3. 'The illustration in MS *L* of song # 8 depicts the soul as a nun, who is present while Jesus carries his cross', Leiden, Universiteitsbibliotheek, MS Ltk. 2058, fol. 26ʳ, *c.* 1470. Reproduced with permission.

Dit bocksen hoert Etheken Bernts dachter toe ende na mijnre doet so gheve icket int ghemeen.

(This book belongs to Etheken Bernts' daughter and after my death I leave it to the community.)[47]

So the bookmark indicates that the manuscript was first in personal possession of a woman called Etheken, and that she intended to pass it on to the community where she lived. But the second part of the bookmark was erased (from *ende* on): so maybe the book never became a part of the collection of the community, or it became private possession afterwards once more. This maybe fits in with another interesting details: in the prose sections the plural forms *susters* and *susterkijns* (sisters) are also changed into the singular *suster* (sister) by erasing a few letters.[48] Evidently, the line between individual and communal use seems to be thin.

In the broader context of other Dutch devotional song collections, there are also manuscripts that show the use of songs for singing in groups, and other sources, in particular the Book of Sisters from St Agnes in Emmerich, describe the singing of devotional songs as a form of recreation.[49] Apparently devotional song could serve different goals and in the entire corpus of Dutch devout song, *Die gheestelicke melody* is a unique cycle with the most explicit indications for an individual use in meditation: elsewhere there are no introductions in prose nor such explicit references to the Bible. Even so, we expect that extended research will lead to further proof that devout songs can be related to the imaginative techniques to arouse affect and elevate the mind to God.

[47] Mertens, 'Die Gheestlicke Melody', pp. 135–36.

[48] De Morreé, *Voor de tijd van het jaar*, p. 294.

[49] Van der Poel, 'Late Medieval Devout Song' and Joldersma, '"Alternative Spiritual Exercises for Weaker Minds"?', pp. 383–86.

Works Cited

Manuscripts

Den Haag, Koninklijke Bibliotheek, MS 75 H 42 (*H*)
Leiden, Universiteitsbibliotheek, MS Ltk. 2058 (*L*)
Wien, Österrreichische Nationalbibliothek, MS s.n. 12875 (*W*)

Primary Sources

David ab Augusta, *De exterioris et interioris hominis compositione*, ed. by the fathers of the
Collegium S. Bonaventurae (Quaracchi: Collegium S. Bonaventurae, 1899)
Die gheestelicke melody. Ms. Leiden, University Library, Ltk 2058 [facsimile edition], intr.
by P. F. J. Obbema (Leiden: New Rhine, 1975)
——, *Kritische editie naar handschrift Leiden, Universiteitsbibliotheek, Ltk 2058*, ed. by
a group of Antwerp students supervised by Johan Oosterman and Frank Willaert
(Antwerpen: UFSIA, 2000) [also available on www.dbnl.org]
*Het geestelijk lied van Noord-Nederland in de vijftiende eeuw. De Nederlandse liederen
van de handschriften Amsterdam (Wenen ÖNB 12875) en Utrecht (Berlijn MG 8°
190)*, ed. by E. Bruning, M. Veldhuyzen and H. Wagenaar-Nolthenius (Amsterdam:
Vereniging voor Nederlandse Muziekgeschiedenis, 1963)
Florent Radewijns, *Petit manuel pour le dévot moderne / Tractatulus devotus*, ed. and trans.
by Francis Joseph Legrand, intr. by Thom Mertens (Turnhout: Brepols, 1999)
Gerard Zerbolt of Zutphen, *De libris teutonicalibus et precibus vernaculis*, in 'The "De
libris teutonicalibus" by Gerard Zerbolt of Zutphen', ed. by A. Hyma, *Nederlandsch
Archief voor Kerkgeschiedenis*, n. s., 17 (1924), 42–70
——, *Manuel de la réforme intérieure. Tractatus devotus de reformacione virium anime*,
ed. by Francis Joseph Legrand (Turnhout: Brepols, 2001)
——, *La montée du cœur / De spiritualibus ascensionibus*, ed. and trans. by Francis Joseph
Legrand, intr. by Nikolaus Staubach (Turnhout: Brepols, 2006)
——, *The Spiritual Ascent: A Devotional Treatise by Gerard of Zutphen, with a Life of the
Author by Thomas à Kempis*, trans. by J. P. Arthur (London: Burns & Oates, 1908)
——, *Van geestelijke opklimmingen. Een aloude vertaling opnieuw gedrukt*, ed. by J. Mahieu
(Brugge: Beyaert, 1941)
——, *The Spiritual Ascents*, in *Devotio Moderna: Basic Writings*, trans. and intr. by John
van Engen (New York: Paulist Press, 1988), pp. 243–315
——, *Geestelijke opklimmingen. Een gids voor de geestelijke weg uit de vroege Moderne
Devotie*, trans., intr. and comm. by R. Th. M. van Dijk (Amsterdam: AUP, 2011)
Guigo II, *Scala claustralium*, trans. by Edmund Colledge and James Wals (Kalamazoo:
Cistercian Publications, 1981)
Hugh of St Victor, *De virtute orandi*, in *L'oeuvre de Hugues de Saint-Victor*, vol. 1: *De
institutione novitiorum, De virtute orandi, De laude caritatis, De arrha animae*, ed. by
Hugh B. Feiss and Patrice Sicard (Turnhout: Brepols, 1997), pp. 115–71

——, *On the Power of Praying*, intr. and trans. by Hugh Feiss, in *Writings on the Spiritual Life: A Selection of Works of Hugh, Adam, Archard, Richard, Walter and Godfrey of St Victor*, ed. by Christopher P. Evans (Turnhout: Brepols, 2013), pp. 315–47

Secondary Sources

Buuren, A. M. J. van, "'Soe wie dit lietdkyn sinct of leest'. De functie van de Laatmiddelnederlandse geestelijke lyriek', in *Een zoet akkoord. Middeleeuwse lyriek in de Lage Landen*, ed. by Frank Willaert and others (Amsterdam: Prometheus, 1992), pp. 234–54 and 399–404

Engen, Hildo van, and Gerrit Verhoeven, eds, *Monastiek observantisme en Moderne Devotie in de Noordelijke Nederlanden* (Hilversum: Verloren, 2008)

Engen, John van, 'Multiple Options: The World of the Fifteenth-Century Church', *Church History*, 77 (2008), 257–84

——, *Sisters and Brothers of the Common Life: The Devotio Moderna and the World of the Later Middle Ages* (Philadelphia: University of Pennsylvania Press, 2008)

Goossens, L. A. M. (Mathias), *De meditatie in de eerste tijd van de Moderne Devotie* (Haarlem: Gottmer, 1952)

Hascher-Burger, Ulrike, *Singen für die Seligkeit. Studien zu einer Liedersammlung der Devotio moderna, Zwolle, Historisch Centrum Overijssel, coll. Emmanuelshuizen, cat. VI. Mit Edition und Faksimile* (Leiden: Brill, 2007)

Hollywood, Amy, 'Song, Experience, and the Book in Benedictine Monasticism', in *The Cambridge Companion to Christian Mysticism*, ed. by Amy Hollywood and Patricia Z. Beckman (Cambridge: Cambridge University Press, 2012), pp. 59–79

Joldersma, Hermina, "'Alternative Spiritual Exercises for Weaker Minds"? Vernacular Religious Song in the Lives of Women of the Devotio Moderna', *Church History and Religious Culture*, 88 (2008), 371–93

Largier, Niklaus, 'The Art of Prayer: Conversions of Interiority and Exteriority in Medieval Contemplative Practice', in *Rethinking Emotion: Interiority and Exteriority in Premodern, Modern, and Contemporary Thought*, ed. by Rüdiger Campe and Julia Weber (Berlin: De Gruyter, 2014), pp. 58–71

——, 'Inner Senses – Outer Senses: The Practice of Emotions in Medieval Mysticism', in *Codierung von Emotionen im Mittelalter / Emotions and Sensibilities in the Middle Ages*, ed. by C. Stephen Jaeger and Ingrid Kasten (Berlin: De Gruyter, 2003), pp. 3–15

McNamer, Sarah, *Affective Meditation and the Invention of Medieval Compassion* (Philadelphia: University of Pennsylvania Press, 2010)

Mertens, Thom, 'Die Gheestelicke Melody: A Programm for the Spiritual Life in a Middle Dutch Song Cycle', in *Women and Experience in Later Medieval Writing: Reading the Book of Life*, ed. by Anneke B. Mulder-Bakker and Liz H. McAvoy (New York: Palgrave MacMillan, 2009), pp. 123–47

Morrée, Cécile de, *Voor de tijd van het jaar. Vervaardiging, organisatie en gebruikscontext van Middelnederlandse devote liedverzamelingen (ca. 1470–1588)* (Hilversum: Verloren, 2017)

Mulder, Herman, 'Een nog onbekend gebedenboek uit het Amersfoortse Sint-Agnesconvent met excerpten uit geestelijke liederen', *Queeste*, 8 (2001), 160–74

Newman, Barbara, 'What Did It Mean to Say "I Saw"? The Clash between Theory and Practice in Medieval Visionary Culture', *Speculum*, 80 (2005), 1–43

Obbema, Pieter F. J., 'Het einde van de Zuster van Gansoirde', in Pieter F. J. Obbema, *De middeleeuwen in handen. Over de boekcultuur in de late middeleeuwen*, (Hilversum: Verloren, 1996), pp. 166–75

Poel, Dieuwke E. van der, 'Late Medieval Devout Song: Repertoire, Manuscripts, Function', *Zeitschrift für deutsche Philologie*, 130 (2011), *Sonderheft*, pp. 67–79

Post, R. R., *The Modern Devotion: Confrontation with Reformation and Humanism* (Leiden: Brill, 1968)

Severus, Emmanuel von, and Aimé Solignac, 'Méditation', *Dictionnaire de Spiritualité*, vol. 10 (Paris: Beauchène, 1980), cols 906–14

Staubach, Nikolaus, ed., *Kirchenreform von unten. Gerhard Zerbolt von Zutphen und die Brüder vom gemeinsamen Leben* (Frankfurt am Main: Lang, 2004)

Online Sources

Digitale bibliotheek voor de Nederlandse letteren: www.dbnl.org

Nederlandse liederenbank: www.liederenbank.nl

ILLUSTRATED INCUNABULA AS MATERIAL OBJECTS: THE CASE OF THE *DEVOUT HOURS ON THE LIFE AND PASSION OF JESUS CHRIST*

Anna Dlabačová*

I n the age of transition from manuscript to print, texts and images circulated in both media and there is ample evidence of cross-fertilization.[1] The *Devout Hours on the Life and Passion of Jesus Christ* (*Devote ghetiden vanden leven ende passie Jesu Christi*) are a telling example of a religious text-and-image-

* The research for this publication has been carried out as part of the projects 'Text and Image on the Printing Press: The Complementarity of the Textual and the Visual in Antwerp's Book Production, 1480-1520' (Marie-Curie Co-fund, Université catholique de Louvain, 2015–2017) and 'Leaving a Lasting Impression. The Impact of Incunabula on Late Medieval Spirituality, Religious Practice and Visual Culture in the Low Countries' (NWO-Veni, 2018–2022). I am grateful to the editor of the present volume, Rijcklof Hofman, for his remarks and suggestions which greatly improved the text.

[1] See especially McKitterick, *Print, Manuscript, and the Search for Order*, and the older work by Sandra Hindman, e.g. Hindman, *Pen to Press*. In the notes below, the following abbreviations are used: *ISTC* (*Incunabula Short Title Catalogue*, British Library: www.bl.uk/catalogues/istc/index.html) and *ILC* (Van Thienen and Goldfinch, *Incunabula Printed in the Low Countries*).

Anna Dlabačová (a.dlabacova@hum.leidenuniv.nl) is Assistant Professor and postdoctoral researcher at Leiden University. She is preparing a monograph on the religious editions published by the printer Gerard Leeu within her NWO (Netherlands Organization for Scientific Research) Veni-project 'Leaving a Lasting Impression. The Impact of Incunabula on Late Medieval Spirituality, Religious Practice and Visual Culture in the Low Countries'. Before that, she conducted a project on text and image on the early printing press at the Université catholique de Louvain.

Inwardness, Individualization, and Religious Agency in the Late Medieval Low Countries, ed. by Rijcklof Hofman, Charles Caspers, Peter Nissen, Mathilde van Dijk, and Johan Oosterman, MCS 43 (Turnhout: Brepols, 2020), pp. 181–221   BREPOLS 🍂 PUBLISHERS   10.1484/M.MCS-EB.5.119395

complex expressly directed at lay readers. The text and images were transmitted in printed editions using woodcuts for illustration and — in varying constellations — in richly decorated manuscripts with painted miniatures and borders, in plainer manuscripts with washed pen-drawings, in a 'hybrid book' that combines engravings with handwritten text, but also in simple manuscripts without any form of illustration at all.[2]

Even though in the latter half of the fifteenth century manuscripts offered most possibilities for the individualization of text and image — keeping in mind that the production of manuscripts and especially books of hours was increasingly large-scale and commercialized —, it is well known that a (cheaper) copy of a printed illustrated book also presented its purchaser with several options to make the book his/her own.[3] The sheets with text and images printed in black ink were sent into a still largely 'handwritten world', dominated by the age-old manuscript culture. Here, the 'naked copy' encountered owners and readers with various interests, preferences, and budgets. Individual copies of incunabula were embellished, used, appropriated, modified, and therefore personalized and individualized. As such, their materiality provides important clues about the dissemination of texts and images, about their reception and consumption, and about personal preferences that shaped the customization of a ready made book. Art historians Graham Larkin and Lisa Pon have already argued the importance of the materiality of printed words *and* images.[4]

The aim of this essay is to test a holistic approach to illustrated religious incunabula as material objects that reflect the interplay between religious developments, book printing, and the devotional practices of their late medieval — in this case lay — users. In doing so, I aim to provide a 'template' for the types of evidence and the way they can be interpreted in connection to each other and to the (presentation of the) text.

Printed in five editions over the course of the 1480s and 1490s, of which currently a total of seven copies are known (see Table 5), the *Devout Hours* offer a relatively small corpus that allows for a close scrutiny of material aspects and a treatment of the copies 'as if they were manuscripts'. The fact that only one of the copies contains a still decipherable inscription by its late medieval owner adds to the interest of this particular case study. Owners' inscriptions are relatively scarce

---

[2] Dlabačová, 'Religious Practice and Experimental Book Production'.

[3] With regard to Leeu's books Goudriaan and Willems, *Gheraert Leeu*, p. 13, speak of 'semi-finished products' ('halffabrikaat').

[4] See the special issue of *Word & Image* and in particular Larkin and Pon, 'Introduction' and Chartier, 'Afterword: Materiality and Meaning'. Cf. Parshall, 'Prints as Objects of Consumption'.

in this kind of small, religious book.[5] Is it possible to distil data about the use of illustrated incunabula from 'circumstantial' material evidence only?

In what follows I will first briefly introduce the text and its presentation in the book as it would have come from the printing press. The major part of this essay is dedicated to a discussion of individual copies and as such to an exploration of how copies of illustrated incunabula can be approached as material artefacts.

Table 5. Extant copies of the *Devout Hours on the Life and Passion of Jesus Christ*.

Editions	Copies
Gerard Leeu, [Gouda, 1483, before 10 December], 8°. *ILC* 1245; *ISTC* ih00433130.	San Marino, CA, Huntington Library, 100989 (wanting leaves 1, blank, and 8) Antwerpen, Ruusbroecgenootschap, L.P. 20/m1099E4 (wanting leaves 16, 24, 58, 63, 64, 84, 85, 121–128, 149, and 150)
Gerard Leeu, [Antwerpen, between 18 September 1484 and 9 July 1485], 8°. *ILC* 1246; *ISTC* ih00433150.	Leiden, Universiteitsbibliotheek, 1498 F 1 (wanting leaf t8)
Jacob Bellaert, [Haarlem, 8 April–20 August 1486], 8°. *ILC* 1431; *ISTC* il00186500.	Amsterdam, Universiteitsbibliotheek, Inc. 421 (wanting leaves a1–2, a7–8, b1, b8, t8)
Claes Leeu, Antwerpen, 29 November 1487, 8°. *ILC* 1247; *ISTC* ih00433200.	London, British Library, IA.49933 (wanting leaves b5; c6; e2, e4, e5, e6, e8; h4; i8; m7, m8; n1–8; p6, p7; r5–8; s1–4; t1, t4–5)
Collaciebroeders, Gouda, 3 October 1496, 8°. *ILC* 1248; *ISTC* ih00433250.	Cambridge, University Library, Inc.5.E.3.10[2890] (wanting leaves n. 3–6) Den Haag, Koninklijke Bibliotheek, 150 E 3 (wanting leaves 1, a3–b1, b6–c5, e3–6, h7–8, n1, p8 and s8)

[5] In folio editions such as the *Boeck van den leven Jhesu Christi* (*Book on the Life of Christ*), a dialogic text based on Ludolf of Saxony's *Vita Christi*, owners' inscriptions seem to be more frequent, see Dlabačová, 'Drukken en publieksgroepen', esp. pp. 341–46.

The Book of Hours Reinvented

With the *Devout Hours*, Gerard Leeu (d. 1492), the Low Countries' most prolific and influential printer of the incunabula period (until 1501), created an innovative and commercially successful product.[6] Right from the start, vernacular religious texts were a vital component of Leeu's business. He started his career in Gouda in the spring of 1477 by printing an edition of the Epistles and Gospels in Dutch.[7] His *Booklet on the office or service of the Mass* (*Boecxken van der officien ofte dienst der missen*), which he published in 1479 in Gouda, became the first ever text (in 1481) to be printed in Antwerp.[8] Three years later, in 1484, Leeu himself moved to the city on the Scheldt where he settled next to the city's art market and became the first printer to join the artists' guild of St Luke (in 1485–1486).[9] Leeu was an important actor in Antwerp's development into the Netherlands' capital of printing in the sixteenth century.[10] Many of the religious texts of which Leeu published the *editio princeps* became relatively successful, if not bestsellers reprinted in numerous editions well into the sixteenth century and sometimes even later, often with the use of Leeu's original woodblocks.[11] Apart from his ability to read the market, Leeu must have maintained an impressive intellectual and creative network that provided guidance and assistance in acquiring copy and illustrational material. Most of his religious editions in the vernacular do not mention the author and/or editor and their relation to Leeu. The edition of the *The Sinner's Consolation* (*Der zondaren troost*) gives a rare indication concerning the acquisition of religious

---

[6] On Leeu see the volume edited by Goudriaan, *Een drukker zoekt publiek*. See also Goudriaan and Willems, *Gheraert Leeu*; Hellinga, 'Gheraert Leeu, Claes Leeu, Jacob Bellaert, Peter van Os van Breda'.

[7] *Epistolae et Evangelia* [Dutch], [Gouda: Gerard Leeu], 24 May 1477 (*ILC* 942; *ISTC* ie00064700).

[8] Leeu published the text on 20 July 1479 in Gouda (*ILC* 1986; *ISTC* is00529000). The text was reprinted by Mathias van der Goes in Antwerp on 8 June 1481 (*ILC* 1987; *ISTC* is00529100). This is the first known book printed in Antwerp. Cf. for example Renaud, 'The emergence of Antwerp as a printing centre', p. 12. Analysis of the text and facsimile edition in Van Venlo, *Boexken van der officien*.

[9] Van der Stock, *Printing Images in Antwerp*, pp. 27–30.

[10] Cf. Goudriaan and Willems, *Gheraert Leeu*, p. 20.

[11] Examples include the *Boeck vanden leven Jhesu Christi* (first edition *ILC* 1503; *ISTC* il00353000) and *Liden ende die passie Ons Heeren Jesu Christi* (first edition *ILC* 1447; *ISTC* il00212900). On the latter text, see Van Moolenbroek, '"Dat liden"'. On the *Boeck* see Dlabačová, 'Chatten met Scriptura'.

texts. The colophon states that the author, Johannes de Reimerswaal, a friar of the Antwerp Franciscan House that adhered to the Observance, finished writing the text on 20 March 1492 and that Leeu printed the book that same week.[12] Apparently, the text was written expressly for the press with Leeu's knowledge. Once the text was finished, he secured a swift publication.

There are no concrete data about how Leeu acquired the *Devout Hours*, however. The voice of the author-compiler who wrote new and collected existing texts — whether or not with the intention of publishing the book with Leeu — can be heard most clearly in the prologue, in which he explains *waer om dattet ghemaect is, hoe dattet gheoerdineert is, ende waer toe dattet profitelick is* (why it [the text/book] is made, how it is structured, and why it is profitable).[13] For the sake of lay people who do not have the time to pray the para-liturgical hours contained in a book of hours, the author-compiler has collected seven short 'hours', penitential psalms, and prayers for each day of the week.[14] The existing book of hours was no longer deemed adequate as a devotional instrument. Lay people required a weekly exercise that was more closely tailored to their needs and the author-compiler sought to satisfy this need. Because of his fairly elaborate description of the priesthood as the exemplary way of life on earth — next to the contemplative life symbolised by Martha's sister Mary (Luke 10:42) on which he spends one sentence only —, Léonce Reypens has suggested that the author-compiler was a priest.[15] The latter's insight into 'what lay people want' certainly points to an active involvement in pastoral care. Was the author-compiler a member of the secular clergy in Gouda or an inhabitant of one of the town's religious communities, for example the Franciscan Observant friary or the Collaciebroeders (a local variant of the Brothers of the Common Life)?[16]

However this may be, the exercise, printed on nineteen quires of eight folia, amounting to a total number of 152 leaves, in small octavo format convenient for private study and meditation offers the reader a well thought-out and richly illustrated programme of spiritual growth. One of Leeu's first and most significant and influential series of religious woodcuts fits only this text and was thus

---

[12] *ILC* 1355; *ISTC* ij00399500. Dlabačová and Prochowski, 'Preken en publiceren', p. 225.

[13] Reypens, 'Belang der "Devote ghetiden"', p. 411. 114–15.

[14] Reypens, 'Belang der "Devote ghetiden"', pp. 410–11. 111–17.

[15] Reypens, 'Belang der "Devote ghetiden"', pp. 406–07.

[16] The Franciscan friary in Gouda was the intellectual center of the Observant movement in the Low Countries, see Dlabačová, *Literatuur en observantie*, esp. pp. 39–42. The Collaciebroeders ran a printing press from the 1490s onward and also issued an edition of the *Devote ghetiden*. On their printing activity see Goudriaan, 'Apostolate and Printing'.

— as a whole — made for this 'alternative layman's book of hours'.[17] In all further editions Leeu's series was reused except for the edition printed in Haarlem in 1486 by Jacob Bellaert. Despite of his close connections to Leeu, Bellaert had a new woodcut series made.[18] Whether or not the illustrational programme was anticipated by the author-compiler and/or whether he was involved in the design of the book, remains an open question. Nevertheless, there is no doubt that the integration of a high number of images into the text — Leeu used no fewer than 68 woodblocks for the first edition — contributed to its success.

The books form a unity of text and image and their users were as much readers as they were viewers. Each chapter starts with a woodcut of, and a meditative exercise on, the subject matter of that day. The reader was to consider Death on Monday, the Last Judgement on Tuesday, and Hell on Wednesday. Thursday was reserved for the love and gifts of God and Friday for the Passion of Jesus Christ. On Saturday the reader focused on confession, followed by the last of the *quattuor novissima*, Heaven, on Sunday. These meditative texts are detailed descriptions in which each section is preceded by an imperative that prompts the reader to internalize the account: think, consider (*dencket, overdencket, aendencket, overlegghet*), notice (*merket*), take or have something in your thoughts (*hebt in uwe ghedachten*) or even to mentally examine (*besiet ende ondersoect*).[19] The devotee's figurative meditation is further stimulated by commanding him/her to see ((*aen*)*siet*), to place something before the eyes or to cast the (inner) eyes onto something (*stelt/settet voer u oghen, slaet uwe inwendighe oghen ende ghedachten op*), to contemplate or envisage something inwardly (*beschouwet inwendelik*), and — with regard to the Passion — to see both with the heart and the eyes (*siet mit harten ende mit oghen*).[20] The meditative texts thus consist of prescriptive sequences of thoughts and visualizations that can be seen as emotional scripts.[21]

[17] Kok, *Woodcuts in Incunabula*, I, p. 172. Conway, *The Woodcutters of the Netherlands*, pp. 46–47. Rosier, 'Gheraert Leeus illustraties'. Dlabačová, 'Religious Practice and Experimental Book Production'.

[18] Kok, 'A Rediscovered *Devote ghetiden*', pp. 167–83; Kok, *Woodcuts in Incunabula*, I, p. 171. Dlabačová, 'Religious Practice and Experimental Book Production'.

[19] Antwerpen, RG, L.P. 20/m1099E4. Examples include fol. a8^v 'overdencket dat die ure des doots sekerlijck ende sonder twivel comen sal'; b1^v 'dencket nu dit'; fol. a8^r 'overlegghe huden in dese ghetide dat ghi cortelick van dit leven moet reysen'. Other examples on fols a8^v–b1^r, b2^v, d2^v, h8^v, i2^v.

[20] Antwerpen, RG, L.P. 20/m1099E4. An example is (fol. d2^r) 'Slaet uwe inwendighe oghen ende ghedachten op dat uterste oerdel'. Other examples on fols d3^v, d5^r, h8^r, l5^{r-v}.

[21] The sequence for Wednesday (fols f5^r–8^r): Meert oeck u inwendighe oghe opten

The images that precede each of these texts — apart from structuring the book — serve as a starting point for the meditation.

The meditations are followed by one of the seven penitential psalms (in an 'extended' version that combines exegesis and meditation, probably an invention by the author-compiler), a prayer to the Trinity and a number of prayers on the history of salvation.[22] In each chapter these prayers are followed by a short penitential psalm taken from the *Psalter of Our Lady* (*Souter OLV*). All texts except for the extended penitential psalms are accompanied by an image. In the prayer cycle on salvation history text and image take on a particularly close relationship as each opening presents the reader with an 'image and text diptych'.[23] Every day the reader should conclude his/her exercise by reciting the *Adoro Te* prayer in Middle Dutch and a prayer to All Saints. Their texts and the accompanying woodcut of the Mass of St Gregory are found only at the end of the chapter intended for Monday. From Tuesday onward a reference at the end of each chapter tells the reader to leaf backward in order to read these prayers (and to view the woodcut of St Gregory).[24]

Due to the nature of the text and the (intended) readership these books would have been kept in private possession and used in households or (lay) confraternities, which might also explain the low number of extant copies.[25] But what can these few copies tell us about the *Devout Hours* as objects handled by reader-viewers and in turn about the impact these lavishly illustrated books had on late medieval spirituality?

---

helschen coninckrijc... Dencket dan ten eersten dat die helle is een gruwelike plaetse ... Siet alsulcke is dese plaets ... Dencket oeck op die veelheyt ende menigherhande pinen die daer sijn inder hellen ... Daer na soe overdencket oeck van die grootticheyt ende swaricheyt der pynen... Dencket in een ghelikenisse oft ghi in die winter alst zeer cout ware... Settet oeck voer u oghen ofte yemant liden mochte die pijn in enen heten barnenden oven... Daer na soe overlegghet wel ende dencket hoe dat die verdoemde vermaledide menschen pijn sullen liden... Dencket daer na op die wreetheyt der duvelen... Dencket oec op die inwendighe pinen... Overdencket dan ten lesten...'

[22] This is also explained in his prologue: Reypens, 'Belang der "Devote ghetiden"', p. 411. 122–27.

[23] Dlabačová, 'Religious Practice and Experimental Book Production'.

[24] Antwerpen, RG, L.P. 20/m1099E4, fol. f4ʳ. On Saturday the Litany of Our Lady is added after the sixth Marian psalm. On Sunday the book concludes with prayers to the name of Jesus and the Virgin.

[25] Cf. Kok, *Woodcuts in Incunabula*, I, p. 172 and Dlabačová, 'Religious Practice and Experimental Book Production'.

Layers of Evidence

The degree to which additions were made by hand differs from copy to copy and it is important to keep in mind that handmade finishes could be made and/or changed over time by several owners and/or craftsmen. One of the two copies of the first edition by Leeu and the only extant copy of his second edition represent the simplest form of handmade finishes: in these copies, rubrication (pilcrows, capital strokes, underlining) and initials have been added with red ink.[26]

The only extant copy of the fourth edition by Claes Leeu, Gerard's brother, also contains rubrication and initials, but here red ink has also been applied — in varying gradations — to eight of the woodcuts. The red colour accentuates contours, details and emphasizes the focus on the central figure(s).[27] Whether a more elaborate adornment of certain woodcuts happened on a random basis or whether the 'choice' of these images (Marriage of Mary and Joseph, Visitation, Christ disputing in the temple) can be seen as an indication of the interest of (a) reader(s) in particular events — and therefore as a kind of pictorial annotation — is thought-provoking, yet difficult to answer. Similarly, in many of the woodcuts in this copy yellow and brownish shades have been added, usually to items of clothing.[28] Again, the colour, nowadays faded, appears to have added focus to the central figures, for example in the sequence of events from the agony in the garden of Gethsemane until Christ is brought before Herod, in which Christ's gown is consequently touched up.[29] Sometimes the addition of yellow shade coincides with the treatment with red ink, as is the case in the Visitation (Plate I).

---

[26] San Marino, CA, Huntington Libr., 100989 and Leiden, UB, 1498 F 1. The rubrication is executed in a consistent quality and was probably added by a professional craftsman. In the San Marino copy, which I have studied in digitized form only, rubrication is more elaborate (more pilcrows and underlining); compare for example fol. c7^v. On fol. c1^v of the Leiden copy a user tried to cover Eve's genitals with brown ink.

[27] London, BL, IA.49933. As several leaves are missing (see table above) the number of woodcuts with red accents might have been higher originally. Elaborate red accents have been added to fols c4^v (Marriage of Mary and St Joseph), e3^v (Visitation) and f2^v (Christ disputing in the temple). A limited number of red accents (mainly blood to wounds) can be found on fols a1^r (title page, Man of Sorrows), d1^v (Last Judgement), e1^v (Throne of grace), g4^v (Throne of grace), and p4^v (Longinus piercing Christ's side). Pen flourishes have been added to two initials (fols a2^r and a8^r).

[28] London, BL, IA.49933, fols e1^v, e3^v, e7^v, g4^v, g6^v, h3^v, h4^v, k1^v–8^v, l1^v, l2^v, l4^v, o1^v, o4^v, p2^v–5^v, p8^v.

[29] London, BL, IA.49933, fols k3^v–l2^v.

Throughout the copy yellow colour has also been added in a fairly crude fashion over the impressions of the woodcut of Mary and the Christ Child clothed with the sun that accompany the short penitential psalms taken from the *Psalter of Our Lady*.[30] The added colour, although unassuming, does make Mary into an illuminated presence. Mary's face and the Child have been left uncoloured, drawing the eye of the reader-viewer effectively toward their intimate embrace. Furthermore, two of these pages are marked with (remnants of) *clavicula* (bookmarks).[31] Together, colour and *clavicula* suggest a particular interest of the reader(s) in these psalms (Fig. 4). Possibly the copy's user(s) read only these short psalms every day of the week. A particular focus on Mary in the devotion of the reader(s) is confirmed by the additions made to the woodcut and very last prayer in the book, a Middle Dutch translation of *Ave Maria, ancilla sanctae Trinitatis* ascribed to St Bernard.[32] The woodcut, showing an image almost identical to the block that accompanies the Marian psalms, is embellished with yellow colour and a red ink that has oxidized and is thus different from the ink used in the other woodcuts. The same ink was used to add a reference to the Hail Mary (*Ave Maria*) after each verse of the prayer.

At the beginning of this copy, the reader is moreover confronted with two extra quires that contain handwritten prayers of which the lion's share is directed at Mary.[33] The first quire also contains communion prayers and the second quire concludes with a prayer to St Peter. The prayers were written by six different

---

[30] London, BL, IA.49933, fols c5ᵛ, f. 3ᵛ, h6ᵛ, l3ᵛ, o3ᵛ, q1ᵛ.

[31] London, BL, IA.49933, fols f3 and l3.

[32] London, BL, IA.49933, fols t7ᵛ–8ʳ.

[33] London, BL, IA.49933. Bound in contemporary brown leather blind-tooled binding on wooden boards with a maculature taken from a twelfth-century liturgical manuscript. I would like to thank Erik Kwakkel (Leiden University) for dating the writing to 1150–1200 (e-mail dd. 5 April 2017). The two quires both count six leaves, not foliated: fols [1ʳ–1ᵛ]: 'dyt gebet lerde onse lieve vrouwe enen mensche...'; [1ᵛ–4ʳ] 'Dit ghebet salmen lesen als men ten heiligen sacrament sal gaen...'; [4ᵛ] 'dit sijn drie paeter noster van der heiliger drivoldicheit...'; [5ʳ–6ᵛ] 'O alre heilichste maghet Maria ghebenedide moeder ons heren Ihesu Christi voer dine heilighe voete val ich neder ...'; [7ʳ–7ᵛ] 'Weest ghegroet ende verblyt gloriose vrouwe, heilighe moder gods Maria...'; [7ᵛ–8ʳ] 'O Maria, ontfermt u mynre, du, dy ghenoemt biste een moder...'; [8ʳ] 'O saele des groten conincks ende blinckende poerte des hemels, coningine alder enghelen...'; [8ʳ⁻ᵛ] 'Och Maria, ic heb tot u gheropen als ic bedroeft was ende sy heeft verhoert...'; [8ᵛ] 'O Maria, sterre des meers, verliechterse alder werelt...'; [8ᵛ] 'Reycke uut tot ons dyn aerme ionffrouwe Maria...'; [9ʳ] 'O coningine des hemels ende vrouwe der enghelen...'; [9ʳ–11ʳ] 'In dien daghe dattu keerdes dyn alder claerste aenghesicht boven ons soe salstu ionffrouwelijke moder ons verblijden...'; [11ʳ–12ʳ] 'O heilige apostel Peter ende vrint gods...'; [12ᵛ] blank.

Figure 4. 'The woodcut of Mary and the Child standing on a crescent moon and clothed with the sun next to the fourth penitential psalm taken from the *Psalter of our Lady*, with yellow colour and bookmark', London, British Library, IA.49933, fol. 13ᵛ. Copy of the edition by Claes Leeu (Antwerpen, 29 November 1487). © The British Library Board.

Plate I. 'The Visitation woodcut. Red ink emphasizes contours and details and Mary's and Elizabeth's garments and halos have been touched up with a yellow hue', London, British Library, IA.49933, fol. e3ᵛ. Copy of the edition by Claes Leeu (Antwerpen, 29 November 1487).
© The British Library Board.

Plate II. 'Start of the meditative text for Monday in one of the copies of the first edition by Gerard Leeu. Coloured woodcut, gold leaf initial and border, and painted upper border with gold leaf details', Antwerpen, Ruusbroecgenootschap, L.P. 20/m1099E4, fols a7ᵛ–a8ʳ. (Gouda, 1483, before 10 December). Reproduced with permission.

Plate III. 'Colouring in the Cambridge copy of the 1496 edition by the Gouda Collaciebroerders. The Incredulity of St Thomas (Plate IIIa) and Pentecost (Plate IIIb). The blue of Thomas's garment and of the ceiling has been added over lighter shades. The Pentecost woodcut represents the 'first stage' of colouring', Cambridge, University Library, Inc.5.E.3.10[2890], fols s2v and s5v. Reproduced by kind permission of the Syndics of Cambridge University Library.

Coninc der glorien o ewyghe onghescapé wijsheyt goods alre goedertierenste heer thesu criste/ ghebenedijt ende ghedanct moet gy wesen van dien pijnliken zueren ganck dien ghy ghinct/ doen gi voer dē coninc herodes gebrocht wort/ daer ghi bespot bespoghen ende myt enen witten cleet als een dwaes bespottet wort/ ende onteert Ic bid v alre zoetste heer thesu criste/ do er alle den laster ende doer al dat verdriet dat v daer is ghescheyet/ dat ick die wijsheyt deser we relt moet versmaden/ ende gaerne om die minne van v bespottet eñ voer een dwaes geacht moet willen wesen Eñ doer die scande eñ scofficrich eit die v den coninc der glorien die bose ioden de den/ als enen dwaes in die langhe witten cleede bespottende/ alsoe bid ick v mijn lieue heer vten gronde mijns herten/ dat ghi mi cleden wilt van den hoofde totten voete/ metten clede der onno selheyt/ ende alle houerdye der cleueré moet scu wen/ op dat ic v mynen heer mynen god/ eñ met allen heilighen enghelen ende heilighen/ nv ende altoes ende ewelic sonder eynde/ moet regneren inder glorien des ewichs leuens Amen

l iij

Plate IV. 'Christ brought before Herod', Antwerpen, Ruusbroecgenootschap, L.P. 20/m1099E4, fol. l2ᵛ (Plate IVa) and Cambridge, University Library, Inc.5.E.3.10[2890], fol. l2ᵛ (Plate IVb). Reproduced by kind permission of the Ruusbroecgenootschap and of the Syndics of Cambridge University Library.

Plate V. 'The agony in the garden of Gethsemane. Coloured woodcut in the Antwerp copy of Leeu's first edition', Antwerpen, Ruusbroecgenootschap, L.P. 20/m1099E4, fols k3ᵛ–k4ʳ. (Gouda, 1483, before 10 December). Reproduced with permission.

Plate VI. 'Entry into Jerusalem. Coloured woodcut with handwritten poem in the only extant copy of Jacob Bellaert's 1486 Haarlem edition. The colouring has been partially removed', Amsterdam, Universiteitsbibliotheek, Bijzondere Collecties, Inc. 421, fols h3ᵛ–h4ʳ. Reproduced with permission.

hands and thus appear to have been either a collective effort and/or collected over time, reflecting the interests (of a group?) of readers with a predominant focus on Marian devotion.[34] The inclusion of communion prayers, often found in books of hours but not incorporated into the *Devout Hours*, reflects a need for these texts and suggests that the copy was also used during Mass. Furthermore, the female form of the Middle Dutch word for sinner (*sondersse*) in these prayers points to a female scribe and setting.[35] Yet another user brought the codex up-to-date in the early sixteenth century by adding a slightly smaller leaf after the *Adoro Te* prayer with the handwritten text of the three extra verses that were added to

[34] Hands: 1 [1ʳ–1ᵛ]; 2 [1ᵛ–4ʳ]; 3 [4ᵛ]; 4 [5ʳ–6ᵛ]; 5 [7ʳ–11ʳ]; 6 [11ʳ–12ʳ].

[35] London, BL, IA.49933, fol. [3r] 'die du gheleden hebste aenden heiligen cruce om mij arme sondersse'.

the prayer in 1503 (Fig. 5).[36] This way she (and other women?) had the latest version at their disposal.

The only extant copy of Claes Leeu's edition thus contains several layers of material evidence that point to a focus on Mary in the devotion of the reader(s): the added quires with predominantly prayers to Mary are consistent with the colour added to the woodcuts of Mary clothed with the sun next to the short psalms, the bookmarks mounted onto some of these leaves and the special attention paid to the Marian prayer ascribed to St Bernard at the end of the book. Due to the various users involved in customizing the book we might think of a small circle of devout urban readers, possibly members of one family or a religious confraternity. In what kind of setting the reader(s) practised their Marian directed devotion exactly, remains uncertain.

Colour

The colouring of woodcuts and other additions to images in religious incunabula from the Low Countries, such as inscriptions, have hitherto not received a lot of attention.[37] More work has been done with regard to colour and other additions to the surface of woodcuts printed on single sheets. Concerning the interpretation, function, and influence on viewing practices of alterations and additions such as colouring and writing in prints, the work by art historians Peter Schmidt and David Areford is seminal.[38] The idea of an 'archaeology of the printed image', which in turn was inspired by the 'archaeology of the manuscript', can also be transferred to incunabula, and illustrated incunabula in particular.[39] As we have seen, layers of handmade additions added to these books by reader-viewers provide clues about the way text and image functioned in readers' hands.[40] Colouring seems to be a particularly important 'reception layer'. The colouring

---

[36] London, BL, IA.49933, after fol. c7. From circa 1483 this prayer consisted of five verses (the text that Leeu put to press). In 1503 three extra verses were added to the prayer. I would like to thank Sanne de Vries (Leiden University) for this information.

[37] Van Delft, 'Illustrations in Early Printed Books', discusses two coloured copies of a Dutch book of hours printed in Paris. General observations in Goedings, *'Afsetters en meester-afsetters'*, pp. 48–52.

[38] Areford, 'Introduction', Areford, 'The Image in the Viewer's Hands' and Areford, *The Viewer and the Printed Image* and, for example, Schmidt, 'Beschrieben, bemalt, zerschnitten'.

[39] Areford, 'Introduction', pp. 2–3.

[40] Cf. Areford, 'The Image in the Viewer's Hands', p. 7.

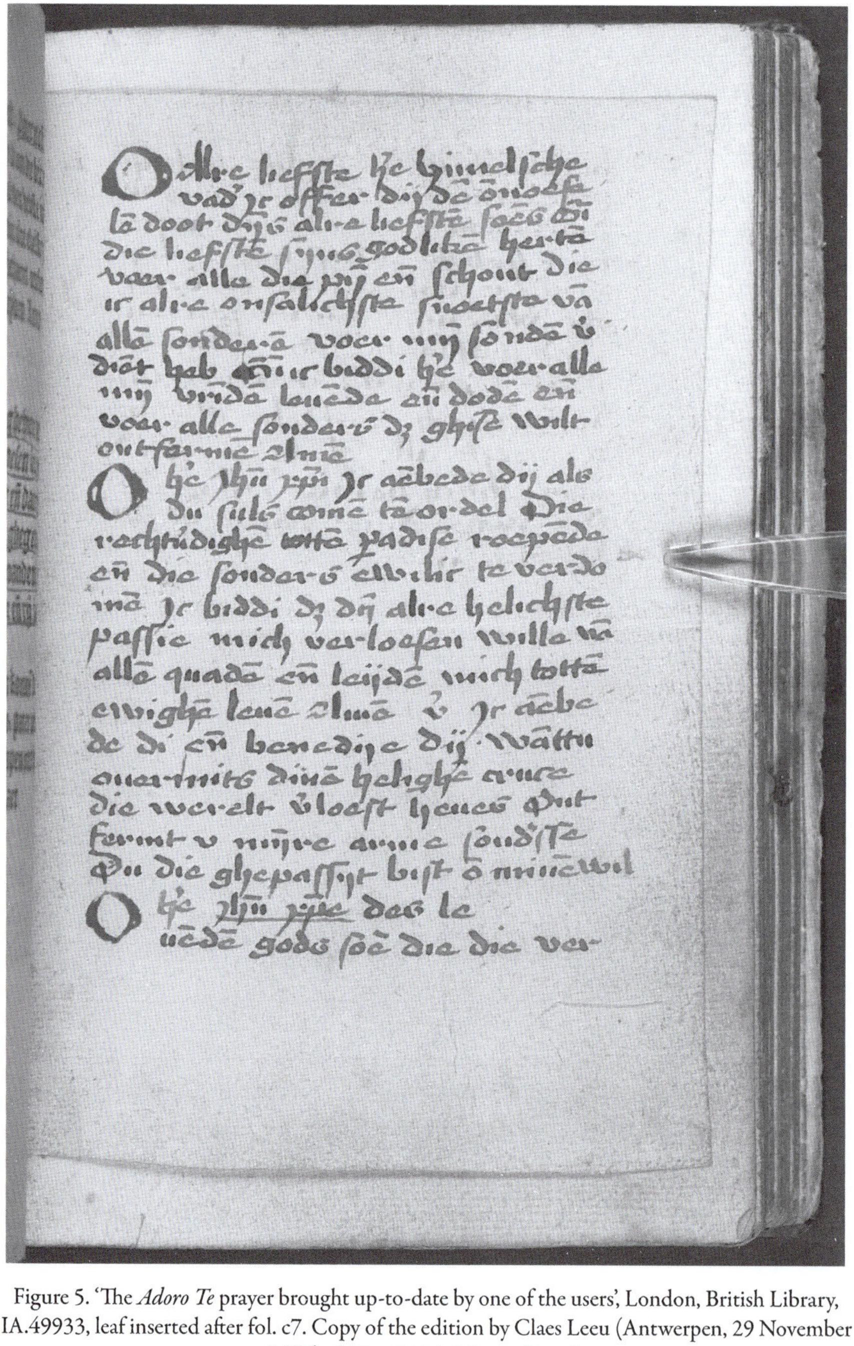

Figure 5. 'The *Adoro Te* prayer brought up-to-date by one of the users', London, British Library, IA.49933, leaf inserted after fol. c7. Copy of the edition by Claes Leeu (Antwerpen, 29 November 1487). © The British Library Board.

we have encountered thus far is simple and in its function seems close to a form of 'pictorial annotation'. Even in works such as the *Devout Hours* colouring was often more sophisticated, however, and although until now largely ignored, essential to the way the book — as a unity of text and image — was experienced by reader-viewers. Out of the total of seven extant copies, five copies contain some form of colouring.[41] The colouring and pallet used differs from copy to copy — there was thus apparently no template that colourists followed —, and in all copies colour has been applied freehand, without the use of stencils.[42]

The oldest copy with coloured woodcuts is one of the two copies of the first edition by Gerard Leeu (Gouda), nowadays in the library of the Ruusbroec Institute in Antwerp.[43] Originally, the copy was bound together with a fifteenth-century parchment manuscript with a Middle Dutch West-Flemish translation of the second book of the *Imitatio Christi*.[44] During restoration manuscript and print were separated, which happened more often when medieval material was made to fit modern distinctions between manuscript and print.[45] This practice ignores, however, late medieval reality and materiality. In the case of the Antwerp copy, the manuscript with the twelve chapters from the work by Thomas a Kempis, bound in front of the printed book, provided a profound introduction to inner life that the reader then could take up further and practice week after week in the *Devout Hours*. At times he would have returned to Kempis's work for a more profound Christocentric contemplation on the withdrawal from the world, purging his conscience and intention and deepening his spiritual growth. Moreover, the manuscript points to a milieu in which these texts circulated and (older) manuscript material was available.[46]

Together with the gold leaf initials, careful rubrication applied with red and blue ink and two handwritten Latin (liturgical) prayers — a rhymed prayer (hymn)

---

[41] Antwerpen, RG, L.P. 20/m1099E4; Amsterdam, UB, Inc. 421; London, BL, IA.49933; Cambridge, UL, Inc.5.E.3.10[2890]; Den Haag, KB, 150 E 3.

[42] On the use of stencils Primeau, 'Colouring within the Lines', and Primeau, 'The Materials and Technology of Renaissance and Baroque Hand-Colored Prints', pp. 66–68.

[43] Antwerpen, RG, L.P. 20/m1099E4. Reypens, 'Rond een Antwerpse druk'.

[44] Nowadays Antwerpen, RG, MS 202. The manuscript is dated to the middle or second half of the fifteenth century. See Reypens, 'Een onbekend vijftiendeeuws handschrift'.

[45] A copy of Gerard Leeu's *Tafel des kersteliken levens* (Den Haag, KB, 169 G 94) was for example bound together with a manuscript of a life of St Jerome, nowadays Den Haag, KB, MS 129 G 8.

[46] Because the recto of the manuscript's first leaf contains the end of a sermon by Goswinus Hex (*Eene oufeninghe vander gracien gods*) it is probable that the owner acquired the second book of the *Imitatio Christi* as an already existing unit.

to Mary added after the end of the penitential psalm for Friday and canticle(s) for the feast of the eleven thousand virgins on the verso of the last leaf, written by the same hand but added over time — the *Imitatio Christi*-manuscript points to a well-to-do and well-educated layman who actively used the *Devout Hours* in his pious practice and looked for material that could function as a supplement to the texts in the printed book.[47] The execution of the gold leaf initials and of the borders on the page where the hours of Death starts (Plate II) is reminiscent of decoration found in devotional manuscripts made in Bruges (Fig. 6). The place of decoration is consistent with the language of the manuscript with the *Imitatio Christi* and we might thus, in all probability, locate our pious layman in Bruges or its surroundings. Leeu's books were sold in Antwerp already in the late 1470s, and in 1484 he registered as a member of the St John's guild in Bruges.[48] In later years he appointed several (international) business agents during the Easter fair at Bergen op Zoom.[49] Thus, it is not surprising that someone from West Flanders bought a copy of the first known edition of the *Devout Hours* and had it decorated in Bruges.

The painting of the woodcuts, executed consistently throughout the copy in yellow, purple, pink, green, dark grey, light red, and brown hues, was probably executed by a different craftsman than the initials and border decoration. Both pigments and technique used are different.[50] Generally, colour has been applied without shading, which is only used sporadically, for example to heighten the folding of cloth. The colourist has consistently added shade to windows in order to add depth to the image. The research by Jan van der Stock has revealed that in 1512 the Antwerp printer Andriaan Janssoens 'de Verlichter' had materials for colouring woodcuts in his workshop.[51] Van der Stock has suggested that Leeu

[47] Antwerpen, RG, L.P. 20/m1099E4. Both handwritten texts have a title in Dutch: fol. m7ʳ 'van onser vrouwe / Stella poli, regina soli, tu proxima soli / Ave maria gratia(?) Digna coli sine nube doli...' (for these lines see Mone, *Hymni Latini*, p. 324, and Blume and Dreves, *Analecta Hymnica*, p. 145. 37–38) and fol. t8ᵛ 'Jhesus Maria Vanden xi dunest[!] maeychden Media autem nocte clamor factus est ecce sponsus venit exite obviam ei prudentes virgines aptate vesteras lampades quia sponsus venit Christus...' (Matthew 25. 6–7, cf. http://cantusindex.org/id/605044a).

[48] Goudriaan and Willems, *Gheraert Leeu*, p. 19 and 23; Hellinga's, *Fifteenth-Century Printing Types*, p. 69; Dewitte, 'Het Brugse St.-Jans en St.-Lucasgilde der librariers 1457, 1469', p. 339; Dlabačová, *Literatuur en observantie*, pp. 210–11, cf. also Hellinga, 'Gheraert Leeu, Claes Leeu, Jacob Bellaert, Peter van Os van Breda', p. 285 n. 7.

[49] Gnirrep, 'Relaties van Leeu', pp. 194–98. Brinkman, 'De *Const* ter perse', p. 161.

[50] Cf. Primeau, 'The Materials and Technology of Renaissance and Baroque Hand-Colored Prints', esp. pp. 63–65 and Oltrogge, 'Illuminating the Print', on different techniques and effects of colour in prints.

[51] Van der Stock, *Printing Images in Antwerp*, p. 98.

Figure 6. 'Book of Hours, use of Rome, Latin. West Flanders, Bruges (?)', 's-Heerenberg, Huis Bergh, MS 29, fols 60ᵛ–61ʳ. Third quarter fifteenth century. Reproduced with permission.

might have become a member of the guild of St Luke because he used materials in his shop that were used by painters.[52] Perhaps some copies of Leeu's editions were coloured under his auspices, as was the case with Hartmann Schedel's *Nuremberg Chronicle* (1493), printed by Anton Koberger in Nuremberg and distributed in coloured and uncoloured copies — the former twice as expensive as the latter.[53] The suggestion that Leeu was somehow involved in colouring might be confirmed if two or more copies with (near) identical (style of) colouring are found. So far, however, colouring seems to differ from copy to copy in Leeu's editions, and in any case in the copies of the *Devout Hours*. The colouring might have been added by a workshop specialized in (manuscript?) illumination or one combining a number of activities linked to book and print production, possibly also in Bruges.[54]

[52] Van der Stock, *Printing Images in Antwerp*, pp. 29–30; 35–43.

[53] Dackerman, ed., *Painted Prints*, cat. 7, pp. 102–04 and Wilson, *Making of the Nuremberg Chronicle*, pp. 229–37. The author owned a magnificently coloured copy (p. 207).

[54] In Antwerp a Jan van den Driele (from 1494 onward) combined his activity as a copyist with book illumination, bookbinding and book selling, see Gnirrep, 'Relaties van Leeu', p. 195. It is likely that someone like van den Driele would also have coloured woodcuts. On print colourists

Both surviving copies of the last known edition of the *Devout Hours* (Collaciebroeders, Gouda, 3 October 1496) have also been coloured. The copy kept in Cambridge, University Library, contains a sixteenth-century owner's inscription by, in all probability, a layman.[55] The images in this copy, bound in an early-sixteenth-century binding,[56] have been coloured with transparent purple, (dark) blue, yellow, brown, (bright) red, and green. The bright red and dark blue are more opaque and similar to the pigments used for rubrication and initials. These two colours are applied more crudely and at times over another, lighter colour (Plate IIIa).[57] Possibly, the red and blue were not part of the original pallet and were added in a later stage (during the process of rubrication?), perhaps because the colouring was deemed too pale. It is also conceivable that the colouring was consciously planned this way in order to make the preparation and use of pigments more efficient — in this case the 'first' colourist, working with pale, transparent colours, deliberately left garments and details uncoloured, as is still the case in for example the Pentecost woodcut (Plate IIIb).[58] This kind of question is difficult to answer yet significant for our understanding of the procedures involved in handmade finishes to incunabula and the meaning of colour. It is important to be aware of the fact that colouring could be the result of the work of more than one person, adding yet more layers to the already collective nature of an illustrated book.[59]

Both the colourists of the Antwerp and Cambridge copies incorporate the colour of the paper into their pallet, usually for skin (faces and hands). One of the most effective uses of the white of the paper in the *Devout Hours* can be found in these copies in the image of Christ before Herod (Plate IV). In the adjacent prayer, the devotee speaks multiple times of the white garment Christ was dressed in:

(*Briefmaler*) in Germany Dackerman, 'Painted Prints in Germany and the Netherlands', pp. 15–26.

[55] On the verso of the flyleaf in the back we read 'Dijt boeck hoert toe Evert (?)'. Although the entire annotation is written in the same ink, the name was probably written by another hand and might therefore use different letterforms inconsistent with the rest of the annotation.

[56] Blind stamped brown leather over wooden boards with images of a pelican wounding its breast to feed its young. Maculature in front (liturgical manuscript, Latin, fifteenth century, Low Countries) and back (liturgical, Latin, twelfth century). McKitterick, 'Tanned Calf over Wooden Boards'.

[57] Examples on fols k2ᵛ (Christ washing the feet of the apostles), n2ᵛ (Christ crowned with thorns), n3ᵛ (Christ disrobed), s2ᵛ (The incredulity of St Thomas), and t4ᵛ (Last Judgment).

[58] Cambridge, UL, Inc.5.E.3.10[2890], fol. s5ᵛ. Other examples include the Agony in the Garden of Gethsemane (k3ᵛ) and the Arrest of Christ (k5ᵛ).

[59] Analysis of the pigments could provide more certainty about the colouring process. See e.g. Primeau, 'The Materials and Technology of Renaissance and Baroque Hand-Colored Prints', pp. 55–63 and Oltrogge, 'Illuminating the Print'. Cf. Chartier, 'Afterword', p. 182.

O coninc der glorien, o ewyghe onghescapen wijsheyt goods, alre goedertierenste
heer ihesu christe, ghebenedijt ende ghedanct moet gy wesen van dien pijnliken,
zueren ganck dien ghy ghinct doen gi voer den coninc herodes gebrocht wort, daer
ghi bespot, bespoghen ende myt enen witten cleet als een dwaes bespottet wort ende
onteert. [...] Ende doer die scande ende scoffiericheit die u, den coninc der glorien,
die bose ioden deden, als enen dwaes in die langhe witten cleede bespottende, alsoe
bid ick u, mijn lieve heer, uten gronde mijns herten, dat ghi mi cleden wilt vanden
hoofde totten voeten metten clede der onnoselheyt.

(Oh King of glory, oh eternal uncreated wisdom of God, most merciful Lord Jesus
Christ, you should be blessed and thanked for your agonizing, grievous journey
that you went when you were brought before king Herod, where you were mocked,
spat at and with a white robe ridiculed and dishonoured as a fool. [...] And through
the disgrace and humiliation that has been done to you, King of glory, by the
wicked Jews, who ridiculed you as a fool dressed in that long white garment, so I
pray to you, my dear Lord, from the bottom of my heart, that you shall dress me
from top to toe with the garment of innocence.)

The colouring augments the meaning of the image and helps the reader to focus
on the garment that is central to the event, the prayer, and to the metaphor used
in the devotee's request. In this case colour strengthens the relationship between
image and text and further assists the reader in emulating Christ's meekness.
The combination of text and image even compelled one of the reader-viewers
of the Antwerp copy to pierce the eyes of the two soldiers (Plate IVa). Thus, he/
she physically interacted with the book in a performative act, altering the image
irreversibly.

In general, colour adds depth and definition to space, makes it easier to
distinguish individuals in groups and to identify them in subsequent images.
St John and Mary, for example, can be located instantly as they are made
recognizable by their blond hair and red robe (St John) and blue garment
(Mary) in sequential images in the second copy of the edition by the Gouda
Collaciebroeders, nowadays kept in the Koninklijke Bibliotheek in The Hague.[60]
Colour thus also strengthens the iconography of woodcuts. Even though a template

---

[60] Den Haag, KB, 150 E 3. This copy can be consulted via Early European Books, http://
eeb.chadwyck.co.uk/. See in particular the prayer sequence for Saturday, starting with the
Crucifixion (fols p3^v–q1^r). With all woodcuts fully coloured in a rich pallet the Den Haag copy
contains the most elaborately executed colouring. The copy has rubrication and red initials with
alternately blue and purple pen flourishes. Small painted borders, executed in a Ghent-Bruges
style, have been added to the impressions of the woodcut of Mary clothed in the sun for which
the Collaciebroeders used a different woodblock from the one use by Leeu (except for the last
prayer on fol. t7^v). See also *De vijfhonderdste verjaring*, pp. 450–52.

was probably not available, colourists clearly followed certain (iconographic) conventions. Other examples include Christ's gown, usually coloured purple, and the image of hell, which is multi-coloured, probably to enhance its confused state and horrors.[61] The possible interaction and discrepancies between woodcut colouring, manuscript miniatures, and even panel painting needs further research. In manuscripts of the *Devout Hours* Christ's gown, for example, is usually painted in a grey(ish) colour instead of the purple colour often found in copies of the printed editions.[62] Moreoever, artists and artisans could work with various media: the well-known Antwerp painter Quentin Massys (*c.* 1466–1530) started his career as a print colourist.[63]

Apart from strengthening the meaning and expressive power of woodcuts, colour can also add pictorial elements to the printed image. Because the medium of the woodcut possessed limited means to portray blood, perhaps the most frequently found addition to impressions of religious woodcuts are drops, streaks, and streams of this bodily liquid.[64] The fact that red ink was frequently at hand for rubrication has resulted in numerous Passion scenes in early printed Netherlandish books overflowing — at times excessively — with blood. In the already discussed copy of Claes Leeu's edition the red ink was occasionally added to Christ's wounds and the *arma Christi*.[65]

In the prayer adjacent to the woodcut of the Agony in the garden of Gethsemane, the devotee thanks Christ for the inexpressible sadness Christ showed when he spoke the words 'My soul is overwhelmed with sorrow to the point of death' (*mijn ziel is bedroevet ter doot toe*) (Matthew 26. 38). In the second half of the prayer the devotee requests to be granted the same fervour in his prayer as Christ:

> Ende doer die onbegripelike banghicheyt die ghi hadt opter aerden legghende ende bevende ende bloedyghen sweet swetende inden lesten strijt laecht ende ghedurich blevet in uwen ghebede. Soe bid ick u, lieve heer, dat ghi mi vuericheit ende aendachticheyt verlenen wilt in mynen ghebeede ende vuerighe ende rouwighe tranen te storten voer mynen sonden daer ghy bloedighe tranen voer ghestort hebt. Amen.

---

[61] The meditative text adjacent to the image of hell starts with the instruction 'Meert oeck u inwendighe oghe opten helschen coninckrijc' (Also cast your inner eye on the kingdom of hell). See n. 20–21 above. Cf. Goedings, 'Afsetters en meester-afsetters', pp. 48–52, on a copy of an edition of *Belial* by Bellaert.

[62] London, British Library, MS Add. 20729; Den Haag, KB, MS BPH 79; Den Haag, KB, MS 135 E 19; Princeton, UL, MS Garrett 63.

[63] Dackerman, 'Painted Prints in Germany and the Netherlands', p. 30.

[64] Cf. Areford, 'The Image in the Viewer's Hands', p. 57. Dackerman, ed., *Painted Prints*, p. 138.

[65] See n. 27 above.

(And through the inconceivable anxiety that you had lying on earth and trembling and sweating bloody sweat in your last agony and persevering in your prayer, so I pray to you, dear Lord, that you may lend me fervour and zeal in my prayer and [that I may] shed ardent and sorrowful tears for my sins for which you have shed tears of blood. Amen.)[66]

The colourist of the copy kept in Antwerp added the bloody sweat to Christ's forehead, a detail that was important in the devotee's prayer (Plate V).[67] In the copy of Bellaert's edition a red hue also seems to have added focus on Christ's bloody sweat and tears, through which the devotee was asking for more passion in his own prayer and which he was to 'mirror' in his prayer.[68] As Christ's agony in the garden of Gethsemane, and in particular his sweating of blood, was also one of the six or seven of Christ's bloodlettings that formed one of the many popular devotional lists in the late medieval period, the red colour might have seemed essential to the image to at least some of the readers. One of the manuscripts that contain the prayers also follows this 'colour-convention', fulfilling the public's expectations (Fig. 7, Plate V).[69] It might even have been the case that designers of woodcuts and/or woodcutters anticipated this kind of colouring.[70]

The coloured woodcuts in the books might not have served only as meditational instruments in relation to the text physically present in the same opening (e.g. as counterparts to the short prayer texts). At the end of the 'hour' on the Passion, to be read on Friday, the reader is encouraged to extend his meditation by literary following Christ during the events from the Last Supper onward:

Ist dat ghi tijt, plaets off stonde hebt dese ghetijde int lang te vertrecken, soe beghintse int avontmael, daer wast u vule voeten myt warm water des berouwes. Soe gaet dan voert int hoeffgen, ende ist moghelic dat god u die kelc des vegheviers off nemen wil, weest oec willich ende bereyt, ghevanghen ende ghebonden te werden om god, tgheloeff, u salicheyt, die penitenci te volharden. Aldus gaet voert ende volghet Jhesum nae die ghebonden gheleyt wort als een dieff in Annas huyse

---

[66] Antwerpen, RG, L.P. 20/m1099E4, fol. k4ʳ.

[67] Antwerpen, RG, L.P. 20/m1099E4, fol. k3ᵛ.

[68] Amsterdam, UB, Inc. 421, fol. k3ᵛ.

[69] Den Haag, KB, MS BPH 79, fol. 57ʳ.

[70] Certain (devotional) woodcuts were intended to be coloured; the addition of blood was required in for example a print of *Christ on the Cross with Angels* in which Christ's blood (to be added by hand) drips into chalices held by angels: Primeau, 'The Materials and Technology of Renaissance and Baroque Hand-Colored Prints', pp. 65--66. Cf. Oltrogge, 'Illuminating the Print', p. 303, and Dackerman, 'Painted Prints in Germany and the Netherlands', pp. 18--19.

Figure 7. 'The agony in the garden of
Gethsemane. Manuscript with the prayer
cycle on salvation history from the *Devout
Hours*, produced by one of the Masters
of Hugo Jansz van Woerden', Den Haag,
Koninklijke Bibliotheek, MS BPH
79, fol. 57ʳ. *c.* 1500. Reproduced with
permission.

[...] ende blijft altijt by hem, waer hy gaet, ter tijt toe dat hi verrijst ende van die
doot weder op staet. Mocht gy aldus dese ghetijde *houwen*, het soude u baten ende
nymmermeer *rouwen*.

(If you have the time, place or occasion to draw out this hour in length, so start
in the [Last] Supper; there wash your soiled feet with warm water of repentance.
And go forth in the garden, and if it is possible that God may want to take the
chalice of purgatory from you, be also willing and prepared to be caught and tied
up [and] to persevere [in] penitence for God, [for] faith and [for] your salvation.
And so continue and follow Jesus who is led tied as a thief to Annas' house [...]
and stay always with him, wherever he goes, until the time that he resurrects and
resuscitates from death. May you thus keep this hour; it would be very helpful and
never distress you.)[71]

To support this meditation, the reader-viewer might have leafed backwards to
the prayers for Thursday (the prayers for Thursday start with an image of the

[71] Antwerpen, RG, L.P. 20/m1099E4, fols 17ᵛ–8ʳ.

Last Supper which is followed by the washing of the disciples' feet and the agony in the garden of Gethsemane and they also include Christ before Annas), and forwards to the chapters that include prayers on Christ's death and resurrection and used the images there as a guideline for this strongly figurative meditation.

Variations in Verse

The only extant copy of the 1486 edition printed by Jacob Bellaert in Haarlem nowadays has subtle colouring in yellow, red, brown, green, and blue hues, but originally the colours would have been much more vivid and intense (Plate VI).[72] The removal and/or alteration of colour in later periods are yet other difficulties one should keep in mind when dealing with colour in incunabula.[73]

Apart from carefully applied rubrication and initials in red, the copy contains several short texts written by a number of users on leaves left — either partially or entirely — blank by the printer. At the end of the chapter for Monday, one of the readers added what seems to be an original poem on the meditative topic of that day, Death (Fig. 8). The poem is divided into two stanzas of sixteen lines. Because of its literary quality, which places the verses close to the sphere of the *rederijkers* (the chambers of rhetoric), it is worthwhile quoting at least the first stanza in full:

> Och god als ic overpeyse
> Die doot die nu niemant en spaert
> Soe duchtic zeer voer myn reyse
> Want ic binder niet op bereyt
> [V]an welcker ic bin soe zeer verwaert

[72] The colours have been removed as much as possible, as has also been done with many of the handwritten texts (see n. 81 below). Possibly this was done by the nineteenth-century owner and antiquarian bookseller F. Olivier (Brussels). The cloak of the father in the Throne of Grace, for example, appears to have been consistently coloured in dark blue, but this colour has been removed almost entirely. Remnants are visible on fols b7ᵛ, c3ᵛ, c5ᵛ, d1ᵛ, e2ᵛ, e3ᵛ, e4ᵛ, f1ᵛ, f3ᵛ, h1ᵛ, k1ᵛ, o4ᵛ, p2ᵛ, p4ᵛ, p5ᵛ, q1ᵛ, r7ᵛ, t4ᵛ. The dark green colour, which originally must have been almost opaque, has also been laboriously removed in most places (see plate VI (= h3v), and for example fols k1ᵛ and k2ᵛ). Cf. Bogaart, *Geleerde kennis in de volkstaal*, on colouring in the copies of Bellaert's edition of *Van den proprieteyten der dinghen*. Bellaert's copy of the *Devout Hours* is discussed in Kok, 'A Rediscovered *Devote ghetiden*', but her focus is on analytical bibliography and she mentions none of the handmade additions.

[73] Cf. Dackerman, 'Introduction', pp. 2–3, on colouring as adultery and the removal of colour from prints. See also Schmidt, 'Beschrieben, bemalt, zerschnitten', p. 245, on the twentieth-century practice of removing any traces left by users from reproductions of prints in publications in order to represent the 'original', clean form of the woodcut. Cf. Jecmen, 'Color Printing and Tonal Etching', pp. 67–68.

[Ic] bidde u, heere god, om respyt
[To]t dat ic myn sonden hebbe verclaert
[W]ant ic en hebbe ure nochte sekeren tijt
[...]aes als ic ga dan overdincken
Die helle ende dat grote torment
Myn herte wil myn van vaere ontsincken
Die ewich is ende niet en eendt
Ic biddu, coninc omnipotent
Wilt my arme sondare niet versmaden
[M]yn ziele die es u testament
Ontfermt myns god doer wuer[? uwer] ghenade

(Oh God, as I ponder upon / death who now spares no one, / so I fear greatly for
my journey / because I am not ready for it / of which I am distressed so deeply / I
pray to you, Lord God, for respite / until I have accounted for my sins / because I
do not have hour nor a sure time / ... thus, when I contemplate upon / hell and that
great torture / my heart wants to sink away because of the terror / that is eternal
and never ends / I pray to you, King almighty / do not scorn me, poor sinner / my
soul is your last will / Have mercy on me, God, through your grace)[74]

It is plausible that the meditative text on Death at the start of the chapter inspired
the reader to write this poem, as it connects closely to the emotional script in the
meditative text.[75] The theme was popular and omnipresent at the time, however,
and is, for example, also expounded in the well-known allegorical play of *Elckerlijc*
(*Everyman*).[76] Furthermore, two lines of the handwritten poem also occur in a
rhymed dialogue between Man and Death, printed in Flanders between 1470 and
1485 as a single leaf, possibly to be hung on a wall.[77] The stanzas in the copy of the
Devout Hours thus seem to be a personal reflection on a familiar theme as much as a
consideration on the meditative topic of that day. In any case, the text was deemed a
useful addition to Monday's chapter, and its addition was well considered: whoever
wrote the poem not only had pen and ink at hand, the verses are neatly written and
the writer anticipated the addition of a decorative initial: he left a space open for an
initial at the beginning of the text, complete with a 'lettre d'attente'.

[74] Amsterdam, UB, Inc. 421, fol. d1ʳ.

[75] The reader has to consider the journey on which he is about to depart, the fact that death
will surely come but unannounced as a thief in the night, etc. Interestingly, the meditative texts
also contain passages set in verse. See Dlabačová, 'Religious Practice and Experimental Book
Production'.

[76] Most recently on this theme in play and painting: Warnar, '*Elckerlijc* in beeld'.

[77] Bax, 'Een onbekend gedicht over de dood als schaakspeler'.

The poem's author followed the same strategy when adding a prayer in prose for a soul in purgatory right after the prologue and immediately before Monday's 'hours of death'.[78] This complementary prayer seems to be a reaction to the exposition in the latter text on the separation of the soul from the body, the soul's individual judgement upon which she has to travel immediately to purgatory, hell or heaven, and chiefly the fact that the deceased are soon forgotten, in particular by their friends and next of kin:

> Ende aldus werden si dicke ende menichwerven vergheten mit lijf ende ziel die nochtan dicwijl langhe inden vaghevier leyt ende biddet grote ghenade, segghende: Ontfermet, ontfermet onser sonderlinge ghi, onse vrienden ende magen die dat goet ende erf ontfanghen hebbet daer om dat ick nu pijn lide.

> (And thus they are often and many a time forgotten with body and soul, which nevertheless often lies in purgatory for a long time and prays for great mercy, saying: Take pity, take pity on me, especially you, our friends and family who have received the goods and estate for which I now suffer pain.)[79]

The added prayer was to remind the reader of the obligation to help the souls residing in purgatory, especially those who were close to him during earthly life.

Another variation in verse was added by the same user beneath the woodcuts of the Entry into Jerusalem and the Purification of the temple (Plate VI): a single poem split in half due to the limited space in the lower margins. The verses relate closely to the former woodcut and the adjacent prayer that expounds on Christ's entry on a donkey as an example of his great love for mankind and of his meekness, which is taken as a starting point in the poem:

> O almachtich god, o oetmoedich van zeeden
> Die op een ezelinne quamt ghereden
> En waert doen ontfanghen met groter eeren
> Mer die eere verghinc in bitterheiden
> Want ghy hebt om ons doerwoenden u seeden
> Och, ghenadich god, wilt my nu doch leeren
> Dat ic myn hertelyck mach touweert keeren
> Ontfermhertich god, verlicht myn van binnen
> opent myn herte, hulpt myn duecht vermeren

---

[78] Amsterdam, UB, Inc. 421, fol. a6ᵛ: 'O eerwardighe heere ende genadighe god, want du een troester der berdroefder herten sijt der ghenre die in dijn gracie stan, soe ontfarmedi over die ziele daer ic arme sonder nu sonderlinghen voer biddende byn. O cristus des levende gods soene... soe verlosse vanden tormenten der pynen ende en laetse niet achter, want sij hevet in di ghehoept'.

[79] Amsterdam, UB, Inc. 421, fol. b2ʳ.

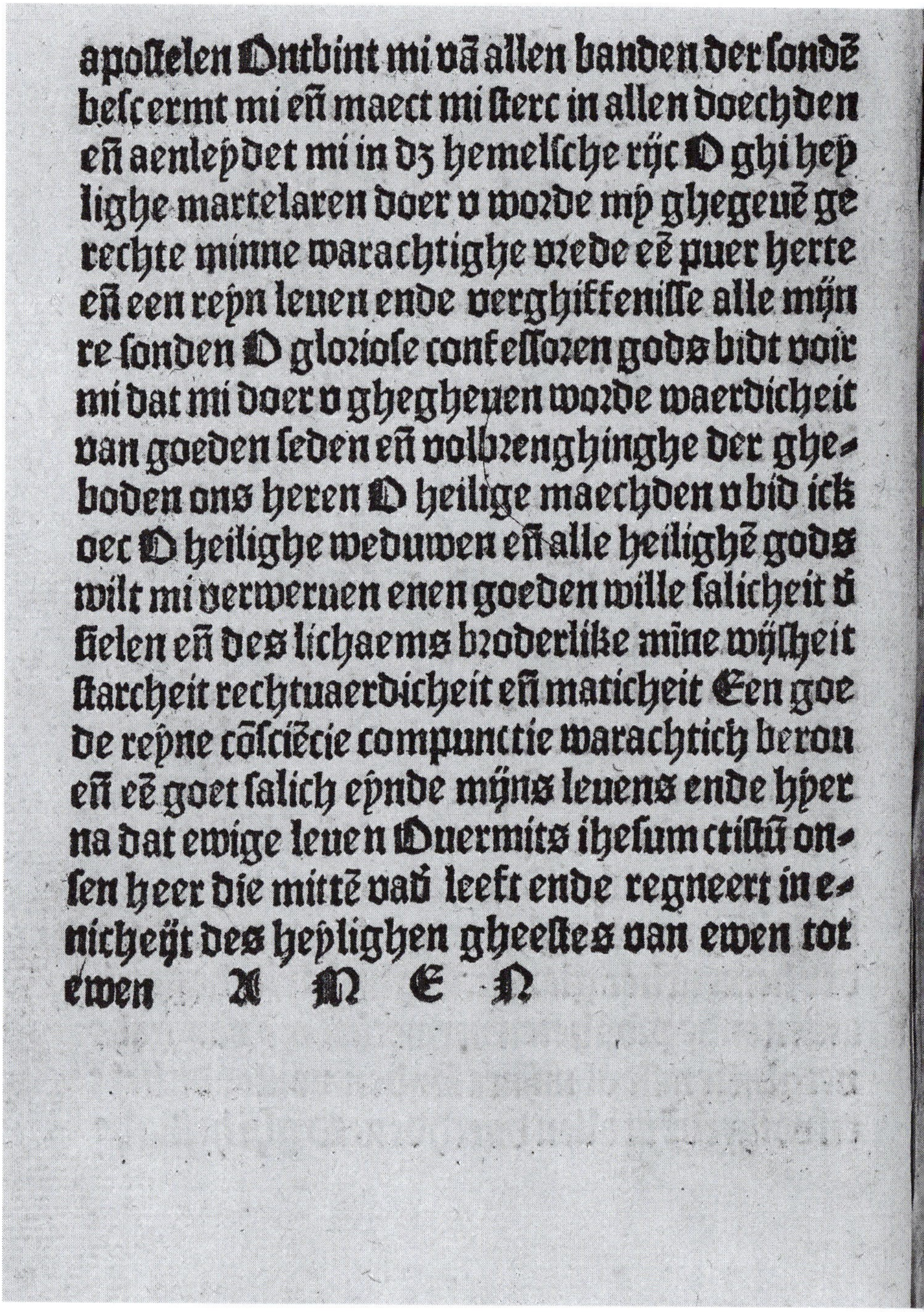

apoſtelen Ontbint mi vã allen banden der ſondẽ
beſcermt mi eñ maect mi ſterc in allen doechden
eñ aenleydet mi in dz hemelſche rÿc O ghi hey
lighe martelaren doer v worde my ghegeuẽ ge
rechte minne warachtighe vrede eẽ puer herte
eñ een reyn leuen ende verghiffeniſſe alle mÿn
re ſonden O glorioſe confeſſoren gods bidt voir
mi dat mi doer v ghegheuen worde waerdicheit
van goeden ſeden eñ volbrenghinghe der ghe
boden ons heren O heilige maechden v bid ick
oec O heilighe weduwen eñ alle heilighẽ gods
wilt mi verweruen enen goeden wille ſalicheit d
ſielen eñ des lichaems broderlike mine wÿſheit
ſtarcheit rechtuaerdicheit eñ maticheit Een goe
de reyne cõſciẽcie compunctie warachtich berou
eñ eẽ goet ſalich eynde mÿns leuens ende hyer
na dat ewige leuen Ouermits iheſum criſtũ on-
ſen heer die mittẽ vað leeft ende regneert in e-
nicheyt des heylighen gheeſtes van ewen tot
ewen   A M E N

Figure 8. 'Poem on death added on a blank leaf after the end of the chapter for Monday in the
only extant copy of Jacob Bellaert's 1486 Haarlem edition', Amsterdam, Universiteitsbibliotheek,
Bijzondere Collecties, Inc. 421, fol. c8ᵛ-d1ʳ. Reproduced with permission.

Och god als ic overpeysse
die doot die mi mochten sprert
soe suchtic zeer voermy deysse
Dant ic onder met op berert
dan welcker ic bin soe zeer verwaert
+ bidda u heere god om respyt
dat ic myn sonden hebbe verclaert
dant ic en hebbe vre nochte scheren tijt
act als ic ga van overdincten
te helle en dat grote torment
myn herte wil mi van vaere ontsincken
te suich is eyde met en eendt
+ biddu conine onpotent
silt my arme sondere met versmaden
U ziele die es u testament
tfernt myns god doer Uuer ghenade
hemeldie conine almachtich god
biddu ghenade verhoert my claecht
hebbe versmact dicke u ghebott
es es u dioulle met hebbe verwaecht
hemeldie vroedie ha ic verpacht
end uminder groeter sonden swaere
Jc bidde u spaert my desen nacht
besoet my voer die helsche saere
Jc biddu heere met traenen lau
staet my in staeden ij desen vaer
etay point maect my my hert soe flau
dat es dat oerdel spanghe ende swaer
saer alle diude coempt mi opewaer
Jc bin vol sonden en weet met vader vliey
Jc waer verloeren te traent het es claer
soude my recht na recht ghesaey

Ende zint myn een woncxken van uweer minnen
So dat ic myn zelven mach leeren kinnen.

(Oh God almighty, oh humility of virtues / who came riding on a donkey / and was
received with great honours / But the honour turned into bitterness / for you have
pierced your virtues with wounds for us / Oh, merciful God, would you still teach
me / that I may turn myself wholeheartedly to you / Kind-hearted God, enlighten
my inner self / open my heart, help to augment my virtue / And send me a small
spark of your love / so that I may learn to know myself.)[80]

This reader-viewer-writer added all three additional texts either at once or within
a limited space of time: the ink and probably also the quill used are the same.
His handwriting does not correspond with any of the two (sixteenth-century)
owner's marks — one in the front and one in the back of the copy — which have
been made largely illegible.[81] We can thus only speculate about his identity. Was
he a member of one of the Chambers of Rhetoric? Judging from the literary form
of his additions and his fine, professional handwriting in a steady cursive it is
fairly certain that he was an educated layman from the upper echelons of society.
It is probable that he fulfilled an administrative function within, for example,
a town government. Similarly to the owner of the Antwerp copy of Leeu's first
edition, he had the means to have the woodcuts richly coloured and rubrication
and initials added.

Another (later?) owner with a less sophisticated hand wrote notes of up to
four lines in the lower margin beneath numerous woodcuts and prayers in the
cycle on salvation history and below the first impression of the woodcut of the
Throne of Grace.[82] Unfortunately his/her elaborations have — together with
the colouring of the woodcuts — been washed out and made largely illegible,
but even their slumbering existence shows that elaborating further on certain
events in salvation history and in the process interweaving text, image, devotion

---

[80] Amsterdam, UB, Inc. 421, fols h4ᵛ and h5ᵛ.

[81] The copy contains two ownership notices, both of them difficult to decipher, one in the
front (fol. a3ʳ: 'Desen boeck hoert toe / klair (?) van sy..y.. en') and one in the back (fol. t7ʳ:
'desen boeck hoert toe / hert huys van s...').

[82] Erased notes appear in the lower margin of fols b5ᵛ (Throne of Grace), b6ᵛ–7ʳ (Creation
of Eve and adjacent prayer), e2ᵛ–3ʳ (Annunciation and adjacent prayer), e3ᵛ (Visitation), e4ᵛ
(Nativity), e5ᵛ (Circumcision), e6ᵛ (Adoration of the Magi), e7ᵛ (Presentation at the temple),
e8ᵛ (Flight to Egypt), f1ᵛ (Massacre of the Innocents), g5ᵛ (Baptism of Christ), g6ᵛ (Temptation
in the Desert), h2ᵛ (Supper at Bethany), h3ᵛ (Raising of Lazarus), k1ᵛ (Last Supper), k4ᵛ (Kiss
of Judas), n4ᵛ (Pilate washing his hands — also contains handwritten note above Pilate: 'rex
Assuerus'), n5ᵛ (Carrying of the Cross), p4ᵛ (Longinus piercing Christ's side).

and creativity, practicing one's literary skill in the context of personal piety, was a current practice in handling illustrated incunabula. Other additions have been inserted by different hands, serving the piety of various readers and subsequent owners: couplets of *Ave pulcherrima regina*, a devotional song relatively popular in the Low Countries, were written on a blank leaf after the end of the penitential psalm for Thursday.[83] A sixteenth-century user from a German-speaking region wrote a prayer on the blank leaf after the penitential psalm for Saturday.[84]

In one of the last woodcuts in the book we find a beautiful example of merging text and image, of mechanical reproduction and handmade addition, and of a reader-viewer actively shaping the meaning *and* function of the image. The white space in the image of Christ in the wine press has been very effectively used for a dictum through which Christ asks the reader to always be mindful of His Passion: 'O cristiane sis cotidie memor passionis nostre — pater noster ave maria' (Oh Christian [believer], be always mindful of our passion) (Fig. 9).[85] Through the addition of these words the reader-viewer transformed the oblong block of wood pressing down on Christ into a banderol through which the Saviour addresses the reader directly.[86] While the major part of the adjacent prayer consists of the devotee's speech to the suffering Christ, the perspective is reversed in the prayer's 'prologue' in which Christ speaks to the reader: 'Ic heb die perse alleen ghetreden' (I have trodden the press alone). The handmade addition fits wonderfully with the first paragraph of the prayer and pulls the reader mentally into the image and the event around which the prayer evolves.

---

[83] Amsterdam, UB, Inc. 421, fol. i8ʳ: 'Ave pulcerrima regina, gracia divina quam trina beavit...Vale Hester per te Judeum salvat Mardacheum Rex regnum comprendit Amon suspendit ...[faded]'. The notation contains stanzas 1–3, 10 and 7 in the edition by Mertens and Van der Poel, *Het liederenhandschrift Berlijn 190*, pp. 281–85. On *Ave pulcherrima regina* see De Loos, *Patronen ontrafeld*, pp. 202–03 and the literature mentioned there. The couplets are followed by four short, contemplations (poems?) in Dutch, written with different ink and faded.

[84] Amsterdam, UB, Inc. 421, fol. p2ʳ: 'Lob matter[?] die tallenheyt[?]. Lob cristi gattigkeyt der reyniget siben misse thod diurch die formlich gnad...'.

[85] Amsterdam, UB, Inc. 421, fol. s8ᵛ ('ave maria' has been added by a different hand).

[86] On inscriptions in prints and similar cases see Schmidt, 'Beschrieben, bemalt, zerschnitten', Areford, 'The Image in the Viewer's Hands', pp. 9–13 and Areford, *The Viewer and the Printed Image*, pp. 69–75. Empty banderoles that could be filled with text by viewers were frequent in prints.

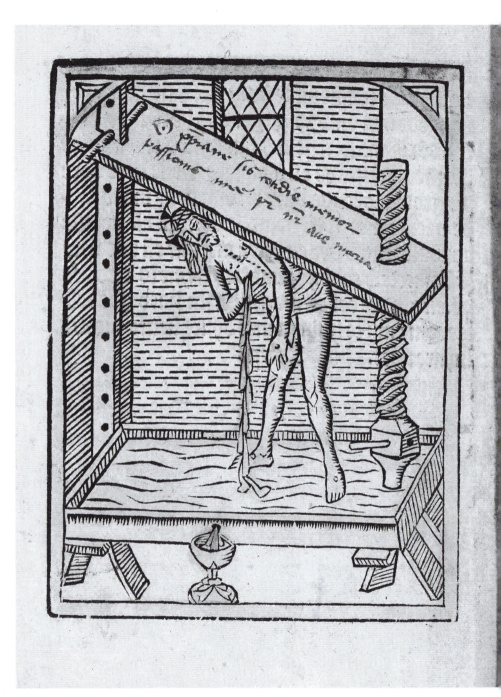

Figure 9. 'The wine press turned into a banderol through which Christ addresses the reader-viewer', Amsterdam, Universiteitsbibliotheek, Bijzondere Collecties, Inc. 421, fols s8ᵛ–t1ʳ. Copy of Jacob Bellaert's 1486 edition. Reproduced with permission.

Ic heb die perse alleē ghetredē spreect dye
heer eñ vādē volcke en was gheē man mit
mi eñ doe mijn hert gedoechde laster verwijt eñ
ōsalicheyt. so verbeyde ic wye mit mi dronich we
sen soude eñ daer en was niemāt eñ wie mi troes
tē soude eñ ic en vāts niet. Mer in minē lidē soe
bē ic alleē gebleuē eñ noch mā noch wijf en was
mit mi waer om ic als een mā vol smartē wel seg
gē mochte.ic heb die perse alleē getredē

O here ihū xpe die gedēckenis dijnre bitter
re passiē eñ die oueruloedige wtstortinge dijns
duerbaren bluedes moet ōs zijn eē salige medi-
cijn eñ boete ōler sondē eñ eē stadige vmaninghe
dijnre soeter minnē

Ic aēbede here ihū xpe dijn gebenedide eer
samige hoeft voer welkē die hemelsce craftē eñ
alle ēgelsche gheestē beuē gecroēt mit doornen
mittē riede geslagē eñ ouer al besmet eñ berōnē
mittē duerbare bluede voer ōs
Ic aenbede dat ouerste vā dinē heyligē hoefde
dat mitter prekelinghen der scherper doernen

t i

Conclusions

At first sight, the *Devout Hours* might be taken as just one of the many vernacular religious texts printed in the Low Countries, lacking a distinct character and easily swallowed by what seems to be a grey mass of similar texts. The sheer volume of these works has hitherto prevented in-depth research and their very existence is still too often explained with an oversimplified reference to the Modern Devotion.[87] The case study shows, however, that the *Devout Hours* are in fact an innovative product that offered lay people new ways to engage in their spiritual growth. It shows the richness of this material for research into developments in religious literature and the use of text and image in (private) piety.

The approach proposed in this essay emphasizes the hybrid and multimedia character of these books and seeks to interpret their materiality as layers of reception. Thus, the extant copies point to a variety of devout settings in which the book was given meaning: by devout women with a particular predilection for the Holy Virgin (copy of Claes Leeu's edition), by well-educated laymen in urban settings who added their preferred prayers (also in Latin) and original, personal variations that show how profoundly they interacted with the printed texts and images. At least one of the copies of Gerard Leeu's first edition printed in Gouda in 1483 soon found its way to West Flanders, possibly to the town of Bruges. Some handmade additions also show the readers' concern for an up-to-date text — e.g. the addition of verses to the *Adoro Te* prayer in the copy of Claes Leeu's edition — simultaneously indicating that these books were actively used in lay devotion over a relatively long period of time and thus had a profound impact on lay religiosity. The conclusions we can draw about the readership of the text are in keeping with the indications provided by the text itself: there are no signs that any of the copies were kept in religious communities, and both men and women engaged with the books.

The colouring of woodcuts is a frequent yet previously little studied addition. While colouring in religious works might be considered embellishment only — as opposed to colouring in 'scientific works' where it is thought vital for the transmission of technical knowledge —, the colouring in incunabula of a religious nature can also be crucial to the image's (symbolic, iconographic) meaning, its expressive power and its cognitive function.[88] The figurative contemplation

---

[87] Pleij, 'The Printing Press as a Long-Term Revolution', p. 290. Van Oostrom, *Wereld in woorden*, p. 495.

[88] On the meaning of colour in 'scientific' texts see McKitterick, *Print, Manuscript and the Search for Order*, pp. 79–80: 'While colour was an embellishment for many books, for others, and especially those in the sciences, it was a vital part of the author's and artist's meaning, and its absence in such books often remains an enigma'.

evoked by the meditative texts and prayers is assisted by the pictorial images that function as meditative tools. This function is enhanced through colour and sometimes by writing onto the image. Apart from making the image livelier and/or its iconography clearer, colour and textual additions can strengthen the relationship between text and image, as we have seen in cases such as Christ before Herod. Even simple forms of colouring can be very effective, such as the yellow shade applied to Mary clothed in the sun in the copy of Claes Leeu's edition. Colouring and other forms of alteration of images in incunabula also show that the way reader-viewers engaged with these images was less distant than in other media and in this sense similar to single-leaf prints — large-scale reproduction, increased accessibility and a more interactive handling of images went hand in hand.[89] Colouring conventions in (Netherlandish) incunabula need to be studied further, not only as an integral part of the images — as has been increasingly acknowledged for prints —, but also in relation to other media. Gathering data on colouring can tell us how many copies were actually coloured, keeping in mind that only a fraction has survived and that the presence of colour might have influenced (positively or negatively) their survival rate. Eventually, it might become possible to locate copies through colouring techniques, as can be done with the help of other forms of decoration, such as painted borders and pen flourishes.

For now I hope to have shown that the study of individual copies of illustrated incunabula as material traces of a multifaceted interplay between printers, religious developments, and devotional, reading and viewing practices does permit a diversified view of these books and the ways they were deployed in — and thus influenced — the readers' personal piety. Ready made books were customized (sometimes in a continuous process over decades) according to personal preferences, which resulted in a devotional personalisation. The process shows an active and reciprocal interaction between the individual and the printed book: while the book encouraged readers to deepen their individual spirituality through an interiorization of both the textual and visual material, users took this individualisation a step further by projecting their own, personal associations and reflections onto the materiality of the book. While deducing data about owners, readers and their interactions with text and image from (circumstantial) material evidence is a labour-intensive and precarious undertaking, it does provide the best — and effectively only — chance of truly gaining insight into the reception and importance of these works, and thus into the impact they had on private piety and visual culture.

---

[89] Schmidt, 'Beschrieben, bemalt, zerschnitten', p. 262.

Works Cited

Manuscripts and Incunabula

Amsterdam, Universiteitsbibliotheek, Inc. 421. *Devote ghetiden vanden leven ende passie Jesu Christi* (Haarlem: Jacob Bellaert, 8 April–20 August 1486, 8°)

Antwerpen, Ruusbroecgenootschap, L.P. 20/m1099E4. *Devote ghetiden vanden leven ende passie Jesu Christi* ([Gouda]: Gerard Leeu, 1483, before 10 December, 8°)

——, MS 202

Cambridge, University Library, Inc.5.E.3.10[2890]. *Devote ghetiden vanden leven ende passie Jesu Christi* (Gouda: Collaciebroeders, 3 October 1496, 8°)

Den Haag, Koninklijke Bibliotheek, 150 E 3. *Devote ghetiden vanden leven ende passie Jesu Christi* (Gouda: Collaciebroeders, 3 October 1496, 8°)

——, 169 G 94. *Tafel des kersteliken levens*. Add: Antonius de Rovere: *Lof van den heiligen sacrament* (Gouda: Gerard Leeu, 20 August 1478, 4°)

——, MS 129 G 8

——, MS 135 E 19

——, MS BPH 79

Leiden, Universiteitsbibliotheek, 1498 F 1. *Devote ghetiden vanden leven ende passie Jesu Christi* (Antwerpen: Gerard Leeu, between 18 September 1484 and 9 July 1485, 8°)

London, British Library, IA.49933. *Devote ghetiden vanden leven ende passie Jesu Christi* (Antwerpen: Claes Leeu, 29 November 1487, 8°)

——, MS Add. 20729

Princeton, University Library, MS Garrett 63

San Marino, Huntington Library, 100989. *Devote ghetiden vanden leven ende passie Jesu Christi* (Gouda: Gerard Leeu, 1483, before 10 December, 8°)

Primary Sources

Simon van Venlo, *Boexken van der officien ofte dienst der missen*, ed. by Ludo Simons, with introductory articles by Jos Andriessen, Elly Cockx-Indestege, and Hendrik D. L. Vervliet, 2 vols (Antwerpen: De Schutter, 1982)

Secondary Sources

Areford, David S., 'Introduction', *Studies in Iconography*, 4 (2003), 1–4

——, 'The Image in the Viewer's Hands: The Reception of Early Prints in Europe', *Studies in Iconography*, 4 (2003), 5–42

——, *The Viewer and the Printed Image in Late Medieval Europe* (Farnham: Ashgate, 2010)

Bax, D., 'Een onbekend gedicht over de dood als schaakspeler', *Tijdschrift voor Nederlandse Taal- en Letterkunde*, 68 (1951), 241–44

Blume, Clemens, and Guido M. Dreves eds, *Analecta Hymnica Medii Aevi*, vol. 33 (Leipzig: Reisland, 1898)

Bogaart, Saskia, *Geleerde kennis in de volkstaal. 'Van den proprieteyten der dinghen' (Haarlem 1485) in perspectief* (Hilversum: Verloren, 2004)

Brinkman, Herman, 'De *Const* ter perse. Publiceren bij de rederijkers voor de Reformatie', in *Geschreven en gedrukt. Boekproductie van handschrift naar druk in de overgang van Middeleeuwen naar moderne tijd*, ed. by Herman Pleij, Joris Reynaert and others (Gent: Academia Press, 2004), pp. 157–75

Chartier, Roger, 'Afterword: Materiality and Meaning', *Word & Image*, 17 (2001), 181–83

Conway, William Martin, *The Woodcutters of the Netherlands in the Fifteenth Century*, 3 vols (Cambridge: Cambridge University Press, 1884)

Dackerman, Susan, 'Introduction', in *Painted Prints: The Revelation of Color in Northern Renaissance & Baroque Engravings, Etchings & Woodcuts*, ed. by Susan Dackerman (Baltimore: The Baltimore Museum of Art, 2002), pp. 1–6

——, 'Painted Prints in Germany and the Netherlands', in *Painted Prints: The Revelation of Color in Northern Renaissance & Baroque Engravings, Etchings & Woodcuts*, ed. by Susan Dackerman (Baltimore: The Baltimore Museum of Art, 2002), pp. 9–47

Dackerman, Susan, ed., *Painted Prints: The Revelation of Color in Northern Renaissance & Baroque Engravings, Etchings & Woodcuts* (Baltimore: The Baltimore Museum of Art, 2002)

Delft, Marieke van, 'Illustrations in Early Printed Books and Manuscript Illumination: The Case of a Dutch Book of Hours printed by Wolfgang Hopyl in Paris in 1500', in *Books in Transition at the Time of Philip the Fair: Manuscripts and Printed Books in the Late Fifteenth and Early Sixteenth Century Low Countries*, ed. by Hanno Wijsman (Turnhout: Brepols, 2010), pp. 131–64

De vijfhonderdste verjaring van de boekdrukkunst in de Nederlanden (Brussel: Koninklijke Bibliotheek Albert I, 1973)

Dewitte, Alfons, 'Het Brugse St.-Jans en St.-Lucasgilde der librariers 1457, 1469', *Biekorf*, 96 (1996), 334–40

Dlabačová, Anna, 'Chatten met Scriptura. Het leven van Jezus in een Antwerpse bestseller', *Boekenwereld*, 33 (2017), 25–29

——, 'Drukken en publieksgroepen. Productie en receptie van gedrukte Middelnederlandse meditatieve Levens van Jezus (ca. 1479–1540)', *Ons Geestelijk Erf*, 79 (2008), 321–68

——, *Literatuur en observantie. De 'Spieghel der volcomenheit' van Hendrik Herp en de dynamiek van laatmiddeleeuwse tekstverspreiding* (Hilversum: Verloren, 2014)

——, 'Religious Practice and Experimental Book Production. Text and Image in an Alternative Layman's "Book of Hours" in Print and Manuscript', *Journal of Historians of Netherlandish Art*, 9.2 (2017), DOI: 10.5092/jhna.2017.9.2.2

Dlabačová, Anna, and Daniëlle Prochowski, 'Preken en publiceren. De franciscaanse observantie als producent en aanjager van religieuze literatuur in de Lage Landen, circa 1490–1560. Ter inleiding', *Ons Geestelijk Erf*, 85 (2014), 225–29

Gnirrep, Kees, 'Relaties van Leeu met andere drukkers en met boekverkopers', in *Een drukker zoekt publiek. Gheraert Leeu te Gouda 1477–1484*, ed. by Koen Goudriaan and others (Delft: Eburon, 1993), pp. 193–203

Goedings, Truusje, *'Afsetters en meester-afsetters'. De kunst van het kleuren 1480–1720* (Nijmegen: Vantilt, 2015)

Goudriaan, Koen, 'Apostolate and Printing: The Collaciebroeders of Gouda and their Press', in *Between Lay Piety and Academic Theology: Studies Presented to Christoph Burger on the Occasion of his 65th Birthday*, ed. by Ulrike Hascher-Burger, August den Hollander and Wim Janse (Leiden: Brill, 2010), pp. 433–52

Goudriaan, K., and G. A. M. Willems, eds, *Gheraert Leeu, meesterprenter ter Goude, 1477–1484* (Gouda: Stedelijk Museum Het Catharina Gasthuis, 1992)

Goudriaan, Koen, and others, eds, *Een drukker zoekt publiek. Gheraert Leeu te Gouda* (Delft: Eburon, 1993)

Hellinga, Lotte, 'Gheraert Leeu, Claes Leeu, Jacob Bellaert, Peter van Os van Breda', in *De vijfhonderdste verjaring van de boekdrukkunst in de Nederlanden* (Brussel: Koninklijke Bibliotheek Albert I, 1973), pp. 283–91

Hellinga, Wytze, and Lotte Hellinga, *The Fifteenth-Century Printing Types of the Low Countries*, vol. I (Amsterdam: Menno Hertzberger, 1966)

Hindman, Sandra, *Pen to Press: Illustrated Manuscripts and Printed Books in the First Century of Printing* (College Park: Art Dept., University of Maryland, 1977)

Jecmen, Gregory, 'Color Printing and Tonal Etching: Innovative Techniques in the Imperial City, 1487–1536', in *Imperial Augsburg: Renaissance Prints and Drawings, 1475–1540*, ed. by Gregory Jecmen and Freyda Spira (Washington, DC: National Gallery of Art, 2012), pp. 67–101

Kok, Ina, 'A Rediscovered *Devote ghetiden* with Interesting Woodcuts (CA 1117)', *Quaerendo*, 13 (1983), 167–90

——, *Woodcuts in Incunabula Printed in the Low Countries*, 4 vols (Houten: Hes & De Graaf, 2013)

Larkin, Graham, and Lisa Pon, 'Introduction: The Materiality of Printed Words and Images', *Word & Image*, 17 (2001), 1–6

Loos, Ike de, *Patronen ontrafeld. Studies over Gregoriaanse gezangen en Middelnederlandse liederen* (Hilversum: Verloren, 2012)

McKitterick, David, *Print, Manuscript and the Search for Order, 1450–1830* (Cambridge: Cambridge University Press, 2003)

——, 'Tanned Calf over Wooden Boards, Early Sixteenth Century', Online exhibition *The Use and Abuse of Books: Private Lives of Print* (Cambridge: Cambridge University Library), https://exhibitions.lib.cam.ac.uk/incunabula/artifacts/tanned-calf-early-sixteenth-century/ [accessed 10 April 2017]

Mertens, Thom, Poel, Dieuwke van der, and others, *Het liederenhandschrift Berlijn 190. Hs. Staatsbibliothek zu Berlin – Preußischer kulturbesitz, germ. oct. 190* (Hilversum: Verloren, 2013)

Mone, F. J., *Hymni Latini Medii Aevi*, vol. 2 (Freiburg im Breisgau: Herder, 1854)

Moolenbroek, Jaap van, '"Dat liden ende die passie ons Heren Jhesu Cristi". Een bestseller uit het fonds van Gheraert Leeu in vijftiende-eeuwse context', in *Een drukker zoekt publiek. Gheraert Leeu te Gouda 1477–1484*, ed. by Koen Goudriaan and others (Delft: Eburon, 1993), pp. 81–110

Oltrogge, Doris, 'Illuminating the Print: The Use of Color in Fifteenth-Century Prints and Book Illumination', in *The Woodcut in Fifteenth-Century Europe*, ed. by Peter Parshall (Washington, DC: National Gallery of Art, 2009), pp. 298–315

Oostrom, Frits van, *Wereld in woorden. Geschiedenis van de Nederlandse literatuur 1300–1400* (Amsterdam: Bert Bakker, 2013)

Parshall, Peter, 'Prints as Objects of Consumption in Early Modern Europe', *Journal of Medieval and Early Modern Studies*, 28 (1998), 19–36

Pleij, Herman, 'The Printing Press as a Long-Term Revolution', in *Books in Transition at the Time of Philip the Fair: Manuscripts and Printed Books in the Late Fifteenth and Early Sixteenth Century Low Countries*, ed. by Hanno Wijsman (Turnhout: Brepols, 2010), pp. 287–307

Primeau, Thomas, 'Coloring Within the Lines: The Use of Stencil in Early Woodcuts', *Art in Print*, 3.3 (2013), http://artinprint.org/article/coloring-within-the-lines-the-use-of-stencil-in-early-woodcuts/ [accessed 10 April 2017]

——, 'The Materials and Technology of Renaissance and Baroque Hand-Colored Prints', in *Painted Prints: The Revelation of Color in Northern Renaissance & Baroque Engravings, Etchings & Woodcuts*, ed. by Susan Dackerman (Baltimore: The Baltimore Museum of Art, 2002), pp. 49–78

Renaud, Adam, 'The Emergence of Antwerp as a Printing Centre: From the Earliest Days of Printing to the Reformation (1481–1520)', *De gulden passer. Tijdschrift voor boekwetenschap*, 92 (2014), pp. 11–28

Reypens, L., 'Belang der "Devote ghetiden" voor de geschiedenis der lekenspiritualiteit', *Ons Geestelijk Erf*, 33 (1959), 406–12

——, 'Een onbekend vijftiendeeuws handschrift met een Westvlaamse vertaling van het tweede boek der Imitatie', *Ons Geestelijk Erf*, 32 (1958), 428–31

——, 'Rond een Antwerpse druk der "Devote ghetiden". Het enige bekende exemplaar weer thuisgewezen en een tweede ontdekt', *Ons Geestelijk Erf*, 33 (1959), 100–06

Rosier, Bart, 'Gheraert Leeus illustraties bij het leven van Jezus', in *Een drukker zoekt publiek. Gheraert Leeu te Gouda 1477–1484*, ed. by Koen Goudriaan and others (Delft: Eburon, 1993), pp. 133–61

Schmidt, Peter, 'Beschrieben, bemalt, zerschnitten. Tegernseer Mönche interpretieren einen Holzschnitt', in *Einblattdrucke des 15. und frühen 16. Jahrhunderts: Probleme, Perspektiven, Fallstudien*, ed. by Volker Honemann, Sabine Griese, Falk Eisermann and Marcus Ostermann (Tübingen: Max Niemeyer, 2000), pp. 245–76

Stock, J. van der, *Printing Images in Antwerp: The Introduction of Printmaking in a City, Fifteenth Century to 1585* (Rotterdam: Sound & Vision Interactive, 1998)

Thienen, G. van, and J. Goldfinch, *Incunabula Printed in the Low Countries: A Census*, Bibliotheca bibliographica Neerlandica, 36 (Nieuwkoop: De Graaf, 1999)

Warnar, Geert, '*Elckerlijc* in beeld. Jan Provoosts "Rijkaard en de dood"', *Spiegel der Letteren*, 57 (2015), 273–89

Wilson, Adrian, assisted by Joyce Lancaster Wilson, *Making of the Nuremberg Chronicle* (Amsterdam: Nico Israel, 1976)

Index of Persons and Literary Works

Persons living up to and including the Middle Ages, and those evidently following the medieval tradition in the sixteenth century, are listed by first name, then title/last name, in the form found on the title page of standard editions. Their literary works are listed in the original language in italic script. For other entries referring to the post-medieval period the last name is given first. Page numbers in italics refer to images and plates.

INDEX OF PLACE NAMES

Index of Manuscripts and Early Printed Editions

MEDIEVAL CHURCH STUDIES

All volumes in this series are evaluated by an Editorial Board, strictly on academic grounds, based on reports prepared by referees who have been commissioned by virtue of their specialism in the appropriate field. The Board ensures that the screening is done independently and without conflicts of interest. The definitive texts supplied by authors are also subject to review by the Board before being approved for publication. Further, the volumes are copyedited to conform to the publisher's stylebook and to the best international academic standards in the field.

Titles in Series

Megan Cassidy-Welch, *Monastic Spaces and their Meanings: Thirteenth-Century English Cistercian Monasteries* (2001)

Elizabeth Freeman, *Narratives of a New Order: Cistercian Historical Writing in England, 1150–1220* (2002)

The Study of the Bible in the Carolingian Era, ed. by Celia Chazelle and Burton Van Name Edwards (2003)

Text and Controversy from Wyclif to Bale: Essays in Honour of Anne Hudson, ed. by Helen Barr and Ann M. Hutchison (2005)

Lena Roos, *'God Wants It!': The Ideology of Martyrdom in the Hebrew Crusade Chronicles and its Jewish and Christian Background* (2006)

Emilia Jamroziak, *Rievaulx Abbey and its Social Context, 1132–1300: Memory, Locality, and Networks* (2004)

The Voice of Silence: Women's Literacy in a Men's Church, ed. by Thérèse de Hemptinne and María Eugenia Góngora (2004)

Perspectives for an Architecture of Solitude: Essays on Cistercians, Art and Architecture in Honour of Peter Fergusson, ed. by Terryl N. Kinder (2004)

Saints, Scholars, and Politicians: Gender as a Tool in Medieval Studies, ed. by Mathilde van Dijk and Renée Nip (2005)

Manuscripts and Monastic Culture: Reform and Renewal in Twelfth-Century Germany, ed. by Alison I. Beach (2007)

Weaving, Veiling, and Dressing : Textiles and their Metaphors in the Late Middle Ages, ed. by Kathryn M. Rudy and Barbara Baert (2007)

James J. Boyce, *Carmelite Liturgy and Spiritual Identity: The Choir Books of Kraków* (2008)

Studies in Carthusian Monasticism in the Late Middle Ages, ed. by Julian M. Luxford (2009)

Kevin J. Alban, *The Teaching and Impact of the 'Doctrinale' of Thomas Netter of Walden (c. 1374–1430)* (2010)

Gunilla Iversen, *Laus angelica: Poetry in the Medieval Mass*, ed. by Jane Flynn, trans. by William Flynn (2010)

Kriston R. Rennie, *Law and Practice in the Age of Reform: The Legatine Work of Hugh of Die (1073–1106)* (2010)

After Arundel: Religious Writing in Fifteenth-Century England, ed. by Vincent Gillespie and Kantik Ghosh (2011)

Federico Botana, *The Works of Mercy in Italian Medieval Art (c. 1050–c. 1400)* (2011)

The Regular Canons in the Medieval British Isles, ed. by Janet Burton and Karen Stöber (2011)

Wycliffite Controversies, ed. by Mishtooni Bose and J. Patrick Hornbeck II (2011)

Nickiphoros I. Tsougarakis, *The Latin Religious Orders in Medieval Greece, 1204–1500* (2012)

Nikolaos G. Chrissis, *Crusading in Frankish Greece: A Study of Byzantine-Western Relations and Attitudes, 1204–1282* (2012)

Demetrio S. Yocum, *Petrarch's Humanist Writing and Carthusian Monasticism: The Secret Language of the Self* (2013)

The Pseudo-Bonaventuran Lives of Christ: Exploring the Middle English Tradition, ed. by Ian Johnson and Allan F. Westphall (2013)

Alice Chapman, *Sacred Authority and Temporal Power in the Writings of Bernard of Clairvaux* (2013)

Religious Controversy in Europe, 1378–1536: Textual Transmission and Networks of Readership, ed. by Michael Van Dussen and Pavel Soukup (2013)

Ian Johnson, *The Middle English Life of Christ: Academic Discourse, Translation, and Vernacular Theology* (2013)

Monasteries on the Borders of Medieval Europe: Conflict and Cultural Interaction, ed. by Emilia Jamroziak and Karen Stöber (2014)

M. J. Toswell, *The Anglo-Saxon Psalter* (2014)

Envisioning the Bishop: Images and the Episcopacy in the Middle Ages, ed. by Sigrid Danielson and Evan A. Gatti (2014)

Kathleen E. Kennedy, *The Courtly and Commercial Art of the Wycliffite Bible* (2014)

David N. Bell, *The Library of the Abbey of La Trappe: A Study of its History from the Twelfth Century to the French Revolution, with an Annotated Edition of the 1752 Catalogue* (2014)

Patronage, Production, and Transmission of Texts in Medieval and Early Modern Jewish Cultures, ed. by Esperanza Alfonso and Jonathan Decter (2014)

Devotional Culture in Late Medieval England and Europe: Diverse Imaginations of Christ's Life, edited by Stephen Kelly and Ryan Perry (2014)

Matthew Cheung Salisbury, *The Secular Liturgical Office in Late Medieval England* (2015)

From Hus to Luther: Visual Culture in the Bohemian Reformation (1380–1620), ed. by Kateřina Horníčková and Michal Šroněk (2016)

Medieval Liège at the Crossroads of Europe: Monastic Society and Culture, 1000–1300, ed. by Steven Vanderputten, Tjamke Snijders, and Jay Diehl (2017)

Episcopal Power and Local Society in Medieval Europe, 900–1400, ed. by Peter Coss, Chris Dennis, Melissa Julian-Jones, and Angelo Silvestri (2017)

Saints of North-East England, 600–1500, ed. by Margaret Coombe, Anne Mouron, and Christiania Whitehead (2017)

Tamás Karáth, *Richard Rolle: The Fifteenth-Century Translations* (2017)

In Preparation

Late Medieval Devotional Compilations in England, ed. by Marleen Cré, Diana Denissen, and Denis Renevey

Episcopal Power and Personality in Medieval Europe, 900–1480, ed. by Peter Coss, Chris Dennis, Melissa Julian-Jones, and Angelo Silvestri

Bishops' Identities, Careers, and Networks in Medieval Europe, ed. by Sarah E. Thomas